Specific Situations
in Effective Oral Communication

Don B. Morlan, University of Dayton

George E. Tuttle, Jr., Illinois State University

Specific Situations
in
Effective Oral
Communication

Bobbs-Merrill Educational Publishing
Indianapolis

The Bobbs-Merrill Company, Inc.
4300 West 62nd Street
Indianapolis, Indiana 46268

First Edition
First Printing 1977

Library of Congress Cataloging in Publication Data
Morlan, Don B
    Specific situations in effective oral
communication.

    Includes bibliographical references and index.
    1. Oral communication.   I. Tuttle, George E.,
joint author.   II. Title.
PN4121.M64   808.5'45   77–1399
ISBN 0–672–61410–3

Contents

Acknowledgments

The authors would like to acknowledge and express their thanks to the following:

Nancy Broom Brown for permission to reprint "Comrades" which first appeared in the 1973 issue of *Vehicle*.

Pathfinder Press for permission to reprint R. L. Moseley's "An Old-Timer Looks at 42 Years Behind Walls" and "An Old-Timer, Inside 42 Years, Sees Outside" and "Testament" by Clarence Harris. Copyright © 1970. Reprinted with permission of Pathfinder Press, Inc.

Broadside Press for permission to reprint "Hard Rock Returns to Prison from the Hospital for the Criminal Insane," "The Idea of Ancestry," and "2 Poems for Black Relocation Centers" from *Poems from Prison*, by Etheridge Knight, copyright © 1968. Reprinted by permission of Broadside Press.

Ray Schmudde for permission to reprint "From Outside Colorado" which first appeared in the Spring 1974 issue of *Vehicle*.

Heather J. Straka for permission to reprint "Madness" which first appeared in the Spring 1971 issue of *Vehicle*.

The Nation for permission to reprint "The Prisoner" by Erica Jong which first appeared in the May 21, 1973 issue. Reprinted with permission.

Harper & Row and **William Peter Blatty** for permission to quote from *The Exorcist* by William Peter Blatty. Reprinted with permission.

Random House and **Neil Simon** for permission to quote from *The Prisoner of Second Avenue*, copyright © 1972 by Nancy Enterprises, Inc. Reprinted by permission of Random House, Inc. and the author. All rights, including the right of reproduction in whole or in part, in any form, are reserved under international and Pan-American Copyright Conventions. Published in the United States by Random House, Inc., New York, and simultaneously in Canada by Random House of Canada Limited, Toronto.

Caution: Professionals and amateurs are hereby warned that *The Prisoner of Second Avenue* is fully protected under the Universal Copyright Convention, Berne Convention and Pan-American Copyright Convention and is subject to royalty. All rights are strictly reserved, including professional, amateur, motion picture, television, radio, recitation, lecturing, public reading and foreign translation, and none of such rights can be exercised or used without written permission from the copyright owner.

All inquiries for licenses and permissions for stock and amateur uses should be addressed to Samuel French, Inc., 25 W. 45th Street, New York, N. Y. 10036. All other inquiries for licenses and permissions should be addressed to Albert I. Da Silva, 4 W. 56th Street, New York, N. Y. 10019.

Prentice-Hall for permission to reprint four letters from *W. C. Fields by Himself* by Ronald J. Fields, editor. Copyright © 1973 by W. C. Fields Productions, Inc. Reprinted with permission.

Chris Benignus for permission to reprint "One Time" which first appeared in the 1973 issue of *Vehicle*.

W. H. Watling, Jr. for permission to reprint "Yellow Fever," copyright © 1975 by W. H. Watling, Jr.

Barnes & Noble for reproducing a sketch of the Globe Theatre by Dr. J. C. Adams from *The Globe Playhouse*, Second Edition, 1961, reprinted 1966. Used on page 106 with permission of Barnes & Noble, a division of Harper & Row, Publishers, Inc.

Delta Psi Omega Playbill for permission to reprint the summary of most produced shows of Delta Psi Omega and Alpha Psi Omega, 1969–74, as it appeared in the November 1975 issue.

Christy Reed for permission to reprint her oration, "What Are We Loyal To?"

Terry Lenhardt for permission to reprint his extemporaneous speech, "Is There Evidence That the United States Is Embroiling Itself Further in Southeast Asia?" which won the Illinois High School Association state final individual events contest in 1971.

The authors would also like to express thanks to **Wanda Wiley** for her careful editing of the manuscript. Appreciation is extended to the following for making valuable materials available and providing assistance in preparation of this text: **Donald P. Garner, R. Glen Wiley,** and **Karolyn Kerr.**

Also, in their memory, a special note of thanks and gratitude is due two of our former teachers now deceased: **Juanita Shearer** and **Dr. Otis J. Aggertt,** who were influential in enabling the authors to produce this text.

Introduction

The study of human oral communication begins with fundamental concepts and fundamental skills. After the study of fundamentals, one can pursue a study of complex theories or a study of complex skills. *Specific Situations in Effective Oral Communication* is a text designed to provide in-depth study of the ways to apply fundamental concepts and skills to situations demanding specialized performance skills. This text is written for several kinds of students and learning situations and will facilitate specialized performance skill development as an aid in effective communication.

Some of the most distinctive features of this text are drawn from contemporary educational theory. First, learning objectives placed at the beginning of each chapter give the student direction and provide awareness of minimum information and skills which the reader should expect to possess when the chapter is completed.

Second, summary probes are placed strategically throughout each chapter rather than just at the end of the chapter. Summary probes throughout the text require immediate review of a few particular concepts; the immediate reinforcement should increase retention. Summary probes found at the end of chapters usually call for synthesis or application of principles or skills from the entire chapter. Some of the end-of-chapter probes will relate specifically to learning objectives stated at the beginning of the chapter.

Third, learning activities are provided, often in somewhat of a sequential order, to facilitate skill exercise, concept discovery, or synthesis. At least some of the learning activities are so closely interrelated with chapter goals that completion of the activity will actually accomplish the stated goal.

Fourth, references located at the ends of chapters will direct the student to a source for further study of a particular concept generalized in the text.

Finally, this text is written with the reader in mind. We have made every effort to prepare a text with a wide range of reading ability as a guiding force. Terms with special meanings are explained while examples and illustrations are provided in a form as simple as possible.

The authors have made two assumptions concerning communication in preparation of this text. It is essential that the student studying this text know and understand those assumptions.

First, the authors assume that all of the specific situations described herein are communicative in nature. That is, each situation primarily involves human beings interacting with the intent of transmitting meaningful messages one to the other.

Second, our view of communication is receiver and message oriented rather than source oriented. It is receiver oriented and message oriented in that the occasions which warrant oral reading, play production, debating, or the various forms of public speaking are those in which it is desirable to transmit a message to receivers. Our view of communication is source—or performance—oriented only in the sense that outstanding performance on the part of the source will enhance the receiver's ability to comprehend the intended message.

I

Oral Reading

ONE

GOALS After completing this chapter you will be able to:

    1. Understand the practice of oral reading as one of many human communicative acts.

    2. Understand the significance of oral reading to the human being.

    3. Distinguish between three types or classifications of material appropriate for oral reading.

Why Should I Read
An Introduction to
Oral Reading

Of all the communication situations available to human beings, every-day conversation is probably the only medium practiced more fre-quently than *oral reading*. As parents, we read aloud to our children; as teachers, we read aloud to students; in work situations, we may read reports aloud to fellow workers. In addition to engaging actively in oral reading, all of us will be listeners in reading situations at countless times in the span of a normal life. As students, we listen to teachers read aloud; as members of various social groups, we listen to the read-ing of minutes of past meetings. If we are regular churchgoers, we spend a great deal of time listening to ministers or liturgists read aloud to us.

While no communication activity is practiced either as sender or receiver as frequently as reading aloud, we might also safely say that no communication situation is taken for granted as much as reading aloud. We learn to read early in our educational career; we, thus, assume that if we can read at all, we can read aloud.

Most of us have experienced a long and dull session of listening to a reader who really didn't read very well. The reader who never looks up from his text, who never varies his voice or volume, who has no concept of effective pause for purposes of enhancing meaning, can be

3

more effective than the most powerful sleeping potion at putting an audience at "complete" ease.

This chapter will introduce you to the process of oral interpretation of the printed word as one of many human communication situations. Definition and analysis of crucial terms in understanding oral reading are a necessary first step. A discussion of the significance of oral reading to the human being and an introduction to various types of literature available to the reader will follow.

DEFINITION AND ANALYSIS

The specific communication process under study in this unit has been called many things throughout its history. Reading aloud can refer to oral interpretation of literature, interpretative reading, oral reading, communicative reading, and—from years past—elocution. We will not become involved in any controversy concerning proper terminology: any of the preceding terms can be used to apply to our subject matter.

For our purposes we will define our study as that process whereby an individual desires to communicate meaning by reading words from a printed page aloud to one or more listeners. Normally the words on those printed pages are those of others; however, many factors in effective oral reading apply equally to reading one's own work. Contained within this definition are four concepts which require further analysis.

Communicate

Our study is one of many areas in the process of human communication. In oral reading the three major components of the communication process are present. A *communicator* desires to transmit a *message* to one or more *receivers*. In the true communicative sense—the emphasis being on the meaning of the message—oral reading is not performance. The following poem relating the trials and tribulations of a communicative reader illustrates our distinction.

AN OVERWORKED ELOCUTIONIST

Carolyn Wells

Once there was a little boy whose name was Robert Reese;
And every Friday afternoon he had to speak a piece.
So many poems thus he learned, that soon he had a store
Of recitations in his head and still kept learning more.

And now this is what happened: He was called upon one week
And totally forgot the piece he was about to speak.
His brain he cudgeled. Not a word remained within his head!
And so he spoke at random, and this is what he said:

"My beautiful, my beautiful, who standest proudly by,
It was the schooner Hesperus—the breaking waves dashed high!
Why is this Forum crowded? What means this stir in Rome?
Under a spreading chestnut tree there is no place like home!

When freedom from her mountain height cried, 'Twinkle, little star,'
Shoot if you must this old gray head, King Henry of Navarre!
Roll on, thou deep and dark blue castled crag of Drachenfels,
My name is Norval, on the Grampian Hills, ring out, wild bells!

If you're waking, call me early, to be or not to be,
The curfew must not ring tonight! Oh, woodman, spare that tree!
Charge, Chester, charge! On, Stanley, on! and let who will be clever!
The boy stood on the burning deck, but I go on forever!"

His elocution was superb, his voice and gestures fine;
His schoolmates all applauded as he finished his last line.
"I see it doesn't matter," Robert thought, "what words I say,
So long as I declaim with oratorical display."

1907

   The young boy depicted in the poem was not communicating; he
was, instead, performing. The center of attention for both sender and
receiver in his communication act was the sender and his ability at
"oratorical display." Virtually no attention was given in this situation
to the message being transmitted.

Our concern rests primarily with the message being transmitted in the reading situation. An immediate question appears when we consider exactly who is the communicator in the reading situation. Obviously, if the reader is rendering his own material, then the communicator is the reader. Rarely does this occur, however. More than likely a reader will be interpreting written material created and set down by some other person.

In an instance where a reader is reading someone else's material, some would say that the author or writer is the communicator and the reader is only a channel of communication. Others would say that because the reader must interpret and extract elements of meaning from a written work, the reader becomes the communicator. Evidence of this theory is illustrated by listening to two individuals read the same piece of writing; most likely, the two interpretations will differ in several respects.

We deny that either the reader or the writer is the sole communicator in a reading situation. Rather, a communicative partnership exists. Most assuredly the writer of the material maintains a high degree of communicative source. However, when an individual other than the writer reads and makes judgments as to intended meaning, we can no longer call the writer the true and only source of the message being transmitted.

In specifying a singular source of the communication involved in oral reading, we would refer to that source as the writer-reader. Those elements of meaning in the written work which remain the same from one reader's interpretation to another are the contributions of the writer; however, those elements of meaning which may vary from one reader to another are the contributions of the reader. The student of oral reading must understand that both parties involved make significant contributions to the process of reading in order to accept oral reading as a specific communicative act.

Reading Words

The usual mode of communicating another person's written message is through reading from the printed text or manuscript. Past controversies have been waged often as to whether or not memorized delivery of a piece of literature or some other form of written message is truly "interpretive reading." Certainly it is not reading in the strictest and most literal sense of the word.

We do not, however, intend in this approach to open the controversy of readers versus memorizers. Interpretation of written messages is usually achieved through reading from a manuscript. If the reader commits the passage to memory and no longer depends on the manuscript, all he has lost is one aspect of the method of delivery.

The essential point of consideration here is that the speaker-reader is engaged in the process of discovering meaning of written material and transmitting that meaning to others. The student in an interpretive contest who does not use a manuscript can be just as much a *reader* in the sense that we have defined the term as the person who holds a manuscript and depends heavily on that manuscript.

Holding and using a manuscript or not doing so is not the determining factor that renders a communicative event interpretive reading. As long as the student speaker-reader focuses primary attention and concern on the message contained within the written work and not the delivery of that message, he is indeed engaging in interpretive reading.

Printed Page

Many authors have traditionally disagreed as to what is included in the domain of appropriate material for interpretive reading. Some have restricted their body of available material to fictitious writing. Jeré Veilleux defined oral interpretation as, "the art of re-creating a literary work (prose-fiction, poetry, or drama) through the medium of oral reading by an interpreter to an audience."[1] In so doing he limits literary work to fictional material.

We do not choose to limit our pool of acceptable material for oral reading. While much of the material selected by student readers will most likely be literature of a fictional nature, other avenues of potential material should be left open. Later in this unit, the student will be presented with examples of excellent reading material consisting of personal letters, and nonfictional material classified as literature.

In order to provide the student with as wide a choice of material as possible, our definition of the printed page will be left virtually unrestricted. It is our belief that far more important measures of criteria in choosing material should be applied than an artificial categorization of what is and what is not *literature*.

Number of Listeners

The number of listeners involved in the interpretive reading situation is immaterial in classifying it as a communicative act. In the broadest sense, one or more listeners must hear a reading. A father, patiently reading a book to a five-year-old child at bedtime, is engaging in interpretive reading just as much as a professional actor interpreting the works of a great author on a national television network.

As long as the primary concern rests with the meaning of the material being read rather than the method of transmission, as it must, either situation is truly interpretive reading.

<table>
<tr><td>SUMMARY
PROBES</td><td>1. What is meant by a communicative partnership relating to the source in the act of reading aloud?
2. Why is oral reading not a performance?
3. How important is the controversy between reading and memorizing material in our study of oral reading?
4. How many listeners must be present for the communicative act of oral reading to exist?</td></tr>
</table>

SIGNIFICANCE

As was stated at the outset of this chapter, perhaps few other communication situations will present themselves more frequently to the average person than the demand for reading aloud in one of a number of settings. No doubt each of you has already, on numerous occasions, been expected to read to one or more people.

Most of us learned to read in early education by reading aloud to others. Throughout our elementary education into junior and senior high and beyond, we have been required to read aloud as part of class participation. Reading aloud is practiced regularly in most homes— from reading bedtime stories to youngsters to mother or father reading a particularly entertaining or well written column or editorial.

The significance of reading aloud to students in terms of relevancy to daily life-style is obvious. Unfortunately by the time a student reaches high school or college, he has often been turned off to oral reading—especially oral reading of literary works.

Many of us have had literature spoiled for our personal use at some early point in our education. The eighth grade teacher who requires all class members to memorize and recite "The Gettysburg Address" or the last few lines of "Thanatopsis" may do a great deal more to destroy the meaning of literature to a student than to enhance it.

Far too often when we are forced to memorize passages with emphasis on ability to stand and regurgitate words in proper order, we fail to read for meaning. Further, it is doubtful that a student should ever be forced to read a *specific* piece of written material in an oral reading situation. It is our belief that the student should be allowed to select from a nearly endless supply of material that has meaning and relevance for him.

TYPES OF MATERIAL

You will recall that we stated earlier that our definition of written material for purposes of oral reading would be virtually unrestricted. We will not, as some have, restrict eligible material to that which is fictional as opposed to that which reports factual or biographical happenings. Our primary criterion determining acceptability of material will be that the writer of the work—whatever form that work might take—had some message to communicate with others.

Even though restrictions on material will be rare in our treatment, we will utilize the three traditional divisions of written works to distinguish between types of material. You as a student reader will be reading either poetry, prose, or drama. Physical structure of the written work normally determines whether the writing is poetry, prose, or drama.

Prose

The great majority of human writing is in the area of *prose*. Simply defined, prose is all forms of recorded human thought in writing which are free of the limitations of verse structure in poetry and the confines of dialogue in drama. Prose may flow in rhythmic pattern much like poetry; yet, verse style is not a necessary component of prose.

Prose comes in wide varieties of packages. Novels, short stories, diaries, letters, memoirs, and narrative description are the most common carriers of prose writing available to the beginning reader. When considering material for a program of prose interpretation, the reader should explore all of these sources.

Following are two samples of prose which are both appropriate for oral reading purposes. The first, from Thoreau's *Walden*, is not fiction—it is a narrative description and explanation of life as experienced by the writer. The second is an actual testament by a prison inmate. Circumstances under which each was written are strikingly different; nonetheless, each is a meaningful communicative expression. Regardless of the differences in the nature of the two samples of prose, both relate a meaningful message from the author.

from WALDEN

Henry David Thoreau

I went to the woods because I wished to live deliberately, to front only the essential facts of life, and see if I could not learn what it had to teach, and not, when I came to die, discover that I had not lived. I did not wish to live what was not life, living is so dear; nor did I wish to practise resignation, unless it was quite necessary. I wanted to live deep and suck out all the marrow of life, to live so sturdily and Spartan-like as to put to rout all that was not life, to cut a broad swath and shave close, to drive life into a corner, and reduce it to its lowest terms, and, if it proved to be mean, why then to get the whole and genuine meanness of it, and publish its meanness to the world; or if it were sublime, to know it by experience, and be able to give a true account of it in my next excursion. For most men, it appears to me, are in a strange uncertainty about it, whether it is of the devil or of God, and have *somewhat hastily* concluded that it is the chief end of man here to 'glorify God and enjoy Him forever.'

1846

TESTAMENT

Clarence Harris

I was born in Mississippi, but my father and mother, being young and the parents of two children, a girl and boy, decided to escape to the promised land. They heard that there were golden opportunities in Memphis, Tennessee, and so they went there. My father acquired a skill as a house painter. His salary was $12 a week. My mother became a housekeeper at $6 a week. We lived in a clapboard shack with an outside toilet. The house set upon four tiers of bricks; inside we had oil lamps, coal stove, and no running water. I spent my time wandering the unpaved streets or playing in our packed-clay yard. I had an old dog, and together we played games of Caucasian heroes and villains. Funny how, as I look back, the villains were always darker than the heroes, with thick mustaches like my father wore, and almost always they were dressed in black clothes. I never realized that I was playing the villain in a much larger and serious game: that of emulation which had been passed on to me in my parents' ignorance and fear.

In the beginning I had very little contact with the white man. However, one particular incident sticks out in my mind even now. A white man, speeding through our street, ran over my dog. I screamed and the man stopped. My dad came out of the house to calm me down and to talk to the man, and that's when I discovered that men were different because of their skin color. The white man told my father: "Nigger, it should have been that little nigger there instead of the dog. You should've kept them both out of the street. And don't you ask me nothing about that dog!" My father shivered, and retreated with me into the house. We never mentioned the incident again. But from that time on I was taught that the white man was king and was to be treated as such; I learned that they were to be idolized, feared, catered to, and also to be emulated as much as possible without stepping out of your place.

Not long after that we prepared to move to another promised land, further North, where we would really be saved. The new state that we were moving to had been a dream, but soon after we arrived there, the bubble burst. The Northern promised land was only a larger plantation with buildings instead of fields. There were more white overseers and exploiters, and even though you didn't come under the domination of one man, you came under the rule of all white men; though they wouldn't physically hold you or punish you, the police were still their legal fist to hold you in line. Still, there were more subtle boundary lines, and the cruelest thing of all was their paternalism.

So I became a part of the black environment in the North that had a smattering of white middle-class bourgeois values, but I couldn't handle the unreality of trying to be white. And I took to the streets. There, we had our own thing, our own language, our own special walks, our hipness and our soul, which we attributed to heart and toughness, and the ability to survive. We wanted to be kings, too, but not kings of rats. By now, I had quit school, and I knew what was happening with whitey.

My father, and others like him, was told to vote for whoever the power structure wanted him to, or no jobs could be had. And those who had jobs were paying taxes for inferior schools, no garbage pickups, no police protection, and on and on and on. So I gave up and withdrew from the whole scene. Why should I follow the rules and conduct of such a hypocritical society? Naturally I ran head on into white power: the police. And eventually I came to prison.

In prison I began to think. I saw myself for what I was, which is completely different from what I am. I saw myself as what whitey had made me, which is completely different from what I am, and I saw society as it really is for making me what I was. And knowing all this, how can I be expected to accept this society that has tried to kill me, or its religion that makes a fool out of any black man.

And prison here is nothing but a smaller version of what's happening outside. There is just as much racism here, both openly and under cover, and just like on the outside, nothing is ever done about it but talk. I've been thinking. All this talking and protesting is just another one of whitey's trick bags, because when you protest and demonstrate and all the rest, it is understood that you believe that the people you're protesting to are really fair and honest and that once you make them see, then they'll apologize and take their feet off your neck. But once that belief fades and protesting ends, then revolution begins. And the belief is fading fast.

1970

Poetry

Our second classification of reading material is that of *poetry*. We will not be concerned with physical structure of poetry but only in terms of the ways it differs from prose and drama. We do not recommend that the beginning student reader attempt to scan poetry or measure its rhythm. Such an effort can provide a nearly insurmountable obstacle to discovery of meaning. Advanced students of literature and oral interpretation may find such activity very useful and meaningful. Our primary concern is with the communicative message expressed by the writer.

The beginning student of oral reading will find a wide variety of styles in poetry. While he may find some styles more conducive to pleasant reading, he should not become tied to any particular stylistic form. Search the poetry for meaning.

Following are two samples of poetry equally suitable for oral reading. The first, by Nancy Broom Brown, is an original student poem; the second is an expression from prison by Etheridge Knight, noted contemporary poet.

COMRADES

Nancy Broom Brown

This old dog could run faster than any rabbits in Kruger's
woods.
Then every night he bounded home to have me pick
cockleburrs from his paws.
My belly is his night-time burrow
as he retraces circles, tailor-marked
with pad prints on my yellowed shawl.
He lifts his head breast level, then nuzzles it into my armpit
and yawns with the corners of his mouth
pulling up to touch his eyes.

We rock into the night and listen to crickets
outside our window squeak tiny rocking chairs.
In his ear, he once had a tick which swelled up like a flashbulb
then finally splashed out on our cement porch.
When I used to bend over tomato plants, pulling weeds,
he'd run past me for the clover field
and stir dust between my legs.

Today I bend less than a fence post in October
and the only field he knows is on my lap.
Now we exchange milk bowls and huddle by the fire-light
spoiling each other with warmth.
Sometimes I think he gives me more
than four sons who forget my birthday
and a man who left me with calloused hands.
I'm a ragdoll as my dangling legs stretch for the floor
to push the chair and our weight again.

We rock with night
invited crickets pull up chairs beside us
and rub their wings together
like sandpaper fingers
to dry them in the warmth.

                                                        1973

HARD ROCK RETURNS TO PRISON FROM THE HOSPITAL FOR THE CRIMINAL INSANE

Etheridge Knight

Hard Rock was "known not to take no shit
From nobody," and he had the scars to prove it:
Split purple lips, lumped ears, welts above
His yellow eyes, and one long scar that cut
Across his temple and plowed through a thick
Canopy of kinky hair.

The WORD was that Hard Rock wasn't a mean nigger
Anymore, that the doctors had bored a hole in his head,
Cut out part of his brain, and shot electricity
Through the rest. When they brought Hard Rock back,
Handcuffed and chained, he was turned loose,
Like a freshly gelded stallion, to try his new status.

And we all waited and watched, like indians at a corral,
To see if the WORD was true.

As we waited we wrapped ourselves in the cloak
Of his exploits: "Man, the last time, it took eight
Screws to put him in the Hole." "Yeah, remember when he
Smacked the captain with his dinner tray?" "He set
The record for time in the Hole—67 straight days!"
"OI Hard Rock! man, that's one crazy nigger."
And then the jewel of a myth that Hard Rock had once bit
A screw on the thumb and poisoned him with syphilitic spit.

The testing came, to see if Hard Rock was really tame.
A hillbilly called him a black son of a bitch
And didn't lose his teeth, a screw who knew Hard Rock
From before shook him down and barked in his face.
And Hard Rock did *nothing*. Just grinned and looked silly,
His eyes empty like knot holes in a fence.

And even after we discovered that it took Hard Rock
Exactly 3 minutes to tell you his first name,
We told ourselves that he had just wised up,
Was being cool; but we could not fool ourselves for long,
And we turned away, our eyes on the ground. Crushed.

He had been our Destroyer, the doer of things
We dreamed of doing but could not bring ourselves to do,
The fears of years, like a biting whip,
Had cut grooves too deeply across our backs.

1970

Drama

Our third category of reading material is drama. *Drama* refers to writing restricted to dialogue or script for one or more characters. The student reader has available to him a wide variety of types of plays which can make excellent oral reading material. Once again, however, our stress is in the communicative message transmitted by the playwright. Certainly classical plays make excellent reading material, but the student should strive to select a play for reading which has meaning he can relate to his own interests and needs.

As a sample of quality material for use in reading drama, we are including below the sleepwalking scene from Shakespeare's *Macbeth*.

from **MACBETH**

William Shakespeare

Act V, scene i: Enter a Doctor of Physic and a Waiting Gentlewoman

DOCTOR   I have two nights watched with you, but can perceive no truth in your report. When was it she last walked?

GENTLEWOMAN   Since his majesty went into the field, I have seen her rise from her bed, throw her night-gown upon her, unlock her closet, take forth paper, fold it, write upon't, read it, afterwards seal it, and again return to bed; yet all this while in a most fast sleep.

DOCTOR   A great perturbation in nature, to receive at once the benefit of sleep and do the effects of watching! In this slumb'ry agitation, besides her walking and other actual performances, what, at any time, have you heard her say?

GENTLEWOMAN   That, sir, which I will not report after her.

DOCTOR   You may to me, and 'tis most meet you should.

GENTLEWOMAN   Neither to you nor anyone, having no witness to confirm my speech.

(Enter Lady Macbeth with a taper)

Lo you, here she comes! This is her very guise, and, upon my life, fast asleep. Observe her; stand close.

DOCTOR   How came she by that light?

GENTLEWOMAN   Why, it stood by her; she has light by her continually, 'tis her command.

DOCTOR   You see her eyes are open.

GENTLEWOMAN   Ay, but their sense are shut.

DOCTOR   What is it she does now? Look how she rubs her hands.

GENTLEWOMAN   It is an accustomed action with her, to seem thus washing her hands. I have known her continue in this a quarter of an hour.

LADY MACBETH   Yet here's a spot.

DOCTOR   Hark! she speaks. I will set down what comes from her, to satisfy my remembrance the more strongly.

LADY MACBETH   Out, damned spot! out, I say!—One; two. Why, then, 'tis time to do't.—Hell is murky.—Fie, my lord, fie! a soldier, and afeard? What need we fear who knows it, when none can call our power to accompt?—Yet who would have thought the old man to have had so much blood in him?

DOCTOR   Do you mark that?

LADY MACBETH   The Thane of Fife had a wife; where is she now?— What, will these hands ne'er be clean?—No more o' that, my lord, no more o' that! You mar all with this starting.

DOCTOR   Go to, go to; you have known what you should not.

GENTLEWOMAN   She has spoke what she should not, I am sure of that. Heaven knows what she has known.

LADY MACBETH   Here's the smell of the blood still: all the perfumes of Arabia will not sweeten this little hand. O, O, O!

DOCTOR   What a sigh is there! The heart is sorely charged.

GENTLEWOMAN   I would not have such a heart in my bosom for the dignity of the whole body.

DOCTOR   Well, well, well.

GENTLEWOMAN   Pray God it be, sir.

DOCTOR	This disease is beyond my practice. Yet I have known those which have walked in their sleep who have died holily in their beds.
LADY MACBETH	Wash your hands, put on your night-gown, look not so pale: I tell you yet again, Banquo's buried; he cannot come out on's grave.
DOCTOR	Even so?
LADY MACBETH	To bed, to bed; there's knocking at the gate. Come, come, come, come, give me your hand. What's done cannot be undone. To bed, to bed, to bed!
DOCTOR	Will she go now to bed?
GENTLEWOMAN	Directly.

Exit.

DOCTOR	Foul whisp'rings are abroad. Unnatural deeds Do breed unnatural troubles. Infected minds To their deaf pillows will discharge their secrets. More needs she the divine than the physician. God, God forgive us all! Look after her, Remove from her the means of all annoyance, And still keep eyes upon her. So, good night. My mind she has mated, and amazed my sight. I think, but dare not speak.

Gentlewoman
Good night, good doctor.

(*Exeunt*)

1606

SUMMARY PROBES

1. Why is it not wise to force a student to read a specified selection?
2. What is the primary criteria determining acceptability of material?
3. What are various types of writing which would qualify as prose?
4. Why shouldn't a beginning reader make an effort to scan poetry for rhythmic or metric measurement?
5. How does drama differ from both prose and poetry?

LEARNING ACTIVITIES

1. Compose a list of all the instances in your memory in which you participated either as a reader or listener in reading situations. From this list attempt to arrive at a personal conclusion as to how significant oral reading has been in your life.

2. Bring several examples of prose, poetry, and drama to class. Be prepared to discuss the differences in the three types of material. How might these differences affect the oral reader?

TWO

GOALS   After completing this chapter you will be able to:

1. Realize why many people possess and display a negative attitude toward reading aloud.

2. Understand how interests of the reader can and should play a major role in the reader's selection of material.

3. Understand that the abilities of the reader impose limitations on selection of material.

4. Realize and practice listener analysis as a primary factor determining selection of material.

5. Understand the importance of honoring copyrights on materials.

What Should I Read

Selecting Material

Let us assume that you have received a class assignment to do an oral reading of a specified length in which you are to select some appropriate material as we have defined it in the preceding chapter. The task of selecting material presents a monumental problem for many students—especially beginning students in oral reading.

Many of us have had our interest and enthusiasm for literature stifled in earlier years of education when forced to memorize passages from literature for recall. Many have not been taught to select literary material for their own personal enjoyment based on relevance and meaning in the material for themselves. Far too often the student in elementary years, high school, or even college, is asked to read and analyze material based on the personal likes and dislikes of the instructor, rather than on the personal likes and dislikes of the reader. Instead, these selections should only be determined after an organized search for material appropriate for the reader.

To illustrate the approach in the past, we can well imagine that an overwhelming majority of Americans who have completed eight years of public education know that the opening words of Lincoln's address in Gettysburg are "Forescore and seven years ago . . .". Yet how many of those same people know that Lincoln was really saying eighty-seven years ago? Memorizing recitations puts the emphasis on words, not meanings.

It is our belief that written words set down by a human being at some point in the past are, in a sense, living entities. As long as they remain as written words enclosed between the covers of a book they fail to possess the degree of life and vibrance accomplished by the oral reader. Words, even those written by others, come to life in full meaning when an interpreter reads them aloud in an effort to retain as much of the original perceived meaning of the writer as well as injecting supplementary meaning.

As a result of early experiences, many of us feel that literature is a dead and dry subject. Some perceive the poet to be an anemic, thin individual who sits under a tree wearing horn-rimmed glasses and writes about the sky, birds, and trees. The unfortunate reality is that a person who has come to feel thus about literature most likely has cause to do so. He or she has probably been taught, perhaps unintentionally, to perceive literature in that manner.

In this chapter we will discuss the problem of selecting material for oral reading situations. Two categories of concerns will be covered: those affecting the reader and those affecting the listener, both as they relate to the reader's eventual choice of material. At the conclusion of the chapter you will find samples of contemporary and more seasoned material which may interest many, but none of which conforms to the "dull and dry" stereotype of literature held by many.

READER CONCERNS

As with selecting a topic for a speech or any other communicative situation, the first and most logical source of topic is within the communicator, or in our case, the reader. Two factors relating to the reader are of crucial concern: the interests of the reader and the abilities of the reader.

Interests of the Reader

In a communication model conceived by Wilbur Schramm[1] we discover that every living person has what Schramm refers to as a field of experience. We also learn that no two human beings have identical fields of experience, and also, that no two human beings have totally differing fields of experience. In simple communicative situations involving social and interactive settings, the message transmitted from one to another must fall into an area of similarity between fields of experiences or communication is nearly impossible.

The concept of a field of experience relates well to the task facing you in selecting material. You must find a piece of writing that falls within your personal field of experience. We all have certain topics that interest us a great deal more than others. The astounding thing about the world of literature is that virtually every topic known to man has been the subject of someone's writing. Our task is to search out that topic or topics which overlap with our personal field of experience.

You might be saying to yourself at this point—"I've read lots of literature in my life and I haven't found any that interests me." Our response would be that you haven't read enough, or that you have been reading in the wrong places.

You who find little interest in topics other than sports would do well to look at some of the recent writings of Howard Cosell.[2] He has provided some quite acceptable prose material for oral reading. Some would no doubt question Howard Cosell as a literary writer; however, in our broad definition of the term (as expressed earlier and as will be expressed again and again), if there is meaningful communication involved in a person's writing, it is indeed literary in the communicative sense of the word.

If outdoor life is your "bag," many writers have spent lifetimes depicting in words outdoor scenes all over the world. If you are a "horror and gore" fan, start with the writing of such recognized literary writers as Edgar Allan Poe and work up to many contemporary writers who have brought numerous stories to the motion-picture screen and television.

The point summarized here is that regardless of what area a person's interests may fall in, someone at some time has written about topics related to that interest. You cannot use the "copout" that nothing interests you as an excuse for not enjoying and participating in oral reading to others.

Your task, then, is twofold. First, you must determine what your interests are. For some this may be an easy task; for others it may require some form of self-inventory. Second, once personal interests are determined, you face the task of a search for material overlapping that interest. Throughout your search keep one point firmly in mind: regardless of your interests, the material to match it exists somewhere in the massive volumes of the printed page.

Abilities of the Reader

Once you have determined your specific interests and have discovered material believed to coincide with those interests, you then face the task of determining if your physical ability will allow you to bring the communicative message of the writer effectively to the listener via reading aloud.

Whether an anticipated reading is intended for a graded classroom assignment or for competition in a reading event, every reader should recognize that he or she is physically incapable of reading some material. Nothing is more disheartening to an instructor in a classroom situation or a judge in a contest situation than to suffer through the experience of listening to a very talented reader struggle through a selection much too difficult for the reader.

We will consider four questions relating to reader abilities that you should ask yourself before making a final selection of material for oral reading.

Are there too many characters in the selection to be interpreted effectively? Not all selections chosen will require considering this question. In such instances, however, when the selection includes multiple characters and a need for the listener to be able to distinguish clearly between those characters, you must resolve this question.

Specific practices and techniques available to the reader in distinguishing characters will be a matter for consideration at this point. The reader has two methods of character differentiation available for his use.

First, you can utilize physical movement and placement of characters with a variety of bodily actions or locations associated with each character. Limitations inherent in this method are obvious. Bodily and physical differentiation of characters can be used effectively for two or, perhaps, three characters. However, if the total goes beyond three, the capacity of the reader to utilize the body for differentiation is severely limited.

Second, the reader can utilize his voice to produce clear differentiation between specific characters. Limitations for application of this method are not as rigid and well fixed. Some readers might very well differentiate between four, five, or six characters by using the voice. Others with a vocal range not so flexible will have difficulty with even two.

The question concerning numbers of characters to be differentiated must eventually be answered by you, the reader, when you fully comprehend your limitations in ability. If you have question concerning your ability with a particular selection, read it aloud for a friend or a group of friends and let them assist you in deciding if you are successful at keeping characters distinguished. If you have serious problems in character differentiation as a beginning reader, then, by all means, select a cutting which requires no character differentiation.

Are vocal emotions required appropriate for you? Expression of emotion required in oral reading will differ greatly from one selection to another. Some beginning readers have a great amount of vocal flexibility in expressing emotions; others do not. Read your selection several times to identify the variety of emotions required. Practice, again on a cooperative friend, expressing those emotions with your voice, assisted by bodily action. Then consider the question as to whether or not you are successful at expressing different emotions in the same selection. If you come to the conclusion that your abilities are insufficient to interpret a specific selection, select another which has emotional content to match your capabilities.

The beginning reader should not feel that a seeming inability to express emotions adequately through the voice indicates a permanent liability in oral reading. One of the most effective methods of voice training in emotional expression is practice and experience at reading various kinds of material. The point to be stressed here is that as a beginning reader, you should not require too much of your vocal and bodily ability. As you continue to read, you may be amazed at what your voice and body can be trained to do.

Does the reading require dialect or accent too difficult for you? Many entertaining and interesting selections may demand interpretation of dialect or nationality accent which is too difficult for the reader. Normally if dialect is used in writing, such dialect is necessary for full meaning of the selection. The reader is not usually free to "localize" the dialect at will.

Once again, the beginning reader should practice reading the selection aloud attempting to employ the dialect as intended in the text. The primary question for the reader to consider in determining his ability to use a dialect is not "Does it sound good when I read it?" Rather the reader should ask himself, "Does the meaning, intended by the writer, emerge when I use the dialect?" A negative answer to this question should set the reader on a renewed search for material.

Do your life experiences "measure up" to life experiences related in the selection? The reader should consider if his or her own personal experiences or field of experience is sufficient to transfer meaning of experiences expressed in the selection. We do not mean to say that a reader should never read a selection expressing reactions to or feelings toward a life experience that he has not personally experienced. We do mean, however, that the reader should be aware of this question and consider it before making a final selection.

If your selection requires that you express human feeling at the time of the death of a close relative and you have never experienced that loss, you may have difficulty in transmitting that feeling. Perhaps, though, you have been sensitive enough to losses of others that you can adequately express that feeling.

If your selection requires that you relate feelings of loneliness experienced by an old and forgotten person, you may have difficulty. If, however, you have made yourself aware of this feeling in others by those close to you or in your reading, you may have little or no difficulty at expressing such loneliness to listeners.

Again, we ask the reader to consider the question of similarity of personal experiences and those expressed in writing. Only the reader can make the final determination as to his ability to transmit those experiences.

SUMMARY PROBES

1. **How does the concept of "field of experience" in the communication process as developed by Wilbur Schramm relate to a reader's selection of material?**
2. **What methods are available to the reader for interpreting clear character differentiation in a selection?**
3. **What special problems may face the reader if his selection requires the use of a dialect?**
4. **Must a reader actually experience all life situations he attempts to interpret for others?**

LISTENER CONCERNS

In addition to being aware of concerns within the self, the reader has the normal communicative obligation to his listener. We have confirmed that oral reading is communication; thus, the reader must be very much aware of his listener and be able to answer certain questions concerning his needs and wishes.

Listener Interest

The reader must consider whether or not the subject matter of his selection will interest the listener. While it is of primary importance that the selection for reading coincide with the reader's interests, the listener's field of experience must be taken into account as well.

Many factors of listener analysis need to be considered by the reader. The age, sex, occupation, economic status, as well as religious and political affiliation are considerations that will assist the reader in making final selection of material for public reading.

Attractive Physical Characteristics

While material utilizing dialogue, multiple characters, and accents may be more difficult for the reader, they are also more attention serving for the listener. Long passages of narrative and description may be physically easy for the reader; however, the listener may find such long passages dull and dry.

You have, no doubt, experienced the feeling of turning a page in a book and finding that both pages have long narratives with few paragraph breaks. Our reaction to this as a silent reader is very different from the situation in which we turn a page to discover the next two abound with quotation marks indicating dialogue between or among several characters. Listeners to oral reading tend to respond in much the same way as a silent reader would to long passages of narrative or description.

Offensive Nature of Selection

It is an obligation of an oral reader in a communicative setting not to offend his listeners through his choice of material. The reader must make some form of mental assessment of his listeners to determine what will or will not offend them. There are three primary dangers facing the reader relating to offending listeners.

Subject Matter. The subject matter of the entire selection may be offensive to members of your listening group. Especially in contemporary literature, the definition of acceptable subject matter has become much more liberal for popular writing. Several years ago one would have had to search long and hard to find articles other than academic or pornographic treating the subject of homosexuality. Novels, dramas, or poetry treating the subject would have been reserved for "adult" book stores.

Such is not the case today. Many meaningful and worthwhile messages on the subject of homosexuality are being transmitted today through the channels of popular writing. Such a selection may be quite appropriate for a specific audience; however, another group may find the subject to be in poor taste and react negatively toward the reader.

Specific Language. A slightly different problem faces the reader in the area of specific language. While the overall subject matter of a selection may be quite appropriate for most audiences, certain specific phrases may be questionable. The use of profanity and vulgarity in a selection presents a problem to the reader that only he can resolve after consideration of the physical and psychological attributes of the audience.

Again, although public acceptance of specific types of language has increased in the recent past, it may not be as agreeable as some readers might think. The reader must make the ultimate decision after careful consideration of the audience. If a selection contains questionable language, such language may not be essential to the meaning. If such is the case the reader may omit or revise such wording providing permission from the copyright holder is granted.

In some cases the use of questionable language may be essential to the selection. If that be the case, the reader should choose another selection if he determines the language inappropriate. The author has been appalled to hear a selection renamed *Darn Yankees* and a famous line in a famous play changed to "Out, darn spot."

Dialect or Accent.   While the use of dialect or accent can present physical problems for the reader, listener problems may also be present. If the use of a dialect or accent ridicules or humiliates a particular group or nationality, it might not be appropriate if members of that group will be in the audience.

The question as to whether a selection will offend listeners or not may be difficult to answer. A good rule of thumb for beginning readers to follow is that if you harbor a reasonable doubt as to the selection's appropriateness, you probably should make another selection.

LITERARY MERIT AND LEGALITIES

Before concluding this chapter, you should consider two additional points concerning our discussion of literature. They are literary quality and copyrights.

Literary Quality

Much is heard concerning the literary quality of material selected for oral reading. Our premise is that literary quality is determined by communicative meaning of the material rather than age of the material or name of the author.

Certainly some famous literary names provide immediate acceptance of writing as "quality" literature. Even though William Shakespeare produced a wealth of poetry and drama, not everything he wrote is either appropriate or meaningful for oral reading experiences.

The essential criterion applied to any writing to establish its literary merit is: "What does this writing say to the reader or listener?" If meaningful communication exists, it is worthy literature for oral reading.

COPYRIGHTS

By now you have certainly deduced that unless you find a selection to fit a specific time limit you will most likely have to cut or extract a segment for your reading purposes. In using any material which is under copyright and certainly in altering any material under copyright, keep in mind that you may have to obtain permission from the copyright holder to do so. Obviously, material that might be used without permission in a classroom situation may require written permission for contest or public performance purposes. A general rule is that if you have any doubts at all concerning copyright of a piece of work, you are obligated to determine if permission is necessary.

Some companies provide catalogues and actual cuttings already prepared for oral reading. Material obtained from these companies is permissible to use for student reading purposes. If, however, you make your own cutting from material which is not listed with such companies, the responsibility of obtaining permission may be solely yours. Do not overlook it.

SUMMARY   1. **What are three ways that a reader's listeners**
PROBES   **might be offended by the chosen material?**
          2. **What are the criteria to be applied to any writing**
             to establish its literary quality?
          3. **What general rule should be followed in relationship to copyrights?**

SAMPLE SELECTIONS

Several selections demonstrating the variety that exists in writing which may be appropriate for oral reading follow. First, we have included original poems by student poets written in an educational setting. Contemporary selections by Erica Jong and Etheridge Knight follow the student poems.

The second sample is a cutting from a contemporary and controversial novel and movie, The Exorcist. The scene relates the priest's first meeting with the possessed girl. Two contemporary narratives concerning contrasting views of prison life follow the selection from The Exorcist. The humorous opening scene from Neil Simon's The Prisoner of Second Avenue depicts modern life in a major city.

Finally, an excerpt from "Poor Richard's Almanack" by Benjamin Franklin and selected letters by W. C. Fields provide examples of materials written in the form of memoirs or personal correspondence. All selections represent a wide variety of types of writing appropriate for oral reading.

FROM OUTSIDE COLORADO

Ray Schmudde

We were camped outside Silverton,
in our tent, prisoners of a four day rain.
Over ten thousand feet
we could see our breath at noon.

Inside our shelter bedrolls were damp
and hot meals remained memories
as we read to pass the time,
cramped and anxious for the slowing of the drops.

Boredom forced us to chance
the roads into town that night
where we ate at the hotel
and bought a newspaper for dessert.

We saw a play at the cafe
and afterwards there was beer and bluegrass
for the tourists and townies.
We were neither so we left.

Stars were out and cold
bounced at us off wet streets.
We saw promise for tomorrow,
would pack and be gone soon.

Halfway back the road was blocked.
There was a wreck. A car
had rolled many times and the sheriff
turned us back toward town.

We crept back to the cafe,
the party still in session.
They were surprised to see us,
the campers, back so soon.

The few who listened to our story
were bored with the party
and with Colorado, as we watched
the sheriff tow the wreck into town.

We left then, driving from town
and past the bend of broken glass.
The road was drying and we saw
the moon for the first time.

The next morning was warm and dry
as we packed to leave, finally moving,
driving north away from town
on a road we had never seen.

1974

MADNESS

Heather J. Straka

Fumbling furiously through
phrases written by other
poets
I pause
close the book
bite my tongue scream
slam my palm on the desk
and rise to the top
of that agitated gesture
undress, swoop into bed
and find my unwritten poem
lying furiously fast asleep
beside me.

I reach to enclose the phrase
we make.
And he creates a parenthesis.

1971

THE PRISONER

Erica Jong

The cage of myself clamps shut.
My words turn the lock.

I am the jailer rattling the keys.
I am the torturer's assistant
who nods & smiles
& pretends not
to be responsible.

I am the clerk who stamps
the death note
affixing the seal, the seal, the seal.

I am the lackey who "follows orders."
"*I have not got the authority.*"

I am the visitor
who brings a cake, baked
with a file.

Pale snail,
I wave between the bars.
I speak of rope with the hangman.
I chatter of sparks & currents
with the electrician.
Direct or alternating,
he is beautiful.

I flatter him.
I say he turns me on.

I tell the cyanide capsules
they have talent
& may fulfill themselves someday.
I read the warden's awful novel
& recommend a publisher.

I sleep with the dietician
who is hungry.
I sleep with the hangman
& reassure him
that he is a good lover.

I am the ideal prisoner

I win prizes on my conduct.
They reduce my sentence.
Now it is only 99 years
with death like a dollop
of whipped cream at the end.
I am so grateful.

No one remembers
that I constructed this jail
& peopled its cells.
No one remembers my blueprints
& my plans,
my steady hammering,
my dreams of fantastic escapes.

& even I,
patiently writing away,
my skin yellowing
like the pages of old paperbacks,
my hair turning gray,
cannot remember the first crime,
the crime
I was born for.

                    1973

THE IDEA OF ANCESTRY

Etheridge Knight

1

Taped to the wall of my cell are 47 pictures: 47 black
faces: my father, mother, grandmothers (1 dead), grand
fathers (both dead), brothers, sisters, uncles, aunts,
cousins (1st & 2nd), nieces, and nephews. They stare
across the space at me sprawling on my bunk. I know

their dark eyes, they know mine. I know their style,
they know mine. I am all of them, they are all of me;
they are farmers, I am a thief, I am me, they are thee.

I have at one time or another been in love with my mother,
1 grandmother, 2 sisters, 2 aunts (1 went to the asylum),
and 5 cousins. I am now in love with a 7 yr old niece
(she sends me letters written in large block print, and
her picture is the only one that smiles at me).

I have the same name as 1 grandfather, 3 cousins, 3 nephews,
and 1 uncle. The uncle disappeared when he was 15, just took
off and caught a freight (they say). He's discussed each year
when the family has a reunion, he causes uneasiness in
the clan, he is an empty space. My father's mother, who is 93
and who keeps the Family Bible with everybody's birth dates
(and death dates) in it, always mentions him. There is no
place in her Bible for "whereabouts unknown."

2

Each Fall the graves of my grandfathers call me, the brown
hills and red gullies of mississippi send out their electric
messages, galvanizing my genes. Last yr/like a salmon quitting
the cold ocean—leaping and bucking up his birthstream/I
hitchhiked my way from L.A. with 16 caps in my pocket and a
monkey on my back. and I almost kicked it with the kinfolks.
I walked barefooted in my grandmother's backyard/I smelled the old
land and the woods/I sipped cornwhiskey from fruit jars with the men/
I flirted with the women/I had a ball till the caps ran out
and my habit came down. That night I looked at my grandmother
and split/my guts were screaming for junk/but I was almost
contented/I had almost caught up with me.
(The next day in Memphis I cracked a croaker's crib for a fix.)

This yr there is a gray stone wall damming my stream, and when
the falling leaves stir my genes, I pace my cell or flop on my bunk
and stare at 47 black faces across the space. I am all of them,
they are all of me, I am me, they are thee, and I have no sons
to float in the space between.

1970

2 POEMS FOR BLACK RELOCATION CENTERS

Etheridge Knight

I

Flukum couldn't stand the strain. Flukum
wanted inner and outer order, so
he joined the army where U.S. Manuals made
everything plain—even how to button his shirt,
and how to kill the yellow men. (If Flukum
ever felt hurt or doubt about who his enemy
was, the Troop Information Officer or the Stars
and Stripes straightened him out.)
Plus, we must not forget
that Flukum was paid well to let the Red
Blood. And sin? If Flukum ever thought about sin
or Hell for squashing the yellow men, the good Chaplain
(Holy by God and by Congress) pointed out with
Devilish skill that to kill the colored men was not
altogether a sin.

Flukum marched back from the war, straight and tall,
and with presents for all: a water pipe for daddy,
teeny tea cups for mama, sheer silk for tittee, and
jade inlaid dagger for me. But, with a smile
on his face in a place just across the bay,
Flukum, the patriot, got shot that same day,
got shot in his great wide chest, bedecked with good
conduct ribbons. He died surprised, he had thought
the enemy far away on the other side of the sea.

(When we received his belongings they took away my dagger.)

II

Dead. He died in Detroit, his beard
was filled with lice; his halo glowed
and his white robe flowed magnificently
over the charred beams and splintered glass;
his stern blue eyes were rimmed with red,
and full of reproach; and the stench: roasted rats
and fat baby rumps swept up his nose that
had lost its arch of triumph. He died outraged,

and indecently, shouting impieties and betrayals.
And he arose out of his own ashes. Stripped.
A faggot in steel boots.

1968

from THE EXORCIST

William Peter Blatty

Quickly reining back his revulsion, he closed the door. Then his eyes locked, stunned, on the thing that was Regan, on the creature that was lying on its back in the bed, head propped against a pillow while eyes bulging wide in their hollow sockets shone with mad cunning and burning intelligence, with interest and with spite as they fixed upon his, as they watched him intently, seething in a face shaped into a skeletal, hideous mask of mind-bending malevolence. Karras shifted his gaze to the tangled, thickly matted hair; to the wasted arms and legs; the distended stomach jutting up so grotesquely; then back to the eyes: they were watching him . . . pinning him . . . shifting now to follow as he moved to a desk and chair near the window.

"Hello, Regan," said the priest in a warm, friendly tone. He picked up the chair and took it over by the bed.

"I'm a friend of your mother's. She tells me that you haven't been feeling too well." He sat down. "Do you think you'd like to tell me what's wrong? I'd like to help you."

The eyes gleamed fiercely, unblinking, and a yellowish saliva dribbled down from a corner of her mouth to her chin. Then her lips stretched taut into a feral grin, into bow-mouthed mockery.

"Well, well, well," gloated Regan sardonically, and hairs prickled on the back of Karras' neck, for the voice was an impossibly deep bass thick with menace and power. "So it's you . . . they sent *you*! Well, we've nothing to fear from you at all."

"Yes, that's right. I'm your friend. I'd like to help," said Karras.

1971

AN OLD-TIMER LOOKS AT 42 YEARS BEHIND WALLS

R. L. Moseley

[Actually R. L. "Whitey" Moseley has been in prison for forty-three years. For the past year he has been a "trusty" outside the walls. Whitey is one of the most respected of the old-timers. He is a well-kept, self-possessed man of sixty-

three, with steely gray hair and a clear gaze. I don't know what crime he was convicted of. One does not ask Whitey Moseley such questions.—E.K.[3]]

The prison crouched between barren sand dunes in a remote and lonely corner of the state, a sprawling collection of unfeeling stone and grim, cold steel. The year was 1924, and I was twenty years old. Many men already knew it as twenty-three acres of venomous hate, surrounded by towering gray walls. As the grisly abode of 1,800 living dead, it seethed with raw, elemental passions spawned of colorless days and endless nights spent in a graveyard of human hope.

When the massive steel gates rolled open and a man was admitted to serve his time, his head was shorn of all hair; he was dressed in a coarse gray uniform and imprisoned in a tiny, almost bare cell. A deathly silence ruled the gloomy corridors of the prison in those days—broken only at given times by the racket of slamming cell doors in a cadence that plainly echoed the resentment stored in embittered hearts. One could feel the crushing weight of prison rule, the total suppression, as the iron jaws of the massive cellblocks worked at their ceaseless grinding on human souls. One strained his ears to catch a human sound, but there was none. All was still as the final grave. The spirit of the stoutest man felt annihilated.

The Silent System in effect then reduced everybody to using signs whenever communication was necessary. It was a piece of wry humor to raise the hand, receive a nod from the glum guard on his little raised dais in the shops, approach him and motion that one had to "go." A wooden paddle hung on a nail at his desk. The "goer" took the paddle and walked with it in hand to a two-closet affair shielded only by a halfway partition and hung the wooden paddle on the outside of the halfway door. The time that the paddle was returned to the desk indicated how long the "goer" had been absent from his task of work. [A task is a prescribed amount of work. E. K.] There was no chance for stalling, or goldbricking, for the paddle "snitched" by its very whereabouts.

The shops, under contract labor, contained many iron-wrought spittoons, for smoking in the shop was not allowed, and cigarettes were unheard of. Prisoners chewed tobacco while at work, and used the spittoons on occasion to clobber some enemy when arguments or differences cropped up. Tension was always at a high peak, as each man literally slaved over his task. Despite the Silent System, men did manage to communicate, for on Saturdays, in season, tier by tier of men marched to the drill ground to watch a baseball game. Under the broiling sun they sat bunched together on wooden benches, unable to smoke because smoking was forbidden anyplace save three times a night in the cells. A kind of cellblock trusty passed a light from cell to cell, carrying a flaming torch like the eternal flame used at the Olympics.

Mail and a weekly newspaper were excessively censored, with items cut out or obliterated by the censors. It was a violation of rules to have a pencil, ink, paper, or anything in the tiny cells, excepting a towel, two library books, comb, and a piece of soap. The walls were barren of pictures—a *rocking* chair, a toilet bowl, and a wash basin were the only fixtures. Attendance at ball games, two-reel movies, and chapel was compulsory.

Everybody worked. The aged mended prisoners' sox, the lame led the blind around the grounds, picking up bits of stray paper and leaves. There was, it seemed, a heartless efficiency about routines, day after endless day, year upon colorless year. There being so little for diversion, the average inmate deteriorated, suffering from mental inertia, frustrated and oppressed by the futility of his daily existence.

The hundreds of ways in which the spirit of man was affected for no good by the negation, suppression, and total regimentation in those early years gradually disappeared, or altered their impact with the passage of time. About 1933 the federal government passed a law forbidding the shipment of prison-made goods out of the state; and that helped to abolish contract labor, and at the same time idled hundreds of men. Adjustments came. The Silent System was broken. Men began to look alive as they called or talked or whistled or sang as they pleased, except in the main dining room. It was 1942 before talking at meals was allowed. Many of the oppressive, petty and irksome rules were dropped—the prison took on an atmosphere of controlled but less rigorous living. Ah, it was still prison, but without the narrowness. By the simple expedient of the turning of official eyes, inmates were allowed to make their cells more livable: put up a few family pictures, secure a table, have pencils, pens, ink, paints, drafting equipment and hobby crafts.

Time has changed many things, but prison is still prison. It still crouches between barren sand dunes and the walls still hem in the men, killing their souls and crushing their spirits.

1970

OLD-TIMER, INSIDE 42 YEARS, SEES OUTSIDE

R. L. Moseley

The first day was a blur. Impressions crowded my mind like a movie screen gone haywire: cars whizzed by, people in street clothes, tall trees, the bright blue free air. All I distinctly remember is that I was nervous and sweating as the officer of the outside dormitory assigned my bunk, and that I spent the remainder of the afternoon at a window in the dormitory, looking down the highway. It was strange, and nice, to be able to see a distance without having my vision broken by walls. I slept well the first night, probably because of nervous exhaustion.

The next morning I reported for work. The boss said, "Whitey, you go with the potato detail today." So I jumped into this snazzy auto and was driven to Zorn's, located downtown. Zorn's is an old brewery, solid as a jail in construction. On the way I saw many homes reminiscent of free days long ago. Hundreds of autos of all shades and colors. Not much traffic, although Michigan City impressed me as a thriving community for its size. Saw one gal on the sidewalks. Weather was cold on this date, only a few people at large. Watched a guy tote a bale of hay to his car and dump it in on the nice upholstery. Passed several churches and a couple schools where the kids' bicycles were parked neatly in rows in the schoolyard.

Later in the day I took a leisurely ride about the limits of the state grounds. Stopped by the prison's cemetery, where about two hundred rest in separate graves, beneath identifying headstones. Did *not* select a lot at this time. Also visited the nearby greenhouse where flowers for the prison are grown. Imagine!

The next outing was to the prison's dairy farm—Summitt Farm, officially. It is located about nine miles from the prison and the ride was eye-filling. Zooming along the highway, past woods and lots, homes and farms, with here and there an auto sales yard floundering in all kinds of bargains for the early bird. Saw a freight train loaded with military equipment for Vietnam. Passed several motels, neon-lighted. The air was bracing, the sky somewhat overcast, but nothing could dampen my interest in the passing scene after forty-two years of bars and steel!

The grounds outside the walls are twice the size of the prison compound. I am assigned to what is called "general custody detail"—which means that you do any and everything. There are a few permanent assignments, but most of the guys out here have made parole and are waiting to go home. And while they wait, they work.

A coal pile as big as a mountain stares the initiate in the face, and with a smile he is handed a nice, big scoop shovel. Get with it, man, get with it! Muscles ache, bones creak, but that coal has got to go. Without it, the prison would have no heat, no lights, and no hot water. Dishes would remain dirty, laundry would go unwashed. Mighty important, yeah man!

There are lawns to mow, trees to plant, flowers to raise, grounds to clear of debris. Trucks fly to and fro, each with a load of sand or dirt or slop and innumerable errands all requiring a conveyance of one sort or another. There are birdhouses to build, squirrels to feed, officers' families to serve.

Is it raining? Snowing? Blowing? Pay it no mind, duty calls and, buddy, you'd better get with it. But actually, it's not as harsh a detail as all that. Time passes quickly with something to do. There are plenty of showers in the dormitory and a cot to flop on when you're beat out. After the day's work, there's television to watch, games to play and reading material to suit every taste. Mail call is important; some guys have been waiting a long time for a letter with the offer or guarantee of a job so that they can go home. It's a terrible mental strain to have made parole and then to be held here for lack of a job.

General custody detail operates under the direction of an outside captain, an outside deputy warden, and two regular officers. The idea of working at such a terrific pace, it is said, is to get the parolee in shape for any job he goes to when he is released. The pay is twenty cents per day, seven days a week. One half of this sum is held back until a man accumulates $35—which is *going home* money.

I was both pleased and saddened when the past month's clemency returns arrived a few days ago. In the first instance, a long-timer finally made the grade. He received a commutation of his life term after serving over thirty years. On the other hand, another lifer with over thirty-six years served was denied a commutation. One wonders what yardstick is used to determine a yea or a nay. Like the Little Fooler in the *Chicago Tribune,* you have to work hard at that one.

The plan to allow selected men to work outside and return to prison at night is gaining momentum in penal circles. I assume that by "selected" is meant those men who have paroles but who cannot secure employment. In any case, working for wages would be a boon and a boost to morale. The average person leaving prison today, unless he has other means, seldom has enough money to get himself a decent start. Men with families will be able to provide for them and also to save a little for themselves if this progressive step jells. I hope it does.

One time in *Reader's Digest* there was an article, written by a businessman, entitled, "Keep Your Convicts." The businessman claimed that inmates are trained on outmoded machines while imprisoned and are unable to operate modern machines when released. There is a great deal of truth in what he says, but what I see is the businessman's attitude toward prisoners who, by force, have to learn on the machines provided in the prisons of the land. In brief, the businessman would not want men released from servitude simply because he feels that they could not function in society. One wonders if he would make an investment in a potential labor pool and donate some modern machines to prison vocational shops?

If and when men reach the moon and it seems possible to establish communities thereon, look for the "drafting" of long-term prisoners. They will be "exiled" to the moon, to build roads, dig ditches, and prepare the land for the erection of buildings and homes. It will be cheap labor, easily commanded. I recall that when England settled Australia, prisoners were sent to that raw land for the very purpose cited. Exile. The oldest form of man's punishment for man. Ask Adam.

1970

from THE PRISONER OF SECOND AVENUE

Neil Simon

ACT 1

MEL   Ohhh, Christ Almighty.
      (*a light goes on in the bedroom. Edna, his wife, appears in her nightgown.*)

EDNA What's wrong?

MEL   Nothing's wrong.

EDNA Huh?

MEL   Nothing's wrong. Go back to bed.

EDNA Are you sure?

MEL   I'm sure. Go back to bed. (*Edna turns and goes back into the bedroom.*) Oh, God, God, God.
      (*Edna returns, putting on her robe. She flips the switch on the wall, lighting the room.*)

EDNA What is it? Can't you sleep?

MEL   If I could sleep, would I be sitting here calling God at two-thirty in the morning?

EDNA What's the matter?

MEL   Do you know it's twelve degrees in there? July twenty-third, the middle of a heat wave, it's twelve degrees in there.

EDNA I told you, turn the air conditioner off.

MEL   And how do we breathe? (*Points to the window*) It's eighty-nine degrees out there ... eighty-nine degrees outside, twelve degrees inside. Either way they're going to get me.

EDNA We could leave the air conditioner on and open the window. (*She goes into the kitchen*)

MEL   They don't work that way. Once the hot air sees an open window, it goes in.

EDNA   We could leave the air conditioner off for an hour. Then when it starts to get hot, we can turn it back on.

(*She comes out, eating from a jar of applesauce*)

MEL   Every hour? Seven times a night? That's a good idea. I can get eight minutes sleep in between working the air conditioner.

EDNA   *I'll* do it. *I'll* get up.

MEL   I asked you a million times to call that office. That air conditioner hasn't worked properly in two years.

EDNA   I called them. A man came. He couldn't find anything wrong.

MEL   What do you mean, nothing wrong? I got it on Low, it's twelve goddamned degrees.

EDNA   (*sits down, sighing*) It's not twelve degrees, Mel. It's cold, but it's not twelve degrees.

MEL   All right, seventeen degrees. Twenty-nine degrees. Thirty-six degrees. It's not sixty-eight, sixty-nine. A temperature for a normal person.

EDNA   (*sits on the sofa*) I'll call them again tomorrow.

MEL   Why do they bother printing on it High, Medium, and Low? It's all High. Low is High. Medium is High. Some night I'm gonna put it on High, they'll have to get a flamethrower to get us out in the morning.

EDNA   What do you want me to do, Mel? You want me to turn it off? You want me to leave it on? Just tell me what to do.

MEL   Go back to sleep.

EDNA   I can't sleep when you're tense like this.

MEL   I'm not tense. I'm frozen stiff. July twenty-third.

(*he sits down on the sofa*)

EDNA   You're tense. You were tense when you walked in the house tonight. You've been tense for a week. Would you rather sleep in here? I could make up the cot.

MEL   You can't even sit in here. (*picks up the small puff pillows from behind him*) Why do you keep these ugly little pillows on here? You spend eight hundred dollars for chairs and then you can't sit on it because you got ugly little pillows shoved up your back.

(*he throws one of the pillows on the floor*)

EDNA   I'll take the pillows off.

MEL   Edna, please go inside, I'll be in later.

EDNA It's not the air conditioner. It's not the pillows. It's something else. Something's bothering you. I've seen you when you get like this. What is it, Mel?

MEL (*rubs his face with his hands*) It's nothing. I'm tired. (*he gets up and goes over to the terrace door*)

EDNA I'm up, Mel, you might as well tell me.

MEL It's nothing, I'm telling you . . . I don't know. It's everything. It's this apartment, it's this building, it's this city. Listen. Listen to this. (*he opens the terrace door. We hear the sounds of traffic, horns, motors, etc.*) Two-thirty in the morning, there's one car driving around in Jackson Heights and we can hear it . . . Fourteen stories up, I thought it would be quiet. I hear the subway up here better than I hear it in the subway . . . We're like some kind of goddamned antenna. All the sound goes up through this apartment and then out to the city.

EDNA We've lived here six years, it never bothered you before.

MEL It's worse now, I don't know why. I'm getting older, more sensitive to sounds, to noise. Everything. (*he closes the door, then looks at himself*) You see this? I had that door opened ten seconds, you gotta wash these pajamas now.

EDNA (*anything to please*) Give them to me, I'll get you clean pajamas.

MEL (*pacing*) Two-thirty in the morning, can you believe that's still going on next door? (*he points to the wall*)

EDNA What's going on?

MEL What are you, trying to be funny? You mean to tell me you don't hear that?

EDNA (*puzzled*) Hear what?

MEL (*closer to the wall, still pointing*) That! That! What are you, deaf? You don't hear that?

EDNA Maybe I'm deaf. I don't hear anything.

MEL *Listen,* for God's sakes . . . You don't hear "Raindrops Falling on His Head?" (*he sings*) Da dum de dum da dum de da . . . "too big for his feet" . . . You don't hear that?

EDNA Not when you're singing, I don't hear it.

MEL (*stares at the wall*) It's those two goddamned German airline hostesses. Every night they got someone else in there. Two basketball players, two hockey players, whatever team is in town, win or lose, they wind up in there . . . Every goddamned night! . . . Somewhere there's a 747 flying around with people serving themselves because those two broads never leave that apartment. (*he grabs Edna, pulls her over to the wall*) Come here. You mean to tell me you don't hear that?

EDNA (*puts her ear against the wall*) Yes, now I hear it.

MEL You see! Is it any wonder I don't sleep at night?

EDNA (*moving away from the wall*) Don't sleep with your head next to the wall. Sleep in the bedroom.

MEL Hey, knock it off in there. It's two damn thirty in the lousy morning. (*he bangs on the wall, then stops and looks at it. He points to the wall*) Look at that, I cracked the wall. I barely touched it, the damned thing is cracked.

EDNA It was starting to crack before. There's a leak somewhere; one of the pipes upstairs is broken.

MEL A two-million-dollar building, you can't touch the walls? It's a good thing I didn't try to hang a picture; we all could have been killed.

EDNA They know about it. They're starting to fix it on Monday.

MEL (*he sits down*) Not Monday. Tomorrow. I want that wall fixed tomorrow, it's a health hazard. And they're going to repaint the whole wall, and if it doesn't match, they'll paint the rest of the room, and if that doesn't match, they'll do the rest of the apartment. And I'm not paying for it, you understand?

EDNA I'll tell them.

MEL And tell them about the air conditioner . . . and the window in the bedroom that doesn't open except when it rains and then you can't shut it until there's a flood and then tell them about our toilet that never stops flushing.

EDNA It stops flushing if you jiggle it.

MEL Why should I have to jiggle it? For the money I'm paying here do I have to stand over a toilet in the middle of the night and have to jiggle every time I go to the bathroom?

EDNA When you're through, get back into bed, tell me and *I'll* jiggle it.

MEL (*turns, glares at her*) Go to bed, Edna. I don't want to talk to you now. Will you please go to sleep.

EDNA I can't sleep if I know you're up here walking around having an anxiety attack.

MEL I'm not having an anxiety attack. I'm a little tense.

EDNA Why don't you take a Valium?

MEL I took one.

EDNA Then take another one.

MEL I took another one. They don't work any more.

(*he sits down in a chair*)

EDNA   *Two* Valiums? They *have* to work.

MEL   They don't work any more, I'm telling you. They're supposed to calm you down, aren't they? All right, am I calm? They don't work. Probably don't put anything in them. Charge you fourteen dollars for the word "Valium." (*he bangs on the wall*) Don't you ever fly anywhere? Keep somebody in Europe awake!

(*he bangs on the wall again with his fist*)

EDNA   Stop it, Mel. You're really getting me nervous now. What's wrong? Has something happened? Is something bothering you?

MEL   Why do we live like this? Why do we pay somebody hundreds of dollars a month to live in an egg box that leaks?

EDNA   You don't look well to me, Mel. You look pale. You look haggard.

MEL   I wasn't planning to be up.

(*he rubs his stomach*)

EDNA   Why are you rubbing your stomach?

MEL   I'm not rubbing it, I'm holding it.

EDNA   Why are you holding your stomach?

MEL   It's nothing. A little indigestion. It's that crap I had for lunch.

EDNA   Where did you eat?

MEL   In a health-food restaurant. If you can't eat health food, what the hell can you eat anymore?

EDNA   You're probably just hungry. Do you want me to make you something?

MEL   Nothing is safe any more. I read in the paper today two white mice at Columbia University got cancer from eating graham crackers. It was in *The New York Times.*

EDNA   Is that what's bothering you? Did you eat graham crackers today?

MEL   Food used to be so good. I used to love food. I haven't eaten food since I was thirteen years old.

EDNA   Do you want some food? I'll make you food. I remember how they made it.

MEL   I haven't had a real piece of bread in thirty years . . . If I knew what was going to happen, I would have saved some rolls when I was a kid. You can't breathe in here. (*he goes out onto the terrace*) Christ, what a stink. Fourteen stories up, you can smell the garbage from here. Why do they put garbage out in eighty-nine degree heat? Edna, come here, I want you to smell the garbage.

EDNA   (*comes to the door of the terrace*) I smell it, I smell it.

MEL   You can't smell it from there. Come here where you can smell it.

EDNA   (*walks to the edge of the terrace and inhales*) You're right. If you really want to smell it, you have to stand right here.

MEL   This country is being buried by its own garbage. It keeps piling up higher and higher. In three years this apartment is going to be the second floor.

EDNA   What can they do, Mel? Save it up and put it out in the winter? They have to throw it out sometime. That's why they call it garbage.

MEL   I can't talk to you. I can't talk to you any more.

EDNA   Mel, I'm a human being the same as you. I get hot, I get cold, I smell garbage, I hear noise. You either live with it or you get out.

         (*suddenly a dog howls and barks*)

MEL   If you're a human being you reserve the right to complain, to protest. When you give up that right, you don't exist any more. I protest to stinking garbage and jiggling toilets . . . and barking dogs. (*yells out*) Shut up, goddamnit.

EDNA   Are you going to stay here and yell at the dog? Because I'm going to sleep.

         (*the dog howls again*)

MEL   How can you sleep with a dog screaming like that? (*the dog howls again. Mel goes to the edge of the terrace and yells down*) Keep that dog quiet. There are human beings sleeping up here. Christ Almighty!!!!

VOICE   (*from above*) Will you be quiet. There are children up here.

MEL   (*yelling up*) What the hell are you yelling at me for? You looking for trouble, go down and keep the dog company.

EDNA   Mel, will you stop it! Stop it, for God's sakes!

MEL   (*comes back in; screams at Edna*) Don't tell *me* to stop it! DON'T TELL ME TO STOP IT!

EDNA   I don't know what's gotten into you. But I'm not going to stand here and let you take it out on me . . . If it's too much for you, take a room in the public library, *but don't take it out on me.* I'm going to sleep, *good night!!*

                                                                    1972

from POOR RICHARD'S ALMANACK

Benjamin Franklin

PREFACE TO POOR RICHARD, 1734

Courteous Readers,

Your kind and charitable Assistance last Year, in purchasing so large an Impression of my Almanacks, has made my Circumstances much more easy in the World, and requires my grateful Acknowledgement. My Wife has been enabled to get a Pot of her own, and is no longer oblig'd to borrow one from a Neighbour; nor have we ever since been without something of our own to put in it. She has also got a pair of Shoes, two new Shifts, and a new warm Petticoat; and for my part, I have bought a second-hand Coat, so good, that I am now not asham'd to go to Town or be seen there. These Things have render'd her Temper so much more pacifick than it us'd to be, that I may say, I have slept more, and more quietly within this last Year, than in the three foregoing Years put together. Accept my hearty Thanks therefor, and my sincere Wishes for your Health and Prosperity.

In the Preface to my last Almanack, I foretold the Death of my dear old Friend and Fellow-Student, the learned and ingenious Mr. *"Titan Leeds,"* which was to be on the 17th of *"October"* 1733, 3 h. 29 m. P.M. at the very Instant of the $\mathcal{O}$ of $\odot$ and $\mathcal{Q}$. By his own Calculation he was to survive till the 26th of the same Month, and expire in the Time of the Eclipse, near 11 o'clock A.M. At which of these Times he died, or whether he be really yet dead, I cannot at this present Writing positively assure my Readers; forasmuch as a Disorder in my own Family demanded my Presence, and would not permit me as I had intended, to be with him in his last Moments, to receive his last Embrace, to close his Eyes, and do the Duty of a Friend in performing the last Offices to the Departed. Therefore it is that I cannot positively affirm whether he be dead or not; for the Stars only show to the Skilful, what will happen in the natural and universal Chain of Causes and Effects, but 'tis well known, that the Events which would otherwise certainly happen at certain Times in the Course of Nature are sometimes set aside or postpon'd for wise and good Reasons by the immediate particular Dispositions of Providence; which particular *dispositions* the Stars can by no Means discover or foreshow. There is however (and I cannot speak it without Sorrow) there is the strongest Probability that my dear Friend is *no more;* for there appears in his Name, as I am assured, an Almanack for the Year 1734, in which I am treated in a very gross and unhandsome Manner; in which I am called a *false Predicter, an Ignorant, a conceited*

Scribler, a Fool, and a Lyar. Mr. *Leeds* was too well bred to use any Man so indecently and so scurrilously, and moreover his Esteem and Affection for me was extraordinary: So that it is to be feared that Pamphlet may be only a Contrivance of somebody or other, who hopes perhaps to sell two or three Year's Almanacks still, by the sole Force and Virtue of Mr. *"Leed's"* Name; but certainly, to put Words into the Mouth of a Gentleman and a Man of Letters, against his Friend, which the meanest and most scandalous of the People might be asham'd to utter even in a drunken Quarrel, is an unpardonable Injury to his Memory, and an Imposition upon the Publick.

Mr. *Leeds* was not only profoundly skilful in the useful Science he profess'd, but he was a Man of *exemplary Sobriety,* a most *sincere Friend,* and an *exact Performer of his Word.* These valuable Qualifications, with many others so much endear'd him to me, that although it should be so, that, contrary to all Probability, contrary to my Prediction and his own, he might possibly be yet alive, yet my Loss of Honour as a Prognosticator, cannot afford me so much Mortification, as his Life, Health and Safety would give me Joy and Satisfaction.

I am, *Courteous and Kind Reader*

Your poor Friend and Servant,
R. Saunders

Octob. 30, 1733   1733

LETTERS

W. C. Fields

January 22, 1940

Mr. Joe Breen,
c/o The Hays' Office,
5504 Hollywood Blvd.
Hollywood, Calif.

Dear Joe Breen:

Thanks for your graciousness and kindly counsel to Charlie Beyer this afternoon concerning the line in "My Little Chickadee": "I know what I'll do, I'll go to India and become a missionary. I hear there's good money in it too."

I'm still prepared to sacrifice a valuable part of my anatomy to keep the line in but if the short-haired women and the long-haired men are back in the driver's seat again, I guess there's nothing to be done.

Will this also have to be deleted from the European version or does that not come under your jurisdiction? I've got to get a laugh out of this picture somewhere even if it's down in India.

My best wishes and sincere thanks.

Bill Fields

P.S. I'm going to have Dave Chasen throw an Indian tsetse fly in your soup the next time you dine there for this overt act.

B. F.

January 25, 1940

Mr. Jack Gross
c/o Universal Studios
Universal City, Calif.

Dear Jack:

I thought the picture needed a little pepping up. There are three sequences which definitely slow up the picture: The whole cabaret scene; Miss West's ride in the carriage with Dick Foran; and the schoolroom scene. With these three out I think you have a picture.

My leaving the hotel, the brief scenes with the manager and the porter should definitely be kept in.

The doffing of my hat with reference to Mrs. Twillie has been eliminated, also where I say: "I sat her on my head so she might get a better view of the fighting." These should be put back in again.

The scene where I look at Bill Wolfe at the bar as they're making me sheriff and Dick Foran comes up, will get a big laugh if they hold it for two or three frames longer. It is unfortunate that there are so few people who know the timing of a laugh.

Can they pep up the line where I say to Zeb in the card game in answer to his question, "Is this a game of chance?" "Not the way I play it."

At the end of the Chicago Molly story, where I say "an elderly lady" just two or three frames more would make the difference between a yell and a titter.

Where I get in bed with the goat, could the caracul coat line be pepped up? I could not hear it.

The bicycle scene is out. It was a big laugh but I can see where you might run into difficulties here.

The scene where I tell them I'll go and get a posse is left hanging in midair, and should be finished inside the bedroom.

The gags about the full-blooded Indian and the cat's eye with Mrs. Gideon are out. Why are these eliminated? They are two big laughs and take up oh so few frames.

Would it be possible to pep up the line after Mrs. Gideon invites me to tea where I say: "Give me that bottle."

In the second poker game where I get one chip for my hundred dollars and where I shuffle the cards and they do not meet, you could almost cut immediately after that to the scene where Badger comes over with his roughs and they take me out to lump me up.

Two or three more people should go through where I try to kiss Mrs. Twillie after the wedding on the train. Here again the cutting ruins the timing and the joke completely where a few frames would have saved it.

If I am going to shoot the slingshot in the train, it is so easy to have an Indian fall off his horse at this juncture.

This is the last suggestion, bleat, will, document and codicil I shall make. Bring on the judges if there is a disagreement.

Bill Fields

February 22, 1940

Mr. Matty Fox
Universal Studios
Universal City, Calif.

Dear Honorable Gentleman:

China Boy would like to call your attention to article on editorial page of the "Evening Press" captioned "Our Neighbors." You will note that in some localities among our dear Latin neighbors to the South, there is more than 90% in some instances illiterate (meaning can't read or write) and yet some [crossed out: son-of-a-bitch] gentleman who is supposed to represent South America objects to my saying "Chiquita" because I do not pronounce the word properly.

This is the God-damndest excuse I have ever heard for cutting a gag out of a picture. I still do not believe that is the reason because it is absurd and it is most disheartening to start a picture knowing that someone is going to tamper with your gags and cut them out for no reason—not only cut them out in South America but to delete them in our U.S.A. and Europe, not to mention the Antipedes and the Coca Islands.

Whilst gazing into my crystal ball this morning I saw Miss West complaining that it might hurt her scene with Calleia if I said "Chiquita." I still contend whoever made up the South American story is a neophyte as a raconteur.

Will you as a special favor to me just to satisfy my girlish curiosity tell me why this gag was cut out of the picture?

I am enclosing in this letter as an extra feature a page from "Click's Guide" showing honorable executives pounding their ear at a preview. The camera doesn't lie.

Best wishes, in which Charlie joins me,

Ever thine and forth hence,
Wilhelmina,
THE LONE STAR

March 21, 1940

Mr. Walter Winchell
c/o New York Daily Mirror
New York, N. Y.

Dear Walter:

Why did you print this?
"W. C. Fields and Mae West ought to go to the woodshed for 'My Little Chickadee.' Each is so busy hogging footage that the story gets stamped to death—not that it doesn't deserve to . . ."

Just to get in the line "the story gets stamped to death—not that it doesn't deserve to . . . ?" Not unfunny. The story of "Chickadee" isn't really so bad but no one can conscientiously object to your saying it is if you don't like it, but there is absolutely no hogging. This is a deliberate, uncalled-for, unjust defamation and a bit of malice, printed probably as a favor to one of your friends.

The ranks of tongue-wagging women and weak men are dwindling fast and will soon become as extinct as the dodo. Can't you see the handwriting on the wall? Haven't you all this time felt like the lowly rodent? If you wish to do some excoriating, tell them about your cowardice—how you carried a big gunman or bodyguard either in your car or on your running board (after Jolson smacked your nose) for fear someone would say, "Boo!" and you'd faint. Don't be a little schmuck all your life. Don't be like that cowardly fish of the jellyfish family (I'm a little rusty on my ichthyology and can't recall the name for the moment) which when it is frightened, runs and exudes a smelly, inky substance to cover up its trail.

You are continually waving the American flag and glorying in our freedom. Let's have a little more freedom from unjust attacks in the newspapers for American citizens who have no power to strike back at you or your ilk in a like manner. Less freedom of the press and more freedom for the people from lies in the press.

I am enclosing some more adolescent scrivening by your worthy contemporary, Jimmy Fidler, who is headed for the limbo. We will not have to tolerate him much longer. Were I or anyone else to mouth such kindergarten drooling, you and Fidler and those other worthies, Hopper and Parsons, would lambaste me to a fare-ye-well and probably throw in as good measure a story about me throwing a baby out of a window.

Please give my best regards to Franklin Delano R. and Eleanor, the King and Queen of England, Jim Farley, Tom Dewey, J. Edgar Hoover and the mob the next time you sit down and deal out gratuitously your sage counsel to them.

Has anyone ever criticised you for bleating over the radio week and two-week-old news, and yelping, "Scoop!" or "Exclusive!"?

I shouldn't dignify you with a letter, but I am up here preparing some stories and this is a little relaxation.

Yours truly,
Bill Fields

LEARNING ACTIVITIES

1. After interviewing at least two other class members to learn all you can about the field of experience of each, bring to class at least three selections to fit the interests of each.

2. Find a selection with at least four very different characters. Bring the selection with you to class and practice reading it aloud. Let the instructor and the students determine how well you differentiate characters.

3. Repeat the second activity, using material containing dialects.

4. Bring a selection to class which involves life experiences completely foreign to your own field of experience. In groups of three or four, discuss these strange experiences and make an effort to determine your ability to effectively communicate the experiences to a group of listeners.

THREE

GOALS After completing this chapter you will be able to:

1. Appreciate the importance of a thorough and conscientious effort at determining the meaning intended in a selection.

2. Recognize the need to acquaint yourself with the life and personality of the author of a selection.

3. Understand the difference between a precis and a paraphrase and know how to write both.

What Should I Read
Discovering Meaning

Once the beginning student of oral reading has made a choice of material, the next step in preparation is making a concerted effort to determine the meaning intended in the selection. We will assume at this point that the student reader has made a selection of material that is suitable to the personality and abilities of the reader.

The importance of discovering the meaning intended in a selection cannot be overemphasized. On the other hand, the student should keep the concept of communicative partnership firmly in mind at this point. It may be impossible to determine exact and undeniable meaning of a given passage or selection. If you have chosen a selection whose author has been dead for 100 years, it is impossible to be definite as to the author's intended meaning. Furthermore, if the author is alive, a reader can never be absolutely certain of intended meaning. If it were possible to contact an author personally and ask him what he meant in a specific phrase or selection, the reader might be surprised to learn that even the author is not absolutely certain of full meaning.

The fact that discovering meaning is a difficult endeavor does not, however, absolve the student from the responsibility of making a concentrated effort to be as sure as possible. You should keep in mind that as you read a selection you are entering into a partnership with the writer. Much of the meaning derived from a selection will be the author's. Nonetheless, it is impossible to avoid a significant degree of reader input into any final determination of meaning. Not only is such input impossible to avoid, but it is undesirable to try.

Various oral interpretation textbooks present numerous steps for you to follow in determining meanings. For our purposes, we will consider three basic steps in discovering meaning. We do not intend to imply that these steps will lead you to a full understanding of meaning in any selection you might choose. They are, however, what we consider to be the essential steps for a beginning reader to take for fuller and richer reading experience.

READ THE SELECTION SEVERAL TIMES FOR MEANING

It is doubtful that you should ever choose a reading selection on the basis of just reading it once. You should, ideally, read a selection through several times pausing after each time to reflect on meaning transmitted by the author. It may be surprising to find that your initial impression or perception of meaning may alter significantly after several times through a selection.

One of the most important points to be made here is that you should be absolutely sure that you understand the literal and contextual meaning of every word in the selection. When we engage in pleasure reading, we often pass over single words of which we do not know the meaning. We don't become confused with unfamiliar words unless they appear in excess, or unless we cannot make contextual jumps in meaning. It may surprise some beginning readers to learn precisely how many words one reads of which he doesn't understand the meaning. It is essential at this early stage in discovering meaning that you search out those unfamiliar words and look up their meaning. A recent dictionary should be considered a standard piece of equipment at this juncture of preparation.

Following are brief excerpts from several selections. None of them appears difficult in meaning on the surface. Read each of them through twice very quickly and then go back over each to determine the words of which you are not absolutely certain. Look up the meanings of each and see if your understanding of the selection is any fuller as a result.

from **THE LEGEND OF SLEEPY HOLLOW**

Washington Irving

POSTSCRIPT, FOUND IN THE HANDWRITING OF MR. KNICKERBOCKER

The preceding Tale is given, almost in the precise words in which I heard it related at a Corporation meeting of the ancient city of Manhattoes, at which were present many of its sagest and most illustrious burghers. The narrator was a pleasant, shabby, gentlemanly old fellow, in pepper-and-salt clothes, with a sadly humorous face; and one whom I strongly suspected of being poor,—he made such efforts to be entertaining. When his story was concluded, there was much laughter and approbation, particularly from two or three deputy aldermen, who had been asleep the greater part of the time. There was, however, one tall, dry-looking old gentleman, with beetling eyebrows, who maintained a grave and rather severe face throughout: now and then folding his arms, inclining his head, and looking down upon the floor, as if turning a doubt over in his mind. He was one of your wary men, who never laugh, but upon good grounds—when they have reason and the law on their side. When the mirth of the rest of the company had subsided, and silence was restored, he leaned one arm on the elbow of his chair, and sticking the other akimbo, demanded, with a slight, but exceedingly sage motion of the head, and contraction of the brow, what was the moral of the story, and what it went to prove?

The story-teller, who was just putting a glass of wine to his lips, as a refreshment after his toils, paused for a moment, looked at his inquirer with an air of infinite deference, and, lowering the glass slowly to the table, observed, that the story was intended most logically to prove:—

"That there is no situation in life but has its advantages and pleasures—providing we will but take a joke as we find it:

"That, therefore, he that runs races with goblin troopers is likely to have rough riding of it.

"Ergo, for a country schoolmaster to be refused the hand of a Dutch heiress, is a certain step to high preferment, in the state."

The cautious old gentleman knit his brows tenfold closer after this explanation, being sorely puzzled by the ratiocination of the syllogism; while, methought, the one in pepper-and-salt eyed him with something of a triumphant leer. At length he observed, that all this was very well, but still he thought the story a little on the extravagant—there were one or two points on which he had his doubts.

"Faith, sir," replied the story-teller, "as to that matter, I don't believe one-half of it myself."

D. K.

1820

SONNET: I SCARCELY GRIEVE

Henry Timrod

I scarcely grieve, O Nature! at the lot
That pent my life within a city's bounds,
And shut me from thy sweetest sights and sounds.
Perhaps I had not learned, if some lone cot
Had nursed a dreamy childhood, what the mart
Taught me amid its turmoil; so my youth
Had missed full many a stern but wholesome truth.
Here, too, O Nature! in this haunt of Art,
Thy power is on me, and I own thy thrall.
There is no unimpressive spot on earth!
The beauty of the stars is over all,
And Day and Darkness visit every hearth.
Clouds do not scorn us: yonder factory's smoke
Looked like a golden mist when morning broke.

1860

ACQUAINT YOURSELF WITH THE AUTHOR

Many uncertainties in meaning or confusion in meaning relationships can be cleared up significantly if you will make an effort to acquaint yourself with the life and personality of the author. While engaging in this step, it is impossible for you not to ask the question, "Why did the author write this?" While it is perfectly all right to raise the question and even attempt to answer it, you should not become obsessed with discovering the answer to this question. As we said earlier, your obligation is to carry your search for meaning as far as possible. However, you should always keep in mind that as a reader you will be expected to insert sizeable amounts of meaning yourself before interpreting the selection to an audience of listeners.

When you launch an investigation into pertinent facts in the life of the author of a selection, some answers may become evident immediately. Perhaps, the general theme of the bulk of an author's work is a direct result of the life of the author. An example of apparent influence on an author's writing is found in the case of Herman Melville: much of the content of his works concerning the sea directly resulted from his life experiences as a seaman.

In many cases the relationship of an author's life and his or her writing may not be so apparent. Emily Dickinson led what appeared to be a life free of startling or unusual events. Making an effort to understand her poetry, based on the physical occurrences surrounding her life can be a difficult task. However, further probing into her alleged character and personality reveals that after her mid-twenties she led a withdrawn and secluded life, and her poetry was in great part her way of communicating with friends and acquaintances. Then, the theme and tone of much of her poetry becomes more meaningful to the reader.

The following poem by Edgar Allan Poe appears to have been written about a specific person. Some have theorized that such is the case, that the poem may refer to a lost childhood sweetheart. We would urge you to acquaint yourself with some of the tragic events in Poe's life and some of his other writing. To do so should enable you to more clearly understand and appreciate both the poem and the poet.

TO ONE IN PARADISE

Edgar Allan Poe

Thou wast all that to me, love,
    For which my soul did pine—
A green isle in the sea, love,
    A fountain and a shrine,
All wreathed with fairy fruits and flowers,
    And all the flowers were mine,

Ah, dream too bright to last!
    Ah, starry Hope! that didst arise
But to be overcast!
    A voice from out the Future cries,
"On! on!"—but o'er the Past
    (Dim gulf!) my spirit hovering lies
Mute, motionless, aghast!

For, alas! alas! with me
    The light of Life is o'er!

No more—no more—no more—
(Such language holds the solemn sea
   To the sands upon the shore)
Shall bloom the thunder-blasted tree,
   Or the stricken eagle soar!

And all my days are trances,
   And all my nightly dreams
Are where thy dark eye glances,
   And where thy footstep gleams—
In what ethereal dances,
   By what eternal streams.

                            1834

A third example of probing the life of a writer for meaningful cues can be found in the writing of Henry David Thoreau. To understand the complexity of the man as manifested in his writing and reflections on his life of hermitage, you must read and appreciate life situations involving Thoreau, a personality who preferred seclusion.

WRITE BOTH A PRECIS AND PARAPHRASE

One of the most effective ways to assure a personal grasp of as much meaning in a selection as possible is first to write a precis of the selection. A precis is a condensed version of a paraphrase providing a brief summary of meaning gleaned from a selection stated in your own words. Some effort should be made in the precis to establish a general or overall theme for the work. Regardless of the length of the selection you should strive to compose a brief precis—perhaps one paragraph. Consider the following two selections and the precis which follows each. The essential meaning of the longer second poem can be stated just as briefly as the shorter selection.

MY AUNT

Oliver Wendell Holmes

My aunt! my dear unmarried aunt!
   Long years have o'er her flown;
Yet still she strains the aching clasp
   That binds her virgin zone;
I know it hurts her,—though she looks
   As cheerful as she can;
Her waist is ampler than her life,
   For life is but a span.

My aunt! my poor deluded aunt!
   Her hair is almost gray;
Why will she train that winter curl
   In such a spring-like way?
How can she lay her glasses down,
   And say she reads as well,
When through a double convex lens
   She just makes out to spell?

Her father—grandpapa! forgive
   This erring lip its smiles—
Vowed she should make the finest girl
   Within a hundred miles;
He sent her to a stylish school;
   'T was in her thirteenth June;
And with her, as the rules required,
   "Two towels and a spoon."

They braced my aunt against a board,
   To make her straight and tall;
They laced her up, they starved her down,
   To make her light and small;
They pinched her feet, they singed her hair,
   They screwed it up with pins;—
Oh, never mortal suffered more
   In penance for her sins.

So, when my precious aunt was done,
   My grandsire brought her back
(By daylight, lest some rabid youth
   Might follow on the track);

"Ah!" said my grandsire, as he shook
  Some powder in his pan,
"What could this lovely creature do
  Against a desperate man!"

Alas! nor chariot, nor barouche,
  Nor bandit cavalcade,
Tore from the trembling father's arms
  His all-accomplished maid.
For her how happy had it been!
  And Heaven had spared to me
To see one sad, ungathered rose
  On my ancestral tree.

1831

Precis: *The poem depicts the comic tragedy of a maiden aunt who was the "apple of her father's eye." All the finishing school touches and preparation by her father could not make the poor creature a salable commodity to a man.*

TELLING THE BEES

John Greenleaf Whittier

Here is the place; right over the hill
  Runs the path I took;
You can see the gap in the old wall still,
  And the stepping-stones in the shallow brook.

There is the house, with the gate red-barred,
  And the poplars tall;
And the barn's brown length, and the cattle-yard,
  And the white horns tossing above the wall.

There are the beehives ranged in the sun;
  And down by the brink
Of the brook are her poor flowers, weed-o'errun,
  Pansy and daffodil, rose and pink.

A year has gone, as the tortoise goes,
  Heavy and slow;
And the same rose blows, and the same sun glows,
  And the same brook sings of a year ago.

There's the same sweet clover-smell in the breeze;
    And the June sun warm
Tangles his wings of fire in the trees,
    Setting, as then, over Fernside farm.

I mind me how with a lover's care
    From my Sunday coat
I brushed off the burrs, and smoothed my hair,
    And cooled at the brookside my brow and throat.

Since we parted, a month had passed,—
    To love, a year;
Down through the beeches I looked at last
    On the little red gate and the well-sweep near.

I can see it all now,—the slantwise rain
    Of light through the leaves,
The sundown's blaze on her window-pane,
    The bloom of her roses under the eaves.

Just the same as a month before,—
    The house and the trees,
The barn's brown gable, the vine by the door,—
    Nothing changed but the hives of bees.

Before them, under the garden wall,
    Forward and back,
Went drearily singing the chore-girl small,
    Draping each hive with a shred of black.

Trembling, I listened: the summer sun
    Had the chill of snow;
For I knew she was telling the bees of one
    Gone on the journey we all must go!

Then I said to myself, "My Mary weeps
    For the dead to-day:
Haply her blind old grandsire sleeps
    The fret and the pain of his age away."

But her dog whined low; on the doorway sill,
    With his cane to his chin,
The old man sat; and the chore-girl still
    Sung to the bees stealing out and in.

And the song she was singing ever since
    In my ear sounds on:—

"Stay at home, pretty bees, fly not hence!
Mistress Mary is dead and gone!"

1858

Precis: *A young man returns to the home of his beloved. As he approaches the house, memories fly before his eyes. Seeing signs of a death in the house he assumes his love's old grandfather has died; however, he soon learns that his love is dead.*

After writing a precis of a selection, you may feel that you understand the selection adequately to render a meaningful interpretation. If you have difficulty coming to absolute agreement in your own mind as to a brief meaning for the selection, you may find it helpful or necessary to write a paraphrase of the selection. In a paraphrase the reader changes the entire selection into his own words. A paraphrase might better be called a complete translation of the selection from the author's language into the reader's language.

Following is a paraphrase of Robert Browning's "My Last Duchess." This particular poem has been interpreted many different ways by various readers. If you were to write your own paraphrase for this selection, you might not agree in every instance with what follows. Keep in mind, though, that the paraphrase forces the reader to make a complete translation and it would be unusual if paraphrases written by several different interpreters would agree in each instance.

MY LAST DUCHESS

Robert Browning

That excellent painting on the wall

That's my last Duchess painted on the wall,

is of my last wife. It is

Looking as if she were alive. I call

Truly a masterpiece. Frà Pandolf

That piece a wonder, now: Frà Pandolf's hands

worked hard for days and, there it is.
Worked busily a day, and there she stands.

why don't you sit down and look at it? I said
Will't please you sit and look at her? I said

Frà Pandolf intentionally, for one who didn't know
"Frà Pandolf" by design, for never read

her has ever looked at the picture and seen
Strangers like you that pictured countenance,

The piercing feeling of its glance
The depth and passion of its earnest glance,

who failed to ask me, (since I determine
But to myself they turned (since none puts by

who does or does not see the picture)
The curtain I have drawn for you, but I)

if they dare be so direct,
And seemed as they would ask me, if they durst,

how that expression came to her face. So
How such a glance came there; so, not the first

you certainly may ask. Sir, she wasn't just
Are you to turn and ask thus. Sir, 'twas not

reacting to my presence at the posing when
Her husband's presence only, called that spot

she displayed that smile. Frà Pandolf might
Of joy into the Duchess' cheek: perhaps

have said something trivial like
Frà Pandolf chanced to say, "Her mantle laps

"Please uncover your wrist a bit, "or
Over my Lady's wrist too much," or "Paint

"Paint can never do justice
Must never hope to reproduce the faint

to your beautiful skin tone." She thought
Half-flush that dies along her throat": such stuff

he was being polite and, Thus, she reacted
Was courtesy, she thought, and cause enough

with that expression. What I mean
For calling up that spot of joy. She had

is that, she was too quick To be
A heart—how shall I say?—too soon made glad,

impressed by others : she liked everything
Too easily impressed: she liked whate'er

she saw and she saw a great deal.
She looked on, and her looks went everywhere.

She was no more impressed with my passionate affection
Sir. 'twas all one! My favour at her breast,

Than she was with the sunset
The dropping of the daylight in the West,

or a gift of orchard cherries
The bough of cherries some officious fool

from a laborer or her favorite
Broke in the orchard for her, the white mule

riding mule - all of those brought
She rode with around the terrace—all and each

the same favorable reaction and beautiful
Would draw from her alike the approving speech,

expressions. She was just as grateful
Or blush, at least. She thanked men,—good! but thanked

for even a simple gift as she was for

Somehow—I know not how—as if she ranked

my gift to her of an old and treasured

My gift of a nine-hundred years-old name

name. So, what's wrong with

With anybody's gift. Who'd stoop to blame

that type of person? Even if had

This sort of trifling? Even had you skill

enough speaking skill to state

In speech—(which I have not)—to make your will

clearly my feelings and tell her

Quite clear to such an one, and say, "Just this

exactly what it was about her

Or that in you disgusts me; here you miss,

that bothered me. And even if

Or there exceed the mark"—and if she let

she had listened and made an

Herself be lessoned so, nor plainly set

effort to change, I would be

Her wits to yours, forsooth, and made excuse,

doing a certain amount of stooping and

—E'en then would be some stooping, and I choose

I never stoop. Yes, she smiled when I

Never to stoop. Oh, Sir, she smiled, no doubt,

passed her, but she smiled equally

When'er I passed her; but who passed without

for everyone. She kept smiling at everyone

Much the same smile? This grew; I gave commands;

and I ordered her to stop. Then, she never smiled again.
Then all smiles stopped together. There she stands

There she is as if alive. Come, let's go
As if alive. Will't please you rise? We'll meet

downstairs. Again, I say that
The company below, then. I repeat,

your master's well-known generosity
The Count your master's known munificence

assures me that no fair request
Is ample warrant that no just pretence

for a dowry will be refused;
Of mine for dowry will be disallowed;

even though his beautiful daughter
Though his fair daughter's self, as I avowed

is my true desire. No, wait, we'll go
At starting, is my object. Nay, we'll go

together, Sir! Notice first though
Together down, Sir. Notice Neptune, though,

this other unusual masterpiece done in
Taming a sea-horse, thought a rarity,

bronze for me by Claus of Innsbruck.
Which Claus of Innsbruck cast in bronze for me!

1868

Keep in mind that the three steps outlined in this chapter are considered preliminary and basic steps for the beginning reader in his effort to discover meaning in selections of others. A reader would have to engage in much more lengthy and complex processes to arrive at a full analytic meaning of a selection. These three steps, however, if completed in entirety will enable the beginning reader to fulfill his share of partnership with the author in bringing written meaning to listeners via oral communication.

SUMMARY   1. Why is it important for a reader to know the mean-
PROBES   ing of every word in a selection before he attempts
                  to read it to others?
               2. Why should the beginning reader avoid an obses-
                  sion with trying to discover why an author wrote a
                  particular work? What benefit will the reader
                  enjoy as a result of acquainting himself with the
                  life and personality of the author?
               3. How does a precis differ from a paraphrase? How
                  can each assist the beginning reader?

LEARNING ACTIVITIES

1. Select two or three of your favorite plays, poems, or stories and read as much as possible about the lives of the authors. Did acquainting yourself with the authors help you to better understand the meaning intended in the selections?

2. Write both a precis and a paraphrase for each of the following selections:

ONE TIME

Chris Benignus

Jamie and I played doctor
In the black of Coles' garage,
Crouching between fenders,
Oil hanging in the air.

A pebble clicked
Behind the teeth of a car.
Its heat made us sticky,
Grit clung.

Shoes crushing gravel,
Marched. The door clattered up.
Jamie dropped his stick.
My eyes wrinkled at the sun.

A hand clenched mine,
Dragging me, like I did my doll.
"Mortal sins," shouted Mother,
"Must be told in confession."

Unfolding sweating hands,
I parted the curtain.
The kneeler was warm,
Muscles tightened.

I crouched in the black,
My voice scratched—
"Jamie and I pulled down pants,
One time."

1973

THE HEIGHT OF THE RIDICULOUS

Oliver Wendell Holmes

I wrote some lines once on a time
   In wondrous merry mood,
And thought, as usual, men would say
   They were exceeding good.

They were so queer, so very queer,
   I laughed as I would die;
Albeit, in the general way,
   A sober man am I.

I called my servant, and he came;
   How kind it was of him
To mind a slender man like me,
   He of the mighty limb!

"These to the printer," I exclaimed,
   And, in my humorous way,
I added (as a trifling jest),
   "There'll be the devil to pay."

He took the paper, and I watched,
   And saw him peep within;
At the first line he read, his face
   Was all upon the grin.

He read the next; the grin grew broad,
    And shot from ear to ear;
He read the third, a chuckling noise
    I now began to hear.

The fourth; he broke into a roar;
    The fifth; his waistband split;
The sixth; he burst five buttons off,
    And tumbled in a fit.

Ten days and nights, with sleepless eye,
    I watched that wretched man,
And since, I never dare to write
    As funny as I can.

1830

from **THE BIGLOW PAPERS, SECOND SERIES**

James Russell Lowell

from the Introduction

THE COURTIN'

God makes sech nights, all white an' still
    Fur'z you can look or listen,
Moonshine an' snow on field an' hill,
    All silence an' all glisten.

Zekle crep' up quite unbeknown
    An' peeked in thru' the winder,
An' there sot Huldy all alone,
    'ith no one nigh to hender.

A fireplace filled the room's one side
    With half a cord o' wood in—
There warn't no stoves (tell comfort died)
    To bake ye to a puddin'.

The wa'nut logs shot sparkles out
    Towards the pootiest, bless her,
An' leetle flames danced all about
    The chiny on the dresser.

Agin the chimbley crook-necks hung,
    An' in amongst 'em rusted
The ole queen's-arm thet gran'ther Young
    Fetched back f'om Concord busted.

The very room, coz she was in,
    Seemed warm f'om floor to ceilin',
An' she looked full ez rosy agin
    Ez the apples she was peelin'.

'Twas kin' o' kingdom-come to look
    On sech a blessed cretur,
A dogrose blushin' to a brook
    Ain't modester nor sweeter.

He was six foot o' man, A 1,
    Clear grit an' human natur'.
None couldn't quicker pitch a ton
    Nor dror a furrer straighter.

He'd sparked it with full twenty gals,
    He'd squired 'em, danced 'em, druv 'em,
Fust this one, an' then thet, by spells—
    All is, he couldn't love 'em.

But long o' her his veins 'ould run
    All crinkly like curled maple,
The side she breshed felt full o' sun
    Ez a south slope in Ap'il.

She thought no v'ice hed sech a swing
    Ez his'n in the choir;
My! when he made Ole Hunderd ring,
    She *knowed* the Lord was nigher.

An' she'd blush scarlit, right in prayer,
    When her new meetin'-bunnet
Felt somehow thru' its crown a pair
    O' blue eyes sot upun it.

Thet night, I tell ye, she looked *some*!
    She seemed to 've gut a new soul,
For she felt sartin-sure he'd come,
    Down to her very shoe-sole.

She heered a foot, an' knowed it tu,
    A-raspin' on the scraper,—

All ways to once her feelin's flew
    Like sparks in burnt-up paper.

He kin' o' l'itered on the mat,
    Some doubtfle o' the sekle,
His heart kep' goin' pity-pat,
    But hern went pity Zekle.

An' yit she gin her cheer a jerk
    Ez though she wished him furder,
An' on her apples kep' to work,
    Parin' away like murder.

"You want to see my Pa, I s'pose?"
    "Wal . . . no . . . I come dasignin' "—
"To see my Ma? She's sprinklin' clo'es
    Agin to-morrer's i'nin'."

To say why gals acts so or so,
    Or don't, 'ould be presumin';
Mebby to mean *yes* an' say *no*
    Comes nateral to women.

He stood a spell on one foot fust,
    Then stood a spell on t'other,
An' on which one he felt the wust
    He couldn't ha' told ye nuther.

Says he, "I'd better call agin!"
    Says she, "Think likely, Mister:"
Thet last word pricked him like a pin,
    An' . . . Wal, he up an' kist her.

When Ma bimeby upon 'em slips,
    Huldy sot pale ez ashes,
All kin' o' smily roun' the lips
    An' teary roun' the lashes.

For she was jes' the quiet kind
    Whose naturs never vary,
Like streams that keep a summer mind
    Snowhid in Jenooary.

The blood clost roun' her heart felt glued
    Too tight for all expressin'
Tell mother see how metters stood,
    An' gin 'em both her blessin'.

Then her red come back like the tide
    Down to the Bay o' Fundy,
An' all I know is they was cried
    In meetin' come nex' Sunday.

1867

YELLOW FEVER

W. H. Watling, Jr.

Finally,
I'm driving Route 53 blacktop northward. Joliet
Overpass
approaches
larger as I near.
With the sun its columns rise, Mercurial spires
in Earth's dustorm
pull. Concrete and iron
slowly consume the firmament.
I push the pedal a notch over the limit, hoping
to pass quickly. Surely too
slight on offence for policing.
A Continental semi trucks east to
the overpass, gears grating up the ramp. Tickets
lose to the greater fears of a stream
in flood, hurrying out from under a
creaking bridge. No more is speed a minor
crime. The cumulous ceiling thunders overhead,
and Martianic rustreaked lightning-thin wall
cracks telescope to meteoric pits. Angry alligator
sucks me down, its steel ribs barring the heavens.
Can I block the all-digesting kick of a hole in
terrestrial space, whose molar wheels grind
planet morsels about me, heartpounding them to
chuckhole dusty arteries? Bluebaby it is!
the spacehole's heart has a hole with
pinlight slipping out and I see the ribs sliding
back, exposing the heavens! And
I'm free and still on the
road, with a firmament
above. Still? Again, but the sky's refracted yellower,

and the highway
bends around and up
to the overpass
roof, banking at the sun. I'm on top, but have
the columns
thickened?
What if
fear of being crushed becomes fear of falling? I
sneeze,
wonder
again:
Could I be allergic to sunlight, or do all lights
have
fangs?

1975

REBUKED

Franklin Baldwin Wiley

In the night there came a voice
Saying, "Despair not, but rejoice!
Life up thy soul in song,
For the day will break ere long."

But I answered, "Why should I
Believe this cunning lie?
Through the watches of the night
Have I not sought for light
Till my eye-strings strained and cracked,
In the search for what they lacked,—
Yet discerned not even a spark
In the starless, ebon dark?
Now that my quest has ceased,
Shall the morning flood the east?
Nay, thou can'st not cheat my sight;
There is no such thing as light."

And even as I spoke,
O'er the hills the bright dawn broke.

1904

References

Aggertt, Otis J., and Bowen, Elbert R. *Communicative Reading*. New York: Macmillan, 1963, Part II.

Bacon, Wallace A. *The Art of Interpretation*. New York: Holt, Rinehart, and Winston, 1966, Part II.

Veilleux, Jere. *Oral Interpretation: The Re-creation of Literature*. New York: Harper and Row, 1967, Chapters 1 and 2.

FOUR

GOALS   After completing this chapter you will be able to:

1. Utilize three suggestions for effectively cutting a segment from a longer selection for oral reading.

2. Appreciate the importance of five elements of voice crucial to effective oral reading.

3. Realize the important but secondary role played by gesture and body movement in oral reading.

4. Mark a manuscript to render it helpful to you in transmitting meaning to your listeners via oral reading.

How Should I Read

Physical Aspects of Oral

Reading

Up to this point our primary interest in preparing for oral reading has been in discovering meaning contained in a piece of writing. Once the beginning reader has arrived at what he believes to be the meaning of a selection, he is ready to begin preparing to read the selection aloud to a group of listeners.

Our primary concern in this chapter includes the physical aspects of oral reading, or those delivery aspects most important to the reading situation. The principles that we will discuss relate to both vocal delivery and bodily movement and are applicable both to classroom reading and contest reading. Specific rules of a contest situation or specific components of a classroom assignment might alter some of the points developed here. Our main concerns in this chapter are three: cutting the selection, vocal aspects of reading, and, bodily aspects of reading.

CUTTING THE SELECTION

Earlier in this unit, we maintained that a beginning reader will usually be faced with the task of cutting a selection for reading from a longer work. Both classroom and competitive situations are normally limited by time parameters. Poetry programs require less cutting due to the shorter length of many poems. However, if the reader chooses to read prose or drama, it is unlikely that time will permit reading of an entire selection.

When you face a time limitation in your reading, you will have to cut the selection. This step in preparation for reading is often taken for granted and often done so in haphazard fashion. We wish to emphasize the importance of this preparation step; three points need your concentrated attention when you attempt to cut a longer selection.

Cut for Maximum Listener Effect

Within the same piece of material the reader will find high points of action, low points, as well as in-between points. The reader should strive to extract a segment of the work which will provide for one of the highest points of action and interest.

The reader should read the selection in its entirety and then determine what part of the selection was most interesting and attention-holding to the reader. Such segments of the work make likely choices for oral reading. Reading the selection entirely is crucial at this point. A beginning reader cannot expect to open a play to Act III, scene 1, and read it meaningfully unless he is well acquainted with the entire play.

In order to achieve maximum listener effect, the selection extracted by the reader should be a self-contained, clear message. Some cuttings the authors have graded and judged in several years of classroom and contest-listening experience have appeared to have been selected by flipping pages and stabbing with pencil. The segment, in itself, should make "sense." Any longer selection such as a play or novel or a short story has parts which are essential to the development of plot, and some sections which are extraneous and secondary to plot development. Obviously secondary or extraneous segments would not be considered adequate or suitable for oral reading.

Cut to Minimize Transitions

The best cutting is normally one that is continuous within itself—that is, it runs continuously with no interruptions within the longer work. If the reader is successful at finding a segment adequate for reading not requiring interruption of content, transitions will not be a problem. In many cases, however, you may find it necessary to take several shorter segments of a work from various locations in the text. When this is necessary you must provide transitional information between segments of the work.

While we recommend that you strive to locate a cutting which does not require transitions—such as a final scene in a play or an internal scene or segment which meets the test of completeness—there will be times when extracting several short pieces of material from various points in the work is necessary. When this happens, you should provide clear and brief transitional statements to assist the listener in making the mental jump from one location or setting to another. Reading several segments from different parts in the work with no transition will leave the listener in a confused and disheveled mental state.

The best transitional statements are ones which meet tests of brevity and clarity. The reader must determine what information should be provided the listener to enable him to move with the reader from one point to another.

Cut to Ease Introductions to Material

All selections need some form of introduction to bring the listeners to the proper frame of mind to hear and enjoy the reading. The length and type of introduction required for a selection is greatly affected by anticipated listener familiarity with the work. A famous work will need less introduction than one less known. For instance, the sleepwalking scene in Shakespeare's *Macbeth* will require less introduction than Shakespeare's sonnets numbers 88, 89, and 90.

The purpose of an introduction to an oral reading selection may vary from one situation to another. Nonetheless, we can generalize that an effective introduction should provide answers to two questions for the listener. First, the introduction should answer the question, "Why this particular selection?" What elements of meaning found in the selection are either relevant or potentially relevant and meaningful to the listener? A second question to be answered is, "How does the particular segment chosen for reading relate to the whole work?" If the cutting begins at a point other than the beginning of the material, what has happened previously? The reader must place the shorter selection chosen in proper context with the whole.

The reader also has an obligation to provide an introduction not only for material that has been taken from longer works, but also for complete materials. The listener will always question communicative material as to why time should be given to listening to a particular message. The reader has a communicative obligation to his receiver to provide an answer to that question.

Following is a sample introduction to Henry Wadsworth Longfellow's "A Psalm of Life." Note the attempt on the part of the reader to provide an answer to the question, "Why should I listen to this particular reading?"

Introduction: We all have no doubt faced periods of time in our existence when we felt life really wasn't worth living. In the following poem Henry Wadsworth Longfellow left us a philosophy to embrace during those periods. He is telling us here that life is really worth living and we must continually strive to make the best of it; someone who follows in a later generation may benefit from our efforts.

A PSALM OF LIFE

Henry Wadsworth Longfellow

WHAT THE HEART OF THE YOUNG MAN
SAID TO THE PSALMIST

Tell me not, in mournful numbers,
    Life is but an empty dream!—
For the soul is dead that slumbers,
    And things are not what they seem.

Life is real! Life is earnest!
    And the grave is not its goal;
Dust thou art, to dust returnest,
    Was not spoken of the soul.

Not enjoyment, and not sorrow,
    Is our destined end or way;
But to act, that each tomorrow
    Find us farther than today.

Art is long, and Time is fleeting,
    And our hearts, though stout and brave,
Still, like muffled drums, are beating
    Funeral marches to the grave.

In the world's broad field of battle,
In the bivouac of Life,
Be not like dumb, driven cattle!
Be a hero in the strife!

Trust no Future, howe'er pleasant!
Let the dead Past bury its dead!
Act,—act in the living Present!
Heart within, and God o'erhead!

Lives of great men all remind us
We can make our lives sublime,
And, departing, leave behind us
Footprints on the sands of time;

Footprints, that perhaps another,
Sailing o'er life's solemn main,
A forlorn and shipwrecked brother,
Seeing, shall take heart again.

Let us, then, be up and doing,
With a heart for any fate;
Still achieving, still pursuing,
Learn to labor and to wait.

1838

SUMMARY PROBES

1. Why should beginning readers read a selection through in its entirety before choosing a segment from it?
2. Why are transitions necessary in many cuttings?
3. What two questions should an introduction to a selection answer for the listener?

VOCAL ASPECTS OF ORAL READING

The reader's use of voice is of primary importance in oral reading situations. The physical presence of a manuscript in oral reading necessarily places bodily movement in a secondary position to the voice. We will consider five aspects of vocal delivery in oral reading.

Vocal Pause

One of the most useful methods for creating maximum effect in oral reading is the meaningful and carefully calculated use of pause. The reader must have a thorough grasp of a selection's meaning if he is to employ pause effectively to enhance that meaning. Listeners can be easily frustrated in their efforts to understand and enjoy a selection by a reader who rushes through the selection with no apparent thought given to proper points for meaningful pause.

Pause can be used for both dramatic and humorous effect. The major task facing the beginning reader is to be confident enough in understanding the meaning of a selection to employ pause properly.

Vocal Emphasis

Not all words in any selection should receive the same degree of stress or emphasis by the reader. Once again the crucial importance of reader understanding of meaning becomes evident. The reader must read through the selection to be certain that words which should receive emphasis to assure proper meaning transmission from reader to listener actually are properly stressed.

The manuscript must be properly marked for vocal pause and emphasis to serve as reminders to the reader as to where both pause and emphasis best be used to enhance meaning. The following manuscript of the last part of William Cullen Bryant's "Thanatopsis" demonstrates effective use of markings to serve as reminders to the reader. While the method employed here is only one of many acceptable schematics for marking manuscripts, it is one that has worked successfully for many readers.

One slash mark (/) indicates a pause to the reader. Two slash marks (/ /) indicates a longer pause. One line under a word indicates that that word should receive heavy emphasis. The reader can underline words two or more times to indicate varying degrees of emphasis.

from **THANATOPSIS**

William Cullen Bryant

Yet <u>not</u> to thine eternal resting-place
Shalt thou retire <u>alone</u>,/nor couldst thou wish
Couch more <u>magnificent</u>.//Thou shalt lie down
With <u>patriarchs</u> of the infant world, with <u>kings</u>,/
The <u>powerful</u> of the earth, the <u>wise</u>, the <u>good</u>,
Fair forms, and <u>hoary</u> <u>seers</u> of ages <u>past</u>,//
All in one <u>mighty</u> <u>sepulchre</u>.//The <u>hills</u>
Rock-<u>ribbed</u> and ancient as the sun,/the <u>vales</u>
Stretching in pensive quietness between;/
The venerable <u>woods</u>/—<u>rivers</u> that move
In <u>majesty</u>, and the complaining <u>brooks</u>
That make the <u>meadows</u> <u>green</u>;//and, poured round all,/
Old Ocean's <u>gray</u> and <u>melancholy</u> waste,/—
Are but the <u>solemn</u> <u>decorations</u> all
Of the <u>great</u> tomb of man.//The <u>golden</u> <u>sun</u>,
The <u>planets</u>, all the <u>infinite</u> host of <u>heaven</u>,/
Are shining on the sad abodes of <u>death</u>,
Through the still <u>lapse</u> of <u>ages</u>.//<u>All</u> that tread
The globe are but a <u>handful</u> to the tribes
That <u>slumber</u> in its <u>bosom</u>.//—Take the <u>wings</u>
Of morning,/<u>pierce</u> the Barcan wilderness,/
Or lose thyself in the continuous <u>woods</u>
Where <u>rolls</u> the <u>Oregon</u>, and hears no sound
Save his <u>own</u> <u>dashings</u>//—yet the <u>dead</u> are <u>there</u>:/
And <u>millions</u> in those <u>solitudes</u>, since first
The flight of years began, have <u>laid</u> them <u>down</u>
In their <u>last</u> <u>sleep</u>/—the <u>dead</u> reign there <u>alone</u>.//
So shalt thou rest,/and what if thou <u>withdraw</u>
In <u>silence</u> from the <u>living</u>, and <u>no</u> friend
Take note of thy <u>departure</u>?//<u>All</u> that breathe
Will <u>share</u> thy <u>destiny</u>./The gay will <u>laugh</u>
When <u>thou</u> are <u>gone</u>,/the solemn <u>brood</u> of care
<u>Plod</u> on, and each one as before will chase
His <u>favorite</u> <u>phantom</u>;/yet <u>all</u> these shall leave
Their <u>mirth</u> and their <u>employments</u>, and shall come
And make <u>their</u> bed with thee.//As the <u>long</u> <u>train</u>
Of ages <u>glide</u> away, the <u>sons</u> of <u>men</u>,/

The <u>youth</u> in life's <u>green</u> <u>spring</u>,/and he who goes
In the <u>full</u> strength of <u>years</u>,/<u>matron</u> and <u>maid</u>,/
The <u>speechless</u> babe, and the <u>gray-headed</u> <u>man</u>—//
Shall one by one be <u>gathered</u> to thy side,
By those, who in their turn shall <u>follow</u> <u>them</u>.//

So live, that when thy <u>summons</u> comes to <u>join</u>
The <u>innumerable</u> <u>caravan</u>, which moves
To that <u>mysterious</u> <u>realm</u>,/where each shall take
His <u>chamber</u> in the <u>silent</u> halls of <u>death</u>,//
Thou go <u>not</u>, like the <u>quarry-slave</u> at night,
<u>Scourged</u> to his <u>dungeon</u>, but,/<u>sustained</u> and <u>soothed</u>
By an <u>unfaltering</u> <u>trust</u>, approach thy <u>grave</u>,
Like one who <u>wraps</u> the <u>drapery</u> of his <u>couch</u>
About him,/and <u>lies</u> down to <u>pleasant</u> <u>dreams</u>.

1811

Vocal Rate

Proper reading rate can do a great deal either to add to or subtract from listener reception of meaning. A normal human tendency when reading aloud is to read faster than one usually speaks in conversation. The reader must be constantly aware of this tendency to read too fast and make concerted efforts to vary reading rate as dictated by intended meaning of the selection.

The best vocal delivery in oral reading is that which does not sound as if it is being read. If the reader has truly engaged in a communicative partnership with the author, the message should sound natural and conversational to the listener. The reader should develop some form of self-serving manner in which to mark his manuscript to indicate the points where vocal rate must be varied for meaningful purpose.

Volume

Regardless of how good a selection might be or of how fully a reader understands the intended meaning or how effectively the reader makes use of vocal pause, emphasis, and rate, the listener must be able to hear what the reader is saying. Then, the reader's first concern is to be certain that every person included in his listener group is able to hear every word of the selection.

Beyond adequacy of volume to enable listeners to hear the selection, the reader has other concerns in the use of volume. Meaning can be greatly altered by proper or improper varying of volume in a selection. Again the reader has an obligation to his listeners to determine those points in the selection where volume should be varied, either upward or downward, to enhance meaning.

The beginning reader should keep in mind that he must often vary volume from one physical setting to another. Many selections contain highly dramatic scenes which require high volume. Even volume used at the same point in the selection must be varied from one physical setting to another. Consider the acoustical nature of the room in which you are to read. If you rehearse a selection at home or in your dormitory with carpeting on the floor, curtains and drapes at the windows, and plush furnishings in the room, the volume level used in this setting may have to be toned down significantly when you stand in a classroom with bare windows, walls, and floors. You must avoid blasting your listeners out of their chairs.

The problem of excessive volume is especially evident in contest situations. A reading given in the bare classroom filled with students all wearing clothing capable of absorbing sound might have to be toned down even more before reading it in a similar classroom with only three other contestants and one judge present. Again, you must avoid excessive volume.

The primary point to remember concerning volume is that proper volume level not only varies greatly within a selection, but it may also vary greatly in terms of physical setting for the reading situation. Regardless of what is needed in the area of volume at a given point, it is the beginning reader's obligation to provide it.

Vocal Rhythm

While vocal rhythm is of great importance in all types of reading, it is perhaps especially critical in effective reading of poetry. Without doubt, the most often observed weakness in our experience of listening to poetry readers is the presence of a distracting "sing-song" rhythm pattern where it is not appropriate. The physical structure of much poetry makes it very difficult for the beginning reader to avoid the trap of the distracting pattern.

In some cases a prominent pattern of rhythm is essential to the meaning of the selection. Some poetry is written with the intention of including a rhythm pattern. Much of the writing of some poets falls into this category. Normally, however, the reader should keep in mind that poetry is a content message—not a performance message. An artificial rhythm pattern will usually distract greatly from the intended effect of a poem. It is the reader's responsibility to eliminate such rhythm pattern from his vocal delivery.

After reading a poem aloud for others several times, if you find that you still have a problem with rhythm pattern, "reconstruct" the poem. You will be amazed at how the rhythm pattern vanishes from a poem when you recast the poem in prose style. Our normal tendency is to read poetry by lines rather than by punctuation. Reading one line at a time leads the reader into establishing a comparable rhythm for each line: when that comparable rhythm is repeated several times, the rhythm pattern occurs.

The most effective method of eliminating the rhythm pattern is to force yourself to read poetry using punctuation, sentence, and thought structure as your guide in pausing and mental patterning. If you must redo a poem into prose style in order to eliminate the pattern, it is your obligation to do so.

The following selections demonstrate both appropriate and inappropriate rhythm pattern in poetry. In "General William Booth Enters Into Heaven," it is impossible to read the poem aloud without a rhythm pattern. The author even instructed the reader to "sing" the poem. "Annabel Lee" by Poe is a poem that lends itself to an improper development of a pronounced rhythm pattern. Here we include the poem in its original structure and then we have written the poem in prose format. Read it through both ways and see for yourself if the rhythm pattern has a tendency to disappear in the second instance.

GENERAL WILLIAM BOOTH ENTERS INTO HEAVEN

Vachel Lindsay

(To be sung to the tune of "The Blood of the Lamb" with indicated instrument)

I

(Bass drum beaten loudly.)

Booth led boldly with his big bass drum—
(Are you washed in the blood of the Lamb?)
The Saints smiled gravely and they said: "He's come."
(Are you washed in the blood of the Lamb?)
Walking lepers followed, rank on rank,
Lurching bravos from the ditches dank,
Drabs from the alleyways and drug fiends pale—
Minds still passion-ridden, soul-powers frail:—
Vermin-eaten saints with moldy breath,
Unwashed legions with the ways of Death—
(Are you washed in the blood of the Lamb?)

(Banjos.)

Every slum had sent its half-a-score
The round world over. (Booth had groaned for more.)
Every banner that the wide world flies
Bloomed with glory and transcendent dyes.
Big-voiced lasses made their banjos bang,
Tranced, fanatical they shrieked and sang:—
"Are you washed in the blood of the Lamb?"
Hallelujah! It was queer to see
Bull-necked convicts with that land make free.
Loons with trumpets blowed a blare, blare, blare
On, on upward thro' the golden air!
(Are you washed in the blood of the Lamb?)

II

(Bass drum slower and softer.)

Booth died blind and still by faith he trod,
Eyes still dazzled by the ways of God.
Booth led boldly, and he looked the chief

Eagle countenance in sharp relief,
Beard a-flying, air of high command
Unabated in that holy land.

(Sweet flute music.)

Jesus came from out the court-house door,
Stretched his hands above the passing poor.
Booth saw not, but led his queer ones there
Round and round the mighty court-house square.
Then, in an instant all that blear review
Marched on spotless, clad in raiment new.
The lame were straightened, withered limbs uncurled
And blind eyes opened on a new, sweet world.

(Bass drum louder.)

Drabs and vixens in a flash made whole!
Gone was the weasel-head, the snout, the jowl!
Sages and sibyls now, and athletes clean,
Rulers of empires, and of forests green!

(Grand chorus of all instruments.)
(Tambourines to the foreground.)

The hosts were sandaled, and their wings were fire!
(Are you washed in the blood of the Lamb?)
But their noise played havoc with the angel-choir.
(Are you washed in the blood of the Lamb?)
Oh, shout Salvation! It was good to see
Kings and Princes by the Lamb set free.
The banjos rattled and the tambourines
Jing-jing-jingled in the hands of the Queens.

(Reverently sung, no instruments.)

And when Booth halted by the curb for prayer
He saw his Master thro' the flag-filled air.
Christ came gently with a robe and crown
For Booth the soldier, while the throng knelt down.
He saw King Jesus. They were face to face,
And he knelt a-weeping in that holy place.
Are you washed in the blood of the Lamb?

1913

ANNABEL LEE

Edgar Allan Poe

It was many and many a year ago,
  In a kingdom by the sea,
That a maiden there lived whom you may know
  By the name of Annabel Lee;—
And this maiden she lived with no other thought
  Than to love and be loved by me.

She was a child and *I* was a child,
  In this kingdom by the sea,
But we loved with a love that was more than love—
  I and my Annabel Lee—
With a love that the wingéd seraphs of Heaven
  Coveted her and me.

And this was the reason that, long ago,
  In this kingdom by the sea,
A wind blew out of a cloud by night
  Chilling my Annabel Lee;
So that her highborn kinsmen came
  And bore her away from me,
To shut her up in a sepulchre
  In this kingdom by the sea.

The angels, not half so happy in Heaven,
  Went envying her and me:—
Yes! that was the reason (as all men know,
  In this kingdom by the sea)
That the wind came out of the cloud, chilling
  And killing my Annabel Lee.

But our love it was stronger by far than the love
  Of those who were older than we—
  Of many far wiser than we—
And neither the angels in Heaven above
  Nor the demons down under the sea,
Can ever dissever my soul from the soul
  Of the beautiful Annabel Lee:—

For the moon never beams without bringing me dreams
  Of the beautiful Annabel Lee;

And the stars never rise but I see the bright eyes
   Of the beautiful Annabel Lee;
And so, all the night-tide, I lie down by the side
Of my darling, my darling, my life and my bride,
   In her sepulchre there by the sea—
   In her tomb by the side of the sea.

                                        1849

ANNABEL LEE

Edgar Allan Poe

It was many and many a year ago, in a kingdom by the sea, that a maiden there lived whom you may know by the name of Annabel Lee; and this maiden she lived with no other thought than to love and be loved by me.

She was a child and *I* was a child, in this kingdom by the sea, but we loved with a love that was more than love—I and my Annabel Lee—with a love that wingéd seraphs of Heaven coveted her and me.

And this was the reason that, long ago, in this kingdom by the sea, a wind blew out of a cloud by night chilling my Annabel Lee; so that her highborn kinsmen came and bore her away from me, to shut her up in a sepulchre in this kingdom by the sea.

The angels, not half so happy in Heaven, went envying her and me: Yes! That was the reason (as all men know, in this kingdom by the sea) that the wind came out of the cloud, chilling and killing my Annabel Lee.

But our love it was stronger by far than the love of those who were older than we—of many far wiser than we—and neither the angels in Heaven above nor the demons down under the sea, can ever dissever my soul from the soul of the beautiful Annabel Lee:

For the moon never beams without bringing me dreams of the beautiful Annabel Lee; and the stars never rise but I see the bright eyes of the beautiful Annabel Lee; and so, all the night-tide, I lie down by the side of my darling, my darling, my life and my bride, in her sepulchre there by the sea. In her tomb by the side of the sea.

SUMMARY   **1. Why might it be necessary to mark a manuscript**
  PROBES   **for pauses and emphasis?**

2. What is the normal human tendency in terms of vocal rate in reading aloud?
3. Why is the problem of volume control in oral reading especially prominent in competitive situations?
4. What is probably the most effective method of eliminating an undesirable rhythm pattern from oral reading when all else fails?

BODILY ASPECTS OF ORAL READING

We said earlier that bodily aspects of oral reading are secondary in importance to vocal aspects. The beginning reader should not assume from this that bodily aspects are so unimportant that they can be overlooked. Certainly the most effective oral reading will be that which makes effective use of the body to assist the listener at receiving the full intended meaning of the selection. Our primary concern is in two areas: (1) gesture and eye contact and (2) use of the manuscript.

Gesture and Eye Contact

The degree and amount of gesturing appropriate in the oral reading situation will be limited significantly by the physical presence of a manuscript. Obviously if the reader is holding a manuscript, his use of hand and arm gestures will be curtailed. To be curtailed, however, does not mean to be eliminated. The oral reader should search his selection for appropriate places to insert gestures and movement which contribute to the overall meaning of the selection. Some caution should be exercised: avoid gestures which become overdone or distract from the meaning of the material.

Eye contact is of crucial importance to the beginning reader. Remember that the beginning reader is not performing; he is, instead, communicating. The oral reader is half of a communicative partnership with the author making up the source in a communication event; the reader's duty is to transmit the message contained in the writing to one or more receivers. Direct and well planned eye contact at appropriate points in the selection will create a communicative atmosphere in the mind of the listener rather than that of a stage presentation.

Use of the Manuscript

We assume at this point that the reader will employ a manuscript for his selection. Keep in mind that we maintained in an earlier chapter that a manuscript is *not* required in a communicative reading situation. Effective use of the manuscript is not to be taken for granted. Certain problems present themselves to the oral reader that require his attention to insure an effective reading situation.

We alert the beginning reader to three helpful suggestions in the preparation of a manuscript for oral reading: he should be very much aware of the typing, marking, and assembling of the manuscript.

Typing the Manuscript. If at all possible the manuscript should be typed to provide maximum reading ease. Some typewriters are capable of producing oversized letters—if such a machine is available to you, use it. Copy for the manuscript should be triple-spaced. Such spacing enables the reader to establish and maintain effective eye contact with his listeners. Multiple spaces between lines make it easy for the reader to find his place again after looking at his listeners.

If it is impossible to type the manuscript, you should print it very legibly, leaving adequate space between lines. Print your copy in dark ink, one that won't smear or smudge.

You should not be concerned with how long your manuscript turns out to be. A poem or short story which can be typed on a single page with wide margins and single spacing may require four or five pages of manuscript. While it may be a good idea generally to conserve paper, preparing a manuscript for oral reading is not one of those times.

Marking the Manuscript. If you leave adequate space between lines of the manuscript, you should have no difficulty in marking the pages. Feel free to make any kind of markings on the manuscript that you feel will assist you in reading. Mark the manuscript for pauses, emphasis, rate, and volume. If you feel that certain points are appropriate for gestures or eye contact with the listener, feel free to indicate so on your manuscript.

Markings on the manuscript should be made with one purpose in mind—to assist you in reading. Your manuscript is a personal item, not to be shared with others. The meaning contained in the manuscript must be shared with others—feel free to do whatever you feel is necessary to the manuscript to make you more able to deliver that meaning.

Be certain in your markings that you don't make it difficult to read the text. Markings should be made neatly and in such a way that they do not distract from the text on the page.

Assembling the Manuscript. Certain points to be considered in terms of assembling the manuscript may save the reader problems during the actual reading of the material. Pages in the manuscript should be numbered. Numbering the pages enables the reader to make last second checks to be certain that the pages are in order. It is indeed an embarrassed reader who turns page 4 in the middle of a selection to find page 6.

Do not staple or paper clip pages together. The pages of the manuscript should not be connected in any way. Leaving each page loose and free will enable the reader to change pages with a minimum amount of disruption. It is probably best to place the pages of the manuscript in some kind of attractive, book-like folder, so that pages can be turned rather than "switched." The manuscript should be held in one hand, like a book, leaving the other hand free to shift pages and gesture when the need arises.

The primary point to remember concerning the use of a manuscript in oral reading is that the manuscript is intended to assist the reader. The reader should feel free to do whatever he deems necessary to the manuscript to promote that help.

SUMMARY PROBES
1. Why is eye contact with listeners critical in oral reading?
2. Why should a manuscript be at least triple-spaced?
3. Why should the beginning reader avoid clipping or stapling pages of a manuscript?

LEARNING ACTIVITIES

1. Select a play or a novel with which you are very familiar. Select segments of the longer work which you feel would make good cuttings. Be prepared to discuss your rationale for each cutting in class.

2. Select a poem and write three different but appropriate introductions. Be prepared to read all three in class and discuss them.

3. Prepare a manuscript for a short selection and mark it for pause and emphasis as done in this chapter.

4. Read something aloud in a variety of physical settings and note the difference in sound and acoustics from one setting to another.

5. Find a poem which gives you a problem with rhythm pattern. Write the poem in prose format and read the poem both ways aloud to the class.

6. Prepare a manuscript for a class reading assignment, following all points suggested in this chapter.

II

Play Production

FIVE

GOALS   After completing this chapter you will be able to:

      1. Understand the difference between the study of drama and the study of dramatics.

      2. Distinguish five historical periods of theater history and identify contributions of each period.

      3. Differentiate tragedy, comedy, and melodrama as traditional types of drama.

      4. Identify the six elements available to the playwright in developing a conflict.

      5. Recognize three crucial points of consideration for a production group in the process of selecting a play.

An Introduction to Play Production

One of the greatest playwrights of all time, William Shakespeare, once wrote, "All the world's a stage, and all the men and women merely players." The meaning of this statement may provide a clue to the mysterious fascination people throughout the ages have shown for the world of drama and playacting. In fact, most of us at one time or another have enjoyed fantasies of appearing on a stage and holding an audience of grateful patrons entranced with our ability.

While the great majority of us will never fulfill our fantasy of performing professionally on stage, no form of communicative entertainment available to man enjoys a more widespread audience of appreciative human beings. We in America have grown to expect to be entertained by playacting—whether it be actual stage performance, television dramatic or comedy series, or the excitement of the motion-picture theater.

The practical application of concepts of play production will be our concern in this section. While most of us will not become professional actors or technical production experts, participation in play production can be one of the most rewarding and beneficial experiences available to the student in various levels of education.

The study of the world of theater can normally be achieved in one of two ways. For the sake of clarity, we will differentiate the study of drama and the study of dramatics, two terms which are often used interchangeably by many and, thus, create confusion. For our purposes we will define drama as the study of the play as communicative literature. While most assuredly the study of the play is crucial to production, it should not become the dominant concern.

Dramatics refers to the actual *production* of the play rather than the play itself. We will explore the area of dramatics or play production to provide the basic knowledge needed by the student who is interested in becoming an active participant in any aspect of play production. Our emphasis throughout our discussion of play production will remain with practical concepts rather than theoretical bases of knowledge.

Since a serious study of practical application should begin with some concern for a theoretical base, this chapter will provide a brief historical sketch of drama in the civilized world. Three basic types and techniques of drama will also be introduced. This chapter will conclude with practical suggestions for selecting plays for production—a first and most crucial step to a successful show.

HISTORY OF DRAMA

Most institutions of higher learning offer complete courses dealing with the history of drama. We are not so naïve as to assume that we can fully provide the student with an understanding and appreciation of the periods in drama history in a brief section of a chapter. We feel, however, that it is possible briefly to cover material from the more significant periods in the history of drama in order to provide a basic understanding of the subject.

For our purposes we will briefly summarize five periods in the history of drama: the Greek, the Roman, the Shakespearean, the Realistic period, and the modern era.

Greek Drama

Throughout the history of drama, the church and, thus, religion has played a greater role in the development of drama than any other institution. The Greek drama had its origin in religious ceremony.

Three clearly defined and recognized types of drama were prominent in ancient Greece. The *tragedy* was the first to develop and generally dealt with heroic legends familiar to the citizenry of the day. Later forms of drama were the *satyr* plays which made sport of the legends presented seriously in tragedy, and the *comedy* which went below the heroic legends to deal with the more base elements of Greek life of that day. All Greek drama, regardless of type, was written in verse. All three forms of drama also made use of a narrator and a chorus between scenes of dramatic action and sometimes within scenes.

Drama was of crucial importance to the average Greek citizen because plays were presented as part of religious rituals and observances. Play festivals were an important element in Athenian life; public interest was so great that competition in play presentation was introduced during the Greek era. In addition to, and in conjunction with, drama festivals, the Greeks were avid participants in drama contests. These contests provided a significant impetus to the development and sustenance of the Greek drama.

Most of the information we have today concerning the Greek drama comes from the manuscripts of the plays themselves. What we know of the physical nature of the Greek theater is somewhat uncertain. Existing information comes from sources such as vase paintings, sketchy contributions of ancient Greek writers, and, of course, the ruins themselves. Most theater history scholars maintain that the Greek playing area was circular and the audience sat in a semicircular pattern around the playing area. Some reports would indicate, however, that from evidence dating years before any written records, other patterns of theater arrangement existed in ancient Greece.

Roman Drama

In many ways the Roman theater was imitative of the Greek drama. Physical structure of Roman theaters was believed to be a mere adaptation of earlier Greek structures. The three types of drama—tragedy, satyr, and comedy—introduced by the Greeks, carried over for the most part to the Roman period.

The Roman era introduced the highly popular pantomime as a drama form. They made extensive use of costumes and physical elements of production which served to please audiences. Original message content for Roman pantomimes was unusual as most of the pantomimes were simply a rehash of myths from ancient Greece.

Roman drama did not hold the religious significance that drama did in Greece. Romans were much more inclined to seek spectacle and frolicking entertainment than they were to seek message inspiration from the drama. While the Greeks were being entertained by the use of drama as a means of religious and life expression, the Romans were more concerned with entertainment as a primary desire. In Roman drama, content and message significance began to take a secondary position to the spectacle of the stage. As a result, the Church ousted drama as immoral and vain.

Shakespearean Drama

Labeling this segment in the history of drama as Shakespearean drama is not an intentional effort to neglect or slight any other prominent writer of the periods surrounding and coinciding with the age of Shakespeare. The plays written by William Shakespeare do, though, provide enough points of distinction to extract certain characteristics as being contributory to later periods of drama.

Two prominent characteristics of Shakespeare's plays were the heavy dependence on the use of servants in plays and the inclusion of the supernatural. While many servants appeared in Shakespearean dramas, their individual parts were normally small. In many cases they were made out to be dumb and ignorant. Supernatural elements— usually manifested in witches, ghosts, or potions—were present in many Shakespearean dramas.

Shakespeare introduced new appeals in drama. A familiar appeal in many of his plays was that of the psychology of the mob. Public speaking before groups of people was intertwined throughout his plots as well as mob murders and instances of human brutality to other humans. The mob scenes in *Julius Caesar* and public reading of proclamations in *Othello* are examples of such appeals.

In many ways other than those already cited, Shakespearean drama served as a mirror of human life in his time. His characters followed the class structure of Elizabethan life. While his plays portrayed servants as dumb and ignorant, his plays flattered the nobility and the ruling classes of the day.

Internal structure of his plays made many innovative contributions to the development of drama. Shakespeare utilized a device called the prologue to introduce scenes and to provide transitional material from one scene to another. In many instances, he included comic scenes in the midst of deep tragedy as an aside to the audience. Shakespeare even developed characters whose main purpose for inclusion in his plays was to provide comic relief from tragic occurrences. Sir John Falstaff is, perhaps, one of the most popular characters of this nature. The practice of including a comical character to provide light relief from more serious subject matter has survived the times and still finds prominence in modern drama. (We are all familiar with serious "whodunit" mysteries in which one policeman investigating the crime provides comic relief through his mental and physical stumbling. Many of our former western heroes always had a comic "sidekick" to provide periodic laughter in the tense action.)

Perhaps, the most famous of all playhouses in Shakespeare's day was the Globe Theater. The physical structure of the playing area had changed drastically from the earlier Greek and Roman theaters. Simply counting the number of different scenes in a typical Shakespeare play confirms a definite need for much greater flexibility in staging than at any earlier time in the history of drama. The typical Shakespearean theater had multiple playing areas—each capable of staging a separate and distinct scene in the course of a play. Audience members were packed into virtually every part of the theater not used for acting. Playing areas are illustrated in Figure 5.1.

The Realists

In the years following Shakespeare, throughout what became known as the Restoration Period and the Eighteenth Century Theater, drama fell into a framework of sentimentalism and artificiality. Realism evolved as a revolt against such tendencies of drama. Realism made an effort to create an illusion of real life by means of material contemporary to the day and time.

The outstanding contributions of the realists were the presentation in dramatic form of contemporary social problems involving language and acting in patterns common to the period. Nonetheless, such an effort at contemporary realism was not a new phenomenon in drama. The Greeks and Romans were known to inject much of contemporary life in their plays, and Shakespeare made many successful efforts to depict life of the various classes of his day in dramatic art form. Thereafter, the period known as that of realism in the late nineteenth century was an effort to return to those principles of earlier years.

While the realism movement was centered primarily in parts of the world other than the United States, the movement was responsible for eventually developing a group of American playwrights who adapted contemporary social significance to the American scene. Eventually a great body of plays dealing with native American problems and depicting native American characters resulted.

The Modernists

Today, some of the most significant work in theater is being done in the United States. Americans spend more time attending and re-

Figure 5.1 Stage area for the Globe Theater

ceive more enjoyment from various forms of dramatic entertainment available to them via the stage, television, and the motion-picture screen than citizens of virtually any other country in the world.

The advent of the motion picture, radio, and television as entertainment media has had a profound effect on the modern theater. While live stage drama has been faced with conditions in this country making it difficult to survive, it has done so. The role of professional theater has diminished to the point of being confined to restricted geographic areas in some of our major cities. Prior to movies, radio, and television, professional stage productions were a part of the local offering of virtually every community in the nation.

Schools and colleges in the United States have played a most significant role in keeping the spoken stage drama alive in the wake of negative conditions. College and university theater programs provide a regular flow of stage productions to their constituent communities. Further, dramatic productions are a part of virtually every community through local elementary and high schools.

Interest in theater via educational means has resulted in a wide and growing popularity for community theater groups. We as a country continue to produce playwrights capable of providing scripts for the stage as well as for the motion-picture screen and the television set.

Drama has never at any time in its history enjoyed a greater and more widespread popularity than it enjoys today in the United States. To cite another famous line from another famous play, "The play's the thing."[1] If the play is truly the thing, our study of techniques of producing the play should find relevance in contemporary society.

SUMMARY PROBES

1. What are the differences between a study of drama and a study of dramatics?
2. What three clearly defined and recognized types of drama were prominent in ancient Greece?
3. Compare and contrast Roman and Greek drama.
4. Cite at least two contributions of Shakespearean drama that appear to be unique and innovative.
5. How did the period of realism in drama history relate to contemporary American drama?
6. How have schools and colleges helped to keep theater alive in America?

TYPES OF DRAMA

Modern drama has drawn from types of plays developed throughout the years of drama history. Most of these forms, however, are offspring of the three basic types of drama: tragedy, comedy, or melodrama.

Tragedy

Most plays whether they be performed on the stage, on the screen, or before television cameras make definite distinctions between the good guys and the bad guys, or, in terms of drama, the protagonists and the antagonists. Simply stated, in tragedy the protagonist, or the good guy, is the eventual loser in the conflict involved in the play.

Historically the protagonist normally lost the basic conflict because of an error in judgment. In early Greek drama the innocent and mortal protagonist usually lost as a result of attempting to take the moral law into his own hands. Shakespearean tragedy followed similar lines.

While one might experience some difficulty in attempting to apply the moral law versus mortal law of early drama to the modern era, we need only consider the barrage of tragic drama on prime-time television in which the good guy often loses because he makes an effort to severely alter the contemporary standard of moral law.

Comedy

In comedy as opposed to tragedy, the protagonist wins in the basic conflict of the play. In Greek and other early eras of drama development, often the only requirement for a production to be labeled a comedy was that the protagonist be the victor.

In modern drama, we have come to associate comedy with laughter and sometimes even raucous entertainment. However, because of our contemporary expectations of laughter associated with the label of comedy, many plays that were once classified as comedies in earlier times would today be judged as tragic by most audiences.

Several variations of the comedy have developed throughout time. If we accept the premise that comedy is the result of some incongruity projected by the dramatist and perceived by the spectator, the nature of that incongruity in large part determines what kind of comedy we are witnessing.

For example, incongruities existing in comedy may either be physical or mental. Physical incongruity—or that kind of comedic situation which requires little thought, such as a man slipping on a banana peel—has been termed *low comedy*. On the other hand, *high comedy* refers to the type of incongruity that requires thought or mental processes on the part of the audience for comprehension and appreciation.

When a play is labeled a *farce*, it contains incongruities so widely separated from the norm or unbelievable as to cause a strain on the human imagination. The imagination accepts the incongruities, however, because of their promise of interest and entertainment to the spectator. Farce and slapstick, therefore, are often confused. While the two types of comedy are similar in some respects, *slapstick* refers to comedy derived solely from the physical and bodily absurdities of the performers. Perhaps the kings of twentieth-century slapstick may prove to be the Three Stooges, who made audiences laugh for years primarily as a result of their physically beating each other around on stage.

Melodrama

Melodrama is a mixed form of drama which combines the victory of the protagonist with the impending disaster of the tragedy. Traditional melodrama is easily distinguished from other forms of drama by its labeled situations, stock characterizations, high emotional levels, and strongly expressed sentiment. A typical melodrama has featured a heroine who is the protagonist, the ever-present villain who fills the role of antagonist, and the hero who saves the day for the heroine.

While the highly exaggerated characteristics of the traditional melodrama are seldom seriously performed today, the dramatic form has survived the times and one often finds the melodrama today used as a classic from the past. Elements of the melodrama can be found in many drama forms in contemporary entertainment. While the situations, stock characters, and high emotions are normally toned down so as to make them acceptable to audiences, the steady diet of soap operas enjoyed by many Americans on daytime television contain many of the elements of the classic melodrama.

TECHNIQUE OF DRAMA

Before analyzing the elements and devices used by the author or playwright to accomplish the dramatic purpose in his writing, one should accept that all drama involves some type of human conflict. The existence of a conflict situation does not mean necessarily that the subject of a play must be serious or heavy. Certainly the conflict in a story like *One Flew Over The Cuckoo's Nest* would be considered serious and complex to understand. The conflict in a W. C. Fields comedy may be much simpler and light, but, nonetheless, it is in fact a human conflict.

The author's purpose then is to develop a conflict. He has at his disposal the tools of plot, theme or thesis, setting, atmosphere, dialogue, and characterization.

Plot

Plot refers to the author's arrangement of incidents by which the conflict is developed to its climax and from there brought to its conclusion. While many people use the terms *plot* and *story* interchangeably, the two concepts are different in meaning. *Story* refers to the original material which the author rearranges to give it special significance. The same story could be written as either a comedy or a tragedy—depending on how the author chooses to plot the story or to arrange the incidents in the conflict.

The author must use exposition for plot development and must include crises from time to time which lead to a high climactic point in the drama and, of course, some solution must normally be provided for audience mental ease. Playwrights must normally be conscious of factors of time, place, and action as necessary unifying elements connecting the independent elements of plot development.

Theme or Theses

A play must have some underlying theme or thesis to act as a unifying force throughout and to which all elements contribute. While a theme or thesis is usually required for a successful play, the theme or thesis should not be the predominant element in the play. If the predominant factor remembered by the audience after seeing a play is the theme at the expense of the characters and plot, the play would not meet the tests of success. The thesis or theme should be apparent in the work but not the overriding or predominant factor.

Setting

The setting of a play is of vital importance in establishing a mood. The setting can also be of assistance in the author's effort to establish the environment and personalities of the characters. The author may utilize change of setting to establish passage of time and change of character.

Atmosphere

Every play has a dominant atmosphere which can be defined as the mood medium through which the play moves. Atmosphere may be established in various ways by the author; however, a common method is by the use of subtle repetition of apparently unimportant details which in the mass create their effect upon the subconscious mind of the spectator.

Production aspects such as setting, lighting, costuming, and props can make significant contributions to the total effect of atmosphere on a production.

Dialogue

Dialogue can be defined as the verbal language used by the characters and written by authors to transmit the communicative message involved in the play. The purpose of dialogue is to establish character, to create atmosphere, and to advance the plot of the play. Effective dialogue will accomplish all three of these purposes. Good dialogue must be in keeping with the type, time, and place represented by the play.

Characterization

The author must provide characterization for his play in order to advance the plot desired. The portrayal of a character is achieved by what the actor says and does, by how he says it and does it, and by the actor's appearance. *Characterization* normally refers to the delineation of people who possess interesting, unusual, or arresting qualities of personality.

SUMMARY   1. **How does the eventual outcome of the protagonist**
PROBES   **and antagonist in a conflict affect the labeling of a**
                    play as either a comedy or a tragedy?

2. What special characteristics are responsible for labeling a comedy as either a farce or slapstick?
3. What good evidence exists in American theater and entertainment that the melodrama is still very much alive?
4. How does the plot of a play differ from the story?
5. What are the primary purposes of dialogue in writing a play?

SELECTING A PLAY FOR PRODUCTION

With a basic discussion of drama history, types and techniques summarized, we are ready to begin our concern for play production. While later chapters will deal with techniques of acting and technical aspects of play production, this introductory chapter is an appropriate point to consider the first and very crucial step in play production—selecting a play to produce.

There are literally thousands of plays in print available to student groups of performers. Such plays range from the historical classics from Greece and Shakespeare's England to lower quality and royalty-free plays produced specifically for the amateur stage. The forty-five plays most often produced from 1969–74 in junior and senior colleges affiliated with two theater fraternities are listed in Table 5.1. (See pgs. 114–115.) A list such as this one is a good starting point for ideas and possibilities for plays to produce.

When faced with the task of selecting a play for stage production, three major considerations should be carefully analyzed by those responsible. First, the communicative message or the play itself should be a major point of criteria. Second, production capabilities of the group are a necessary qualifying factor. And, third, as in any communicative situation, the anticipated audience must be given careful consideration.

The Play's Message

Our approach to play production is to consider the written play as a communicative message to be transmitted to others. The author is the original communicator in the situation: he structures his message into the format of the dramatic script using language to develop characters, theme, plot, and stage instructions as supplementary message material.

The communicative message is solely the author's if the receiver in the communication act only reads the play.

When a group of interested individuals chooses to produce the play on stage, however, those people become a vital segment in a communicative partnership with the author to transmit the message. Given the opportunity to view the same play produced by several different groups, one will see different components of meaning emerge from one production to another. Certain meaning components will remain constant; these are more than likely the unique contributions of the author. Those components that change, however, are the result of contributions from many individuals involved in one of several areas of play production.

The first question, then, to be answered by a group selecting a play for production is, "What is the message being transmitted in this play?" If the message is deemed worthy of several weeks of rehearsal and preparation, and if the group feels that they can adequately bring to the message the needed components of meaning to complete the partnership, then the play may very well be appropriate for the group. While this step in play selection may sound matter of fact, it should not be taken lightly. Woe is the group of aspiring dramatists who select a play in haste to discover general disenchantment with the play's message after committing themselves to from four to eight weeks of intense rehearsal.

Production Capabilities

Determining that a play has a significant and suitable message to communicate is a major step in play selection. However, the selection process must not stop here. Assuming that a group has found a play suitable to them for presentation in terms of message, the group must next determine for itself if it can meet the challenges required by the script for good production.

Cast. Depending on the nature of the specific group preparing for play production, the number called for in the cast of a show may be a big factor. If the pool of available and willing talent is estimated to be small, select a play with a small cast. If the group anticipates that large numbers of students will aspire to acting positions, select a play to accommodate as many as possible.

Factors other than number of available personnel may be a major consideration. Some schools are more successful at getting females to try out for roles than males—other schools may find the opposite situa-

Table 5.1   Plays most often produced in junior, four-year colleges from 1969–74.

SHOW	RANK ORDER JR.	RANK ORDER SR.	AUTHOR	TYPE	MEN	WOMEN
Androcles and the Lion	0	12	Bernard Shaw	Comedy	14	2
Antigone	9	3	Jean Anouilh	Tragedy	8	4
Armes And The Man	9	17	G. B. Shaw	Comedy	5	3
Arsenic And Old Lace	8	17	Joseph Kesselring	Comedy	11	3
Barefoot In The Park	11	10	Neil Simon	Comedy	4	2
Black Comedy	0	15	Peter Shaffer	Farce	5	3
Blithe Spirit	7	16	Noel Coward	Farce	2	5
Come Blow Your Horn	6	0	Neil Simon	Comedy	3	4
Crucible, The	3	4	Arthur Miller	Drama	10	10
Dark Of The Moon	8	5	Richardson-Berney	Drama	1	27
Death Of A Salesman	11	0	Arthur Miller	Drama	8	5
Diary Of Anne Frank	11	0	Goodrich-Hackett	Drama	5	5
Don't Drink The Water	11	0	Woody Allen	Farce	12	4
Effect of Gamma Rays On Man In The Moon Marigolds	0	12	Paul Zindel	Drama	0	5
Fantasticks, The	4	2	Jones and Schmidt	Musical	3	2
Funny Thing Happened On The Way To The Forum, A	8	11	Stephen Sundheim	Comedy	4	3
Glass Menagerie, The	2	7	Tennessee Williams	Drama	2	2
Harvey	8	0	Mary Chase	Comedy	6	6
Hello Dolly	11	0	Wilder-Herman	Musical		
Imaginary Invalid, The	11	15	Moliere	Comedy	8	4
Importance of Being Earnest	5	8	Oscar Wilde	Farce	5	4
J.B.	3	10	Archibald Macleish	Drama	12	9
Land Of The Dragon	11	0	Madge Miller	Comedy	5	5
Lion In Winter, The	0	9	James Goldman	Comedy	5	2
Little Foxes, The	11	0	Lillian Hellman	Drama	6	4
Little Mary Sunshine	11	0	Rick Besovan	Musical	17	3
Madwoman of Challiot	0	14	Jean Giraudoux	Comedy		8
Man of LaMancha	11	17	Dale Wasserman	Musical	21	5

SHOW	RANK ORDER		AUTHOR	TYPE	MEN	WOMEN
	JR.	SR.				
Midsummer Night's Dream, A	0	10	Wm. Shakespeare	Comedy	13	10
Miracle Worker, The	7	0	Wm. Gibson	Drama	7	7
Night Thoreau Spent In Jail	11	17	Lawrence and Lee	Comedy	11	14
Odd Couple, The	7	6	Neil Simon	Comedy	6	2
Our Town	9	15	Thornton Wilder	Drama	17	7
Skin Of Our Teeth	11	12	Thornton Wilder	Farce	4-5	4-5
Spoon River Anthology	11	12	Charles Aidman	Revue	3	2
Star Spangled Girl	0	16	Neil Simon	Comedy	3	1
Stop The World I Want To Get Off	0	16	Anthony Newley	Musical	1	3
Streetcar Named Desire, A	9	11	Tennessee Williams	Drama	6	6
Summertree	11	8	Ron Cowen	Drama	4	2
Taming Of The Shrew, The	11	8	Wm. Shakespeare	Comedy	17	4
Tartuffe	11	13	Moliere	Commedy	7	5
Trojan Women, The	0	14	Euripides	Tragedy	3	5
Waiting For Godot	0	16	Thomas Becket	Tragedy	5	0
You Know I Can't Hear You When The Waters Running	11	0	Robert Anderson	Comedy	7	6
You're A Good Man Charlie Brown	1	1	Charles M. Schultz	Comedy	4	3

tion to be true. Anticipated difficulties in getting the proper proportion and types of performers must be considered. Failure to consider possible difficulties in casting brought about by play selection can lead the performing group to disastrous situations in play preparation.

Technical Capabilities. Even if the group determines that a sufficient cast exists in the available student pool, the script may present insurmountable technical problems when physical facilities are considered. If the play is to be performed in a cafeteria or in the middle of a gymnasium floor, a Shakespearean play requiring an excess of thirty-five scenes may be too much to handle. There are excellent plays which make use of only one setting. For ease in production and dramatic effect, some groups might do well to select one of them.

A script that calls for elaborate lighting scenes to create atmosphere and quick scene changes may be impossible for a production group who is saddled with a stage with twelve-foot ceilings and no backstage area.

Methods and suggestions for producing plays with inferior or substandard facilities will be presented in a later chapter. At this point, it suffices to say that the production group must be very much aware of the technical limitations in play production and that they must weigh these limitations carefully when selecting a play.

Audience. If we consider the production of a play as a form of human communication, we as communicators in the production group must keep the interests of the audience as receivers in the total communication process in mind. While our primary concern in play production is to provide an educational experience for student participants, we cannot afford to disregard totally preferences of the audience in selecting a play.

If your school or group has a past history of play production, you should be able to discover without too much difficulty what kind of plays have met with audience favor in the past. If you are providing your audience with what may be their first exposure to local stage performance, it would be best to select a play with general appeal— perhaps one that will strike a note of familiarity with the audience.

While the amateur production group should strive to avoid the professional and commercial attitude of giving an audience only what it wants, the group cannot disregard known preferences of the audience. Even though our primary concern is educational experiences for participants, the play production is not complete without a reasonably large and satisfied audience in the theater.

SUMMARY   1. How is the performance of a play by a production
PROBES   group a communicative partnership?
             2. What special questions concerning casting
                capabilities must be raised before selecting a play
                for production purposes?
             3. How can technical capacities affect a production
                group's choice of a play?
             4. Why must the audience be a major factor in choos-
                ing a play for production?

LEARNING ACTIVITIES

1. Read a play from each of the five periods in the history of theater in this chapter. Your instructor will provide you with a suggested
list of possible plays. Write a report on each play with the primary
intent of comparing and contrasting the five plays in terms of plot,
theme or thesis, setting, atmosphere, dialogue, and characterization.
2. Do further reading on each of the five periods in the history of
drama discussed in the chapter as well as on other eras falling between
those discussed. Be prepared to discuss your report in class.
3. Read a classic melodrama and then attempt to identify elements
of melodrama in a contemporary form of entertainment.
4. Compile a list of five plays that meet the tests of play selection
discussed in this chapter. When evaluating the plays use your own
production capabilities as a criteria. Be prepared to compare and discuss your lists in class.

References

Berthold, Margot. *A History of World Theater.* New York: Frederick Ungar, 1972.
Hughes, Glen. *The Story of the Theatre.* New York: Samuel French, 1947.
MacGowan, Kenneth, and Melnitz, William. *Golden Ages of the Theater.* En-
    glewood Cliffs: Prentice-Hall, 1959.

SIX

GOALS   After completing this chapter you will be able to:

1. Identify four basic steps in character analysis.

2. Understand the importance of maintaining character to the overall success of the performance.

3. Identify basic stage directions and acting areas.

4. Relate the importance of speaking to sound acting technique.

5. Comprehend the importance of clear motivation for every on-stage movement.

6. Define fourteen essential terms in basic acting technique.

Technique and Principles of Acting

Many people enjoy daydreams of being a great actor or actress and enthralling audiences with their stage expertise. Of course, very few such daydreams ever become a reality. However, the authors would hope that any student in an educational setting who desires to portray a character in a play on stage would realize the opportunity to do so. The self-discipline and rigid training necessary to bring a character to life on stage can be of benefit to the student in many more ways than simply contributing to a successful stage production.

This chapter will investigate some of the most fundamental and basic concepts involved in acting. We fully realize that semester or year-long courses meant to train actors are offered in many institutions. Further, many specialized schools in the country offer full four-year courses of study in acting. Our purpose here is simply to acquaint the amateur student with some fundamental concepts of acting technique that should enable him to understand the intricacies of stage performance.

The student will be introduced to three major concerns facing the beginning actor or actress. They are characterization, stage directions, and basic acting technique.

CHARACTERIZATION

We will define *characterization* as that process whereby a person becomes another person temporarily for stage portrayal. The aspiring actor or actress must lose his or her own personality for the purpose of portraying another personality in a simulated real-life situation.

Characterization is the single most important factor in determining varying degrees of quality of an acting performance. All traits of the actor's own personality not appropriate to the character being portrayed—a person's voice, movement, bodily action, and reaction—must be sublimated.

Obviously, some acting parts present much greater difficulties to actors than others. The term *typecasting* is used to indicate a situation in which an actor must portray a character with personality traits similar to the actor's own personality. For instance, when a college age, athletically inclined male is assigned the task of portraying a college age, athletically inclined male in a stage production, his task is simpler than if he had been assigned the part of a fifty-five-year-old skid-row derelict. In the first instance we might say that the student had been typecast into a part. His task of characterization will be partially fulfilled before he reads the play. Another form of typecasting occurs when the same person always plays a similar role. An example would be a performer such as the late Marjorie Main who not only was cast as Ma Kettle in nine films, but also portrayed similar characters in other pictures she made.

One of the true marks of outstanding acting is the degree of versatility that an individual is able to inject into portraying various kinds of stage personalities. In order to be a truly versatile actor or actress the student must master all the fine points of developing and maintaining a character.

Our primary aim in a discussion of characterization is twofold. First, the actor must be concerned with a careful and progressional system of character analysis and, secondly, once the character has been developed to the satisfaction of the actor, the character must be maintained.

Character Analysis

The degree of character analysis required of an actor will depend directly on the degree of contrast the actual personality displays from the stage personality required. If you are to portray a character greatly different from your own personality, it may be necessary for you to undergo actual field observation of living people in addition to the progressional steps detailed here. Professional actors who have played a biographical role often report that they may spend a year or more studying the life habits of the person to be portrayed.

There are four basic steps in developing character that every performer should consider as soon as a part has been assigned him.

Read the Entire Play. It is impossible to understand fully the assigned character and accompanying expectations of that character until the entire play has been read through. Even if a character only appears in one or two scenes of the production, a full and thorough understanding of the character's relationship to other characters and overall plot of the play is essential.

It may be necessary to read the play through several times to receive full understanding of the personality of an assigned character. In the one or more readings of the entire play, a concentrated effort should be made to determine as many personality traits of a character as possible. Also, relationships between an assigned character and others in the play should be determined.

It can sometimes be helpful to construct a personality inventory of a character after an actor feels he understands it. He should pose questions about the person he will portray and answer those questions based on the understanding of him. Appropriate questions will be variant from one character to another—however, an actor should raise some of the same questions about his character that he might raise about an actual person. He should begin with such questions as, "Would strangers like this person if they were to meet him? Would he be liberal or conservative on political issues?" Any type of standardized or self-constructed personality inventory or measurement can be applied to the character—often with very helpful results to the aspiring actor or actress.

Position the Character in the Basic Conflict. In the preceding chapter, we established that every play contains a basic conflict to which all characters of the play relate in some manner. Whether the play is a farcical comedy or a very serious and heavy drama makes no difference: a basic conflict is a mandatory element in all plays. (However, it may take more than one reading to fully comprehend the basic conflict of the play.) After the actor feels that he fully understands the conflict, he should determine where his character stands in relation to it. Is his character a protagonist or an antagonist? If he is an antagonist, who are his fellow antagonists, and who are those in the play who will most likely oppose him as protagonists?

Regardless of the size of the part the actor is to portray, the character will more than likely be on one side or the other of the basic conflict.

Rarely do we find a part in a play that is neutral to the conflict or a part that holds no relationship to the conflict. Even a one line walk on and walk off is written into the script for a reason and that reason probably relates to the basic conflict. It is his task to determine that reason. If a part is truly neutral and holds no relationship to the conflict, we should question the worth of the playwright who would include such a part in a script.

Relate the Character to the Traditional Stock Characters of the Drama. Several stereotyped, stock characters exist in the minds of audiences of stage productions. Certainly we have some idea in mind as to how a villain should act. Other stock characters are the interfering mother-in-law, the hen-pecked husband, spinster aunt, dizzy blonde, and misguided youth. We could go on and on listing stock characters which have developed in people's minds from real-life situations. While the practice of stereotyping is not normally acceptable, we must face the reality that people do cling to stereotypes and certain personality traits and mannerisms are expected of characters fitting one of the stock positions.

If the character the actor is to portray fits one of the stock character molds, such audience and public expectations can assist him in character development. The actor should, however, make a concentrated effort to inject some original elements of personality into the portrayal of even the most stereotyped character that might raise it above the stock part. An actor or actress who copies or mimics just those elements of personality an audience is likely to expect in a stock part has not met his or her obligation to the practice of character development.

Raise and Answer Specific Questions Relating to Character. Once the performer has satisfied the general points of character analysis raised thus far, he or she is obligated to raise and answer specific questions concerning the character to be portrayed.

The actor should determine if there is a general physical mask that should be assumed by the character. Should the character be a happy person with a pleasant smile? Should the general mask of the person be gruff and grouchy? Perhaps one general physical mask is not appropriate for the character throughout the play. In that case the student must know when and why the general mask should change.

Is there a particular posture that should be used for the character? Obviously, if the character is eighty-five years old, some form of posture indicating old age should be employed. Relating to posture, the student should also consider if there are characteristic walks or movements that will add to audience appreciation and understanding of the character.

The student should consider if there is a particular style or color of costume which would be more appropriate for developing the personality desired. Other factors such as properties to be carried or used by the character and appropriate make-up should be considered. While many of these questions will be answered definitely by production and technical staffs later in the progression of play production, the performer has an obligation to his part to consider these now and to provide input for decisions which might be made later.

Maintaining Character

Once the performer has arrived at what he or she considers to be the proper characterization for the part to be portrayed, the next task facing the performer throughout rehearsal and performance is maintaining that character at all times on the stage. Nothing is more disconcerting to an audience than to witness an actor or actress "break character" while on stage and suddenly become John or Jane Doe rather than the person being portrayed.

When on stage, the performer must lose himself in the mood and tempo of the scene or play. The actor should submerge himself long before he comes on stage, and while on stage follow the action of the play even if there are long periods of time when the actor has no lines. Characterization is a constant on-stage process—not just when you are speaking lines. It is easy to become mentally distracted by things such as your next line, the heat of the lights, the torn garment of another performer. Nonetheless, the seasoned actor must be consciously aware of the demand for constant characterization. When you go on stage, leave yourself behind, become the person you are portraying and remain that person until you are well off stage.

It might be a good idea to practice "getting into character" several pages in the script before you actually make a stage entrance. You should also remain in character for a specified time after you exit. To do so will prevent the assuming of character after entrance—rather than before—or the shedding of character before the exit is accomplished.

SUMMARY   1. What is meant by typecasting? How does it relate
PROBES   to the importance of versatility in acting?
            2. How can a personality inventory of the character
               to be portrayed assist the actor or actress?

3. What is meant by stock characters in acting? How can an understanding of them assist in developing character?

4. What is meant when it is said that the actor must lose himself in the mood and tempo of the scene or play in order to maintain character?

STAGE DIRECTIONS

The beginning actor or actress will, of necessity, familiarize himself with the universal language of stage directions at once. Playscripts normally include directions for each part for movement within a scene, placement at the beginning of a scene, and entrances and exits. The director of the show may wish to change stage directions provided in the script in order to facilitate blocking for a particular stage. *Blocking* refers to the arrangement and placement of characters, furniture, and properties on the stage so that all the essential action of the script can be seen and understood by the audience. The beginning performer should consider a pencil a standard piece of equipment at all rehearsals in order to mark the script according to the director's instructions.

Stage directions are always written from the position of the performer on stage as he or she faces the audience. Thus, right stage means

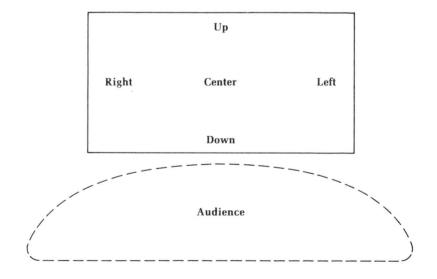

Figure 6.1   Five basic playing areas on stage

the actor's right as he faces the audience, and left stage means the actor's left. There are five basic descriptive terms for any total stage area from which several different playing areas can derive. We speak of right stage, left stage, center stage, upstage, and downstage, as illustrated in Figure 6.1. While right and left stage are determined by the actor as he faces the audience, upstage and downstage are determined by distance from the audience.

During the seventeenth century, stages were built in England with raked floors, that is, the stage was angled with the lowest point nearest the audience and the highest point farthest away from the audience. From these raked stages came the terms *upstage* and *downstage*. To tell an actor to go upstage meant literally what it said. The actor turned away from the audience and walked up the incline of the stage floor. The actor came downstage when he walked down the same incline to be nearer the audience.

The terms *upstage* and *downstage* have survived in the language of stage directions even though raked stages are no longer built. Modern theater architects found it much more convenient and more conducive to audience ease in seeing all the action to rake the auditorium floor and build the stage on a level plane. Thus today the back rows in auditoriums are higher than rows closer to the audience.

The total number of playing areas for any particular play is determined by the nature of the requirements for furniture and set. Actually, a stage can have as many as fifteen different playing areas. Figure 6.2 illustrates a typical stage floor with fifteen playing areas. It is essential that the performer memorize the fifteen areas and be able to move to any one of them from any other when directed. Movement from one area to another should be smooth and spontaneous and with no hesitation or pause for thought.

It will be necessary for the student actor to commit the following stage abbreviations to memory. The first five abbreviations indicate stage areas from which the various combinations in Figure 6.2 are derived. The last four abbreviations are others most often used in marking scripts and directing performers:

R	Right Stage	St	Stage
L	Left Stage	X	Cross
U	Upstage	T	Table
D	Downstage	Ch	Chair
C	Center Stage		

The beginning actor will also be required to learn and use certain written symbols which direct movement by actors on stage. For example, within the script the actor should place a mark (/) to indicate a

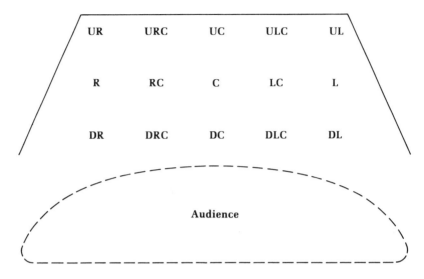

Figure 6.2 Typical stage floor with fifteen playing areas

pause between words. In addition, he may be asked to make any of the markings on his script listed below to enable him to move more freely and meaningfully on the stage:

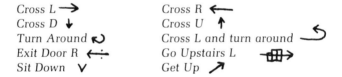

Cross L →	Cross R ←
Cross D ↓	Cross U ↑
Turn Around ↻	Cross L and turn around ↰
Exit Door R ←┆	Go Upstairs L ⊞→
Sit Down V	Get Up ↗

SUMMARY PROBES

1. **What do the terms** right stage, left stage, upstage, **and** downstage **mean to the performer on stage?**
2. **List the fifteen possible playing areas on a typical stage.**

ACTING TECHNIQUE

While specific and fine points of acting may differ greatly from one director to another or from one school of acting to another, we believe that there are several points of acting technique which would receive general acceptance from most authorities. The approach in presenting these principles of technique is practical in nature: our effort here is not to be concerned with why these concepts are accepted, but rather that they are concepts with widespread acceptance and the serious student of acting should know them.

There is a first rule of acting that supercedes all other rules or statements of technique: An actor MUST speak loudly enough and distinctly enough to be heard by every member of his audience—even the people in the very back row of the auditorium or theater setting. The principle involved here is audience awareness—one that is of primary concern in every form of human communication. The actor or actress who cannot be heard at any point in the auditorium can easily destroy the total effect of an otherwise successful production.

Acting technique can be divided into two areas for ease of study: we are concerned with speaking technique and also the technique of movement.

Speaking Technique

An actor should make a careful and detailed study of the script and especially his own lines to determine which words are most important in terms of delivering meaning to the audience. Those words, crucial to full understanding, should be emphasized more heavily than other incidental words. The actor should always remember that the play was written by a professional writer and that as an actor he is never free to paraphrase ideas. Lines should be memorized and delivered exactly as written.

In addition to emphasis by using voice, the actor should be sure that his lips are turned toward the audience when he utters the more important parts of his speeches. The probability of full understanding by the audience is much greater if the lips are turned to the audience rather than being turned away from or in profile to the audience.

When two actors are engaging in a conversation with each other, they should stand facing one another and in profile to the audience. If one of the actors is doing most of the talking and the other is doing most of the listening, the one talking should, perhaps, be a bit upstage of the one not talking. Such an arrangement will force the actor not talking to turn slightly toward the speaker and the speaker will be more turned toward the audience. Such an arrangement will successfully draw desired attention to the person speaking.

One of the most common errors made by amateur performers is failure to pick up cues instantly. A cue refers to the line or action of the person who speaks or moves just before your line. Actually there should normally be no pause at all between lines in a stage production. Unless the particular scene calls for pause to create desired effect, an actor should almost interrupt the lines immediately preceding his.

A fast pace resulting from quick pick up of cues is especially crucial in most comedy presentations. When the play calls for exceedingly fast pace to be provided by rapidly picking up cues, the performers may find it necessary to begin speaking a line when the actor utters the next to last word of the line immediately preceding his speech. The split second that it takes your brain to engage your mouth in speaking will be just right to create the situation whereby absolutely no pause exists between lines.

While normally an actor on stage should not be aware of the audience's physical presence, there are times when it becomes necessary to adapt to confusion in the audience and to speak louder. Some points of confusion in the audience can be easily predicted; others cannot.

Performers on stage should talk louder at the beginning of an act, after a laugh, and at every entrance. When an act opens, audience members may still be trying to get settled to watch the show; they may be hurriedly trying to finish conversation started before the curtain. An audience is likely to miss important lines at the very opening of an act or scene. Until the actor senses a "settling down" in the audience, volume of lines should be increased slightly.

While the actor can expect an audience not to be settled at the opening of an act, there may be points in the middle of scenes when confusion occurs in the audience. A child crying, a spectator leaving hurriedly, or any loud and unexpected noise can temporarily distract even the most entranced audience member away from the action. When actors become aware of a disturbance in the audience, they are obligated to win them back. Volume should be increased in such situations slightly until the sense of settling down is apparent.

Next to being slow at picking up cues, the second most frequent problem with amateur actors is a failure to wait for audience laughs. Audiences come to see plays and to be entertained. If they are expected to laugh after a humorous line, let them laugh. Nothing will kill audience laughter faster than inexperienced actors and actresses who hurry on to the next line while the audience is laughing at the last line. One or two instances of failing to wait for laughs will tend to make audiences avoid laughing at later points in the play. If they are conditioned to the frustrating experience of missing a part of the play because they laughed at something funny, the obvious solution is to restrain laughter.

Actors should remember that laughter in an audience normally comes in two waves. At the instant a line is spoken a large wave of laughter will appear; however, a few seconds after the large wave you may expect a smaller wave of laughter. Some people don't get punch lines as quickly as others—some don't hear them and have to ask the person next to them what was said. When that person is told what was said that was so funny, he will probably want to laugh too.

Directors and performers must learn to anticipate laughs in the script. One problem facing play production is that many times we don't know what lines audiences will think are funny until an actual audience is present. Some lines that a director and performers might think hilariously funny may bring only a titter from an audience, while a line rehearsed for weeks with no anticipation of laughter may stop the show.

One should also keep the inherent differences in audiences in mind: no two audiences are alike. A line that produced uproarious and prolonged laughter in one performance may be passed lightly by another audience. The point that must be kept firmly in mind is that the director and performers have an obligation to the audience to allow them to be entertained. If the play is funny—let them laugh.

Technique of Movement

Regardless of how many lines a part provides for a performer in a play, the job of acting is a constant one, equally important the entire time an actor is in view of the audience. Thus, while speaking lines are of crucial importance to transmitting the message of the script accurately, equally important to the overall effect of the show is every movement, position, and facial expression in which an actor engages on a stage.

The first rule of movement on the stage is that it MUST be motivated. In normal situations, people don't just walk across a room to stand on the other side. We have a definite reason or motivating force which causes us to move from one point to another.

Sometimes, movement in a play is motivated by the script. Many times, however, to work out blocking problems for later lines, actors may have to be moved from position to position without a reason provided by the script. The actor must provide that reason if the script does not.

Consider the following two situations. First, assume that an actor standing at right stage suddenly walks across the stage to stand at left stage. When he arrives at his destination, he simply turns and faces the other actors as he was doing on the other side of the stage. Such a movement lacks motivation and is likely to be noticed as such by the audience.

Second, let us assume that an actor standing at right stage suddenly walks across the stage to stand at left stage. Before he turns to face the other actors, he picks up a magazine on the table, glances at the cover, nods his head, replaces it on the table, and then turns to face the actors. Picking up the magazine provided the reason to the audience for the movement. The magazine may have absolutely nothing to do with the action underway at the time. Nonetheless, it provides logical reason for the actor to move other than that the director told him to do so.

With the notion of motivation for every movement on stage firmly in mind, we will consider three aspects of stage movement. First, the beginning actor should be introduced to the concept of "business," second, factors involved in changing stage positions should be considered, and finally, stage poise is an important concept for beginning actors.

Business.   Stage business refers to the actor or actress doing intelligent and meaningful actions with hands, feet, hips, shoulders, and any other part of the body which contributes to the fulfillment of the purpose of the show. The actor, as a part of character analysis, should strive to develop appropriate business for his character, adding to the scene being played.

Study your lines carefully to determine how business can further enhance their meaning. The director of the show will no doubt direct you to use certain points of business; however, some of the best and most meaningful business is that developed by the performer as study of the part progresses through rehearsals.

The student actor should be cautious to avoid "mugging" when developing business to use with his part. Business is appropriate and meaningful only when it contributes to the overall effect of the show. If an actor's movements become distracting to the point that attention is drawn to the movement away from his lines and the lines of others, it is no longer business—it then becomes mugging. Mugging normally refers to the actor who responds too violently with physical actions to what is happening on the stage. The actor who mugs consistently is a greater hindrance than he is an asset to the total production.

Changing Stage Positions.   Unless directed otherwise for a very good reason, an actor should always move on his own lines rather than on lines of others. The human eye tends to follow a moving object. If you move from one point to another or simply move your arms about during the lines of another actor, the audience is likely to look at you, thus, missing the other's lines.

When an actor is required to turn on stage, he should normally turn so as not to turn his back to the audience. In other words, turn facing the audience. It is permissible to turn with your back to the audience only when it is significantly quicker and appears more natural and relaxed than to turn facing the audience. The most common turn is the turn from one profile to the other profile. In this situation the time it takes to turn is normally the same whether the actor turns toward or away from the audience. In such cases the actor should always turn facing the audience.

Let action precede voice when a line calls for both spoken words and some gesture or movement. Again, keep in mind that the audience tends to follow the moving object at the expense of the spoken word. To speak first and then move can distract the spectator from the more important line being spoken.

For some unexplained reason, amateur actors have a tendency to look down at their feet when moving about on stage. DON'T. You learned to walk many years ago, and you can be assured that your feet will work on stage the same way they do in real-life situations. When stage directions call for you to move from one point to another on the stage, look straight ahead and walk—don't look down at your feet.

To achieve balance on the stage and to assure that one actor doesn't steal a scene from another, the concept of supporting a cross is very important. Supporting a cross means if an actor moves one way, the person to whom he is talking has to move the opposite way. If an actor fails to support a cross, the attention will be drawn to the person who doesn't move, thus causing him to steal the scene from the actor who did move. The concept of supporting a cross is illustrated in the three diagrams in Figure 6.3.

Stage Poise. When an actor is required to gesture as part of a line he should use the hand farthest away from the audience. To use the hand closest to the audience is likely to cause the actor's hand or arm to block part of his face, possibly causing part of the spoken line accompanying the gesture to be lost.

When several actors are on stage together, the best stage picture is normally achieved through arranging them in a triangle. Straight lines, circles, or semicircles appear artificial and uninteresting. Triangles can and should be used with nearly endless variations as illustrated in Figure 6.4.

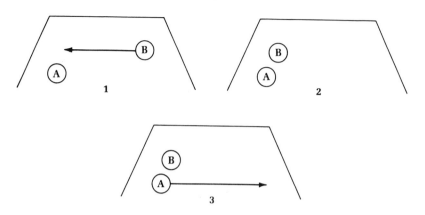

Figure 6.3   In diagram **1**, performer **B** crosses to a point very near performer **A**. The result, seen in diagram **2**, is a stage picture lacking balance. By moving, as depicted in diagram **3**, performer **A** supports the cross of performer **B** and provides the stage picture with balance. The movement of both performers must be accomplished with motivation obvious to audience members.

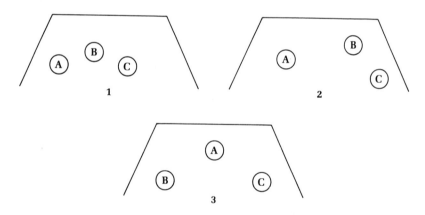

Figure 6.4   Diagram **1** shows the rather uninteresting and unrealistic semicircle pattern. Diagrams **2** and **3** demonstrate just two of many variations possible for use of the triangle in forming stage pictures. The nature of the triangular pattern is directly related to the desired relationship of the performers to each other.

If a scene requires an actor to kneel, he should normally kneel in the profile position to the audience and on the knee closest to the audience. Kneeling on the knee closest to the audience will cause his body to be turned slightly toward the audience just as gesturing with the hand farthest away from the audience does. When standing in profile position, the foot farthest away from the audience should be slightly in advance of the one closest. This, too, will cause the actor's body to be turned toward the audience rather than away from it.

If an actor finds himself on stage with a group of other actors and only one or two are actually speaking in the scene, those not speaking should follow the dialogue and keep their attention focused on the speaking actors. Supporting actors in a scene can do a great deal to assure that the audience attention will remain where it should be—on those actors speaking lines.

While many hours and several rehearsals will be devoted to the problem of blocking the action on stage, the actor must be constantly aware of the problem during each scene. A good actor will keep one point constantly in mind during a show: don't block other performers and don't allow yourself to get blocked.

GLOSSARY OF COMMON TERMS IN ACTING TECHNIQUE

Every beginning actor should commit to memory the several terms used in acting technique which are listed below.

Turn in	Turn the body in toward center stage from whatever point you are currently positioned.
Full front	The body and head should face the audience.
Quarter position	45° away from the audience.
Profile	A 90° turn from full front.
Three quarter position	135° turn from full front.
Open up	Turn more of the body around toward the audience.
Ad lib	Make up lines appropriate to the situation. The performer should ad lib when someone forgets or something goes wrong.
On the same level, or On the same plane	Two actors or an actor and an object the same distance from the audience.

Flatten out	Take a full front position and take a step back so that an actor can pass in front of you.
Share a scene	Two actors have a quarter or profile position on the same plane.
Giving a scene	An actor gives a scene to another actor by moving downstage from him.
Upstaging	An actor upstages (weakens) another actor if he moves upstage from him.
Stealing a scene	Through any of various methods, drawing attention to yourself at the expense of other actors on stage.

**SUMMARY
PROBES**

1. What is the first rule of acting superceding all other rules or statements of technique?
2. Why is it important for actors and actresses to pick up cues promptly?
3. What will audiences tend to do if the performers on stage fail to give them sufficient time to laugh?
4. Why is motivation so important to effective movement on stage?
5. What is meant by business in acting technique? What is meant by mugging?
6. What is meant by supporting a cross? Why is it important?
7. Why must the actor be constantly aware of blocking?

LEARNING ACTIVITIES

1. Select at least three characters in a play and undergo a detailed character analysis for each, using all the suggestions provided in this chapter. What special techniques could you employ to assure maintaining character in each instance?

2. Practice finding all fifteen acting areas on a stage with a friend. If a stage is not available to you, use a large room with a stage area drawn in chalk. Stand in center stage and have your friend call off areas at random and then move quickly and without hesitation to that area. Switch positions with your friend and continue the exercise until you can both move to any acting area on command.

3. With a group of classmates, read lines from a play with special emphasis on picking up cues. Keep practicing until there is no pause or lag whatsoever between lines.

4. Observe mannerisms and movements of people in a group setting such as at a party. Note the existence of motivation for movement. If you detect movement that did not have apparent motivation, analyze it in terms of naturalness.

5. Select a character in a play and after having developed points of characterization, create as much business as possible for the character.

6. Practice all the points of acting technique discussed in this chapter until you are familiar with them.

SEVEN

GOALS   After completing this chapter you will be able to:

1. Define basic terms essential to an understanding of staging a production.

2. Appreciate the importance of sketching a set.

3. Grasp some basic steps and processes in constructing and using scenery.

4. Understand the importance of stage lighting to the total effect of a dramatic production.

5. Identify the various purposes stage lights serve.

6. Know how to compensate for problems encountered in staging a play with inadequate facilities.

Staging the Play

Technical aspects of staging the play vary more from one play to another and from one stage facility to the next than any other aspect of play production. For schools or institutions with unlimited budgetary support and the best of professional facilities, staging the play comes as an easy routine. Unfortunately many—if not most—institutions do not enjoy unlimited financing; staging a production can present massive problems.

While facilities that are less than desirable can create definite hardships on production groups, the tendency is usually to exaggerate those problems. Many aspiring dramatists are amazed at what can be done on a shoestring budget. A great part of the living stage is audience imagination; sometimes we are surprised at an audience's willingness and ability to imagine.

The purpose of this chapter is to introduce the student to basic fundamentals involved in staging the play. We will first examine some terms and definitions basic to set construction and creation. With the definitions in mind as a base, we will examine concepts of set construction and set design. A vital part of staging a production is lighting, another topic for our concern. We will conclude with some discussion of alternative methods of staging productions for those groups with little or no facilities.

COMMON TERMS

Both the quality and quantity of equipment available to production groups will vary widely. Listed below are some of the most common objects and basic terms relevant to staging productions.

The *proscenium arch* refers to the opening in the stage through which the audience views the play. In earlier periods of theater the arch represented the fourth wall which supposedly had been removed to allow the audience to look in on the action. While the fourth-wall concept is becoming obsolete, the term proscenium arch is still used to refer to the stage opening in an auditorium setting.

The *oleo curtain* is the main curtain which denotes the beginning and the end of an act or scene by its rise and fall or its opening and closing. Several interesting stories exist in the history of the theater as to how the oleo curtain was so named. Perhaps the most curious is that in the early days of theater in America, one particular theater had a man named Leo whose job was to open and close the curtain. Leo often went to sleep on the job and the director would shout, "Oh, Leo." Thus—the oleo curtain.

The part of the stage that extends in front of the lowered or closed oleo curtain is referred to as the *apron*. The apron is often used as a playing area for a short scene. The advantage of such use is that crew work in changing scenery can be conducted behind the closed curtain while the play goes on.

A *flat* is a piece of canvas stretched over a wooden frame. Flats, used for construction of walls for interior sets, are built in varying sizes—normally from one to seven feet in width and as high as twelve feet. Narrow flats are fastened together to make a wall by means of *stage braces* which hold flats straight and erect; *cleats* are metal pieces of hardware on the back of flats used in *lashing* flats. Lashing flats involves a technique similar to lacing shoes.

With several narrow flats lashed and braced together, cracks would appear in the wall between flats if it were not for the use of the *dutch-man*. A dutchman is a small piece of canvas glued over the crack between flats to give several connected flats the appearance of a solid wall.

Back and side curtains on a stage are referred to as the *cyclorama* or *cyc* for short. The cyc is usually constructed of heavy material and should normally be a dark color. Entire productions can be staged without flats and other forms of scenery by the use of the cyclorama as walls for interior sets and imaginary parameters for exterior sets. Production groups lacking other facilities may find it necessary to make imaginative use of the cyclorama to stage a show. In such a situation the audience can normally be depended upon to utilize their imaginative powers.

There are other types of scenery which are often used to construct exterior sets or provide backing for windows and doors in a room set:

Batten	A strip of wood or metal on which scenery or lights are fastened and used sometimes to drop scenery from above the stage.
Wing	Two flats of equal width hinged together from top to bottom and capable of standing on its own like a book with no back support.
Tormenter	A flat or wing used at the sides of the set to complete the frame effect of the set and to conceal the mechanics of the back stage area.
Border	A piece of material hanging from a batten that may be raised or lowered from the flies.
Flies	All the stage equipment above the floor of the stage. Some stages have no flies at all—simply a twelve-foot ceiling. Such stages severely reduce flexibility in staging procedures.
Teaser	The border that makes the top of the picture frame of the stage. (You recall that the tormenter makes up the sides of the picture frame.)
Drop	A piece of canvas with battens at the top and bottom that may be raised and lowered from the flies. Such pieces of scenery are especially useful in making fast set changes.
Profile Piece	A flat with one irregular side which is painted to represent foliage—shubbery or leaves. Such pieces of scenery are used for outdoor scenes or backing behind windows and doors.

SET DESIGN AND CONSTRUCTION

Regardless of the facilities available to a production group, the two steps of set design and set construction must be completed. As soon as a play has been selected for production, the technical director should draw a scaled sketch of the set or sets demanded by the script. Obviously the work of the staff will be simplified if the script calls for a single set for all scenes and acts. The great advantage to such an arrangement is that once the set is in place, it need not be changed or moved until the show is a matter of history.

In designing a set, the technical director must take several things into consideration. First, the script will call for certain specific dimensions and arrangement of objects for the set. If facilities and equipment at hand permit using the set called for in the script, the task is simple. Usually, though, some variations will have to be made in the set designated by the script to adapt it to the local physical facility.

If a great deal of adaptation becomes necessary in set design, the technical director must consider the capability of the production group to make the necessary adaptation. How much scenery will have to be constructed to stage the show successfully? Are financial resources available for the necessary materials for construction of scenery? It may be necessary after consideration of these items to take drastic steps—in some cases to select another play for production.

When designing the set, the technical director must work closely with the individual who will direct the performers on stage. Problems in blocking and arranging scenes can be greatly reduced by minor changes in set design suggested by the director at this stage of planning.

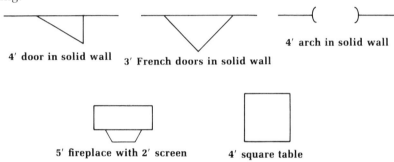

4' door in solid wall   3' French doors in solid wall   4' arch in solid wall

5' fireplace with 2' screen   4' square table

Figure 7.1   Most frequently used symbols for set design

When the technical director is ready to draw the plan for the setting, he should do so using a scale such as $\frac{1}{4}'' = 1'$. In Figure 7.1 you will find some of the most often used symbols for set design. In Figure 7.2 an actual scale drawing for a set is illustrated. From this scale drawing you should be able to see the importance of carefully preparing and planning at this stage of production to avoid problems of blocking in later rehearsals.

CONSTRUCTING THE SET

Once the set has been designed on paper the next great task is to make the set a reality—to construct it. If the production group has a supply of stage equipment such as flats, braces, wings, books, etc., they

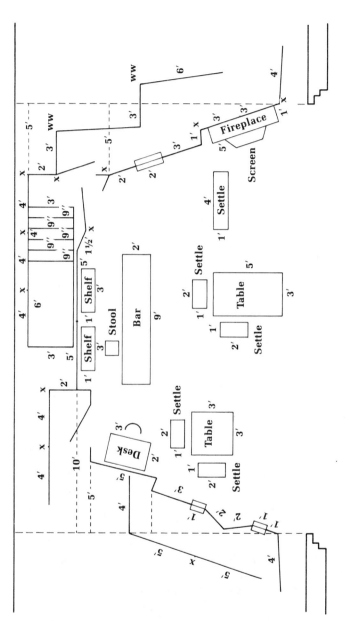

Figure 7.2 Actual scale drawing of a set

can normally be used many times with new paint. Water base paints should be used on stage scenery in order to facilitate repainting several times.

Color of the set will be determined in part by the nature of the play and the specific details of the room or surroundings to be portrayed. Generally a light color should be used: one that will reflect lighting rather than absorb it. Flecking—a process of spotting brighter colors on the scenery over the base color—is normally recommended in order to gain full advantage of the available stage lighting. It is impossible to specify exact suggestions as to painting sets. Such specifications must depend on the nature of the particular stage facility and lighting capacity.

More than likely a production group will find that all the necessary bits of equipment to stage a play are not available. If such is the case, the group may have to improvise by the use of the cyclorama or perhaps construct some scenery.

The greatest cost involved in constructing flats and other items of scenery is usually labor. Scrap lumber, cheap canvas (muslin), and water base paint can usually be secured with a minimum outlay of money. Scenery that appears to be relatively professional can be produced by amateur carpenters through a group effort. Several excellent handbooks on constructing scenery are available to production groups.

If no financial resources are available the group may still rely on the amazing imaginative powers of the audience. Excellent productions have occurred where no flats or elaborate scenery of any kind have been used. Window frames hung on the cyclorama, and door frames erected in a curtain opening can create the illusion of a four-walled room.

The primary point for the production group to keep in mind when designing and constructing a set is that they have an obligation to do as much to create reality for the audience as resources will allow. Normally, though, audiences are more than cooperative and will respond perfectly to what may appear to be the most remote suggestion.

SUMMARY PROBES

1. What is a flat? How are they used to construct a set for a play?
2. What must a technical director consider when designing a set?
3. Why are water-base paints recommended for painting stage scenery?
4. How can the imaginative powers of the audience

assist a production group with limited capacity for designing and constructing a set?

LIGHTING THE SET

Lighting has been called the single most effective element of play production because it can change or alter virtually every other element. A set can be made or broken with proper or improper lighting. Costumes are completely dependent on lighting for total effect. An actor's make-up can be rendered totally inappropriate and distracting by improper lighting. Last but certainly not least, the greatest performer in the world can have a performance destroyed by poor illumination in critical scenes.

While stage lighting can be the most important element of play production, it is also often the most problematic for many production groups. Rarely does any stage except the most professional come equipped to perform all lighting demands for any show. If a group lacks adequate lighting facilities they may have difficulty acquiring them. Lighting is also the most expensive element of play production. Lack of lighting equipment is also most difficult to have to modify or for which to improvise.

If all the above problems aren't enough, lighting also requires more skilled expertise than any other element of play production. Amateurs can construct passable sets, apply make-up, sew costumes—but amateurs should not tinker with electricity. It may be necessary to call in expert help if such knowledge does not exist in the group.

Let us examine some principles of good stage lighting, basic stage lighting devices, and classifications of stage lighting. While much of what we will discuss may be out of reach of many production groups, we will conclude with those elements essential for a production.

Principles of Stage Lighting

The set itself will provide sources from which light should normally come in real-life situations. These should not be overlooked by the technical group or realism is likely to be destroyed. Obviously if there are lamps sitting on tables we would expect light from that area—more than from other areas of the stage. Windows and doors would be sources of more light. If a fireplace is part of the set and there is to be fire in it, light should come from the fireplace. Thus, the first principle: provide light from sources where audiences would expect light.

Both underlighting and overlighting a set should be avoided but to most audiences, underlighting is more annoying. If the script calls for dark scenes or if a scene is to be played in a dark area of the stage, it should be of short duration. If lighting facilities are lacking, the director may find some areas of the stage better lit than others. When blocking scenes, those scenes which will draw the audience's attention should be played in the areas with better illumination. Avoid the dark areas.

Be very careful to avoid single, glaring lights. Such lights are distracting to an audience and can spoil the total effect of a scene or an entire show. The places most likely to offend with glaring lights are lamps, windows, and doors. While lighting is essential at these points for realism, avoid at all costs any glares or sharp contrasts in degree of illumination.

Lighting Devices

The three most common lighting devices are strip lights, spotlights, and floodlights. An entire acting area can be illuminated adequately with the use of these three types.

Strip Lights. Footlights and border lights are the most common stage uses of strip lights. Strip lights differ from other types in that they normally consist of several bulbs of varying colors in a straight line or row. Footlights are strip lights in a trough working from the floor at the edge of the stage nearest the audience. While most stages are equipped with footlight capability, they are seldom used in most contemporary stage productions.

Border lights are strips of bulbs backed with reflectors hanging from the flies above the stage. They are used to light the stage evenly and brightly. Border lights are often depended upon to fill the darker areas of overlap created by using several spotlights to illuminate acting areas.

Spotlights. As the name implies a spotlight throws a spot of light. The light is normally concentrated by a lens at its opening and is usually used in play production to illuminate a specific area of the stage. By using several spotlights beamed at different stage areas, several acting areas can be created as seen in Figure 7.3.

Floodlights. Floodlights throw a more diffused light over a larger area than the other types of light. The most common use for floodlights is for throwing light onto the set through an open door or window. Backing effects are often created by using floodlights.

In Figure 7.3 you see a stage with six acting areas all being illuminated from different sources. In addition to the spotlights creating the areas of light, border lights and floodlights add to the total illumination of the set. Various moods can be created by altering the amount and degree of illumination provided on the set to match the tone of the scene.

Classifications of Lighting

We will examine four classifications of lighting which are necessary for the success of most productions. Some of these may present difficulties for production groups; however, attention should be given to each.

Acting Area Lighting. Acting area lighting refers to the illumination needed to light that part of the stage that will be used by the performers. As we see in Figure 7.3, the acting area can be broken into a variant number of small areas with separate sources of light provided for each. Of all the classifications of lighting, this is the one area that a production group cannot slight. The actors and actresses must be seen by the audience.

If several acting areas are illuminated from independent sources, the lighting designer should provide for a significant amount of light overlap from one area to another. If overlap does not exist, actors will hit dark pockets when they move from one area to another. If dark pockets do exist in the stage and efforts to overlap areas fail, blending lighting, our second classification, may be necessary.

Blending Lighting. Border lights are most frequently used for blending lighting and the primary purpose of this classification is to eliminate dark sections between acting areas illuminated by spotlights. While many stages are not equipped with overhead border lights, the lighting designer should rig some kind of overhead light if dark pockets exist between acting areas.

Effect Lighting. Effect lighting differs from the first two classifica-

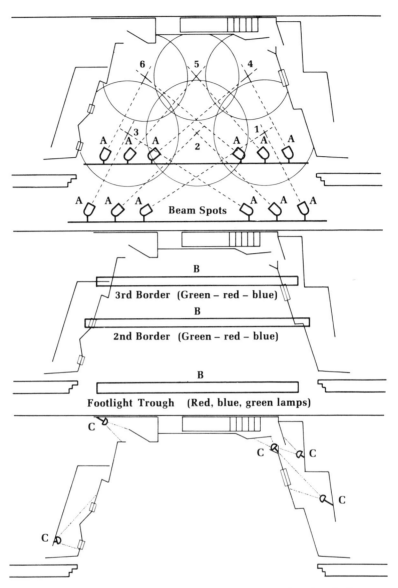

6 5 4

A A A 2 A A A
3

1

A A A Beam Spots A A A

B

3rd Border (Green – red – blue)

B

2nd Border (Green – red – blue)

B

Footlight Trough (Red, blue, green lamps)

C

C C

C

C

C

Figure 7.3 Lights **A** represent spotlights, **B** are border lights, **C** are spotlights for backing effects. By following the indicated beams of the twelve spotlights you will see two lights for each of the six playing areas. The three border lights provide illumination which eliminates dark areas and shadows between acting areas. Spotlights are placed behind windows and doors to provide light from areas where the audience would normally expect it.

tions in that such lighting is normally not used to illuminate the acting area. Rather, effect lighting is used to enhance the proper mood of a scene. For instance, if a scene occurs at sunrise, some effort to effect a sunrise glow outside a window should be achieved.

Other common demands for effect lighting occur in instances calling for lighting outside a window, a distant forest fire or explosion, or the disappearance of outside light such as the sun going behind a cloud.

Motivating Lights.   Motivating lights refer to light sources which are actually visible to the audience. A table lamp being used in a scene is a form of motivating light. A much dimmer source should be provided for motivating light than would normally be expected. For instance, a desk lamp might carry only a fifteen-watt bulb for stage use. The realistic illusion of light from the expected source is there; however, the glare that would occur with the use of a sixty- or seventy-five-watt bulb is avoided.

A fire in a fireplace is another form of motivating light. Audiences expect to see a glow of light coming from a fireplace if an actor is warming his hands over the supposed fire. Lighting units are available to provide needed light for fireplaces. Such lighting units should, however, be connected to a dimmer if realism is to be preserved. The light from a fireplace should not remain constant throughout a scene. Intermittent raising and lowering of the glow from the fireplace will enhance the realistic effect.

While stage lighting can be a severe problem for production groups with inferior facilities, it should not be considered an insurmountable obstacle. Again, trust the audience's willingness and ability to imagine. First and foremost, however, you must—regardless of facilities—provide proper illumination for the performers. Few audiences are willing to imagine that they can see a person's face. While perfecting an elaborate lighting scheme may be beyond the reach of many groups, those groups can provide shadow-free illumination for the action on stage.

SUMMARY   1. In what ways can stage lighting be the most
PROBES   difficult problem to face a production group?
          2. Why is underlighting generally more annoying to
              an audience than overlighting?

3. What are the differences between strip lights, spotlights, and floodlights? How are each used?
4. How is effect lighting used in a production?

STAGING A PLAY WITH
INADEQUATE FACILITIES

Most books on play production are written presupposing that
groups performing plays have certain basic stage facilities at their disposal. Much of the information included so far in this chapter assumes
the existence of a stage and very little else. We have been active in
drama and theater long enough to realize that even a stage is beyond
the grasp of many groups who are active in play production.

We now offer several basic production problems facing those
groups who produce shows in an enclosure other than on an actual
stage. No doubt the two most common alternative settings for most
groups are the cafeteria and the gymnasium. Listed below are the most
frustrating disadvantages to such arrangements and suggestions as to
ways that will compensate for those disadvantages.

Before exploring such disadvantages, however, one definite advantage should be pointed out to the absence of a stage. If a group must
perform a show in a cafeteria or gymnasium and use some form of
alternative staging such as audience on three sides or audience on four
sides, the expectations of a well-constructed box set are nil. Arena style
staging (audience surrounding the playing area) or a variation of the
same alleviates some concern for set design and construction.

Problems in Alternative Staging

While the director of a show who faces the task of staging the
production in a 4,000 seat gymnasium may believe the problems to be
solved unending, such is usually not the case. Acoustics, blocking, and
lighting pose the greatest challenge to the successful staging of a show.

Acoustics. A common misconception that many production
groups have is that they must use all the area provided in the room
where the play will be presented. Neither gymnasiums nor cafeterias
were constructed with the needs of dramatists in mind. Acoustics are

normally terrible in such structures and amateur performers may find it impossible to project enough to fill the entire area.

Rather than stage the show in the center of the gymnasium floor with the audience seated in basketball seats or bleachers, it would be wiser to create an entire theater area in some smaller portion of the larger structure. Such planning can enable the areas not in use to be blocked or screened off, thus improving acoustics and setting up a "little" theater within a gymnasium or cafeteria. Figures 7.4 and 7.5 demonstrate this concept.

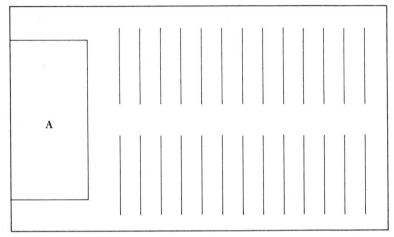

Figure 7.4 Utilizing a stage (**A**) located at the end of a gymnasium floor with audience members seated in the entire area makes production very difficult.

Blocking. If an audience is seated on three or four sides of the acting area, blocking will be a special problem for the director. With an audience surrounding the acting area it is impossible to have every actor in full view of all audience members. Furniture and properties will also block actors and actresses from view of some audience members. Special blocking concerns, here, will involve spreading the necessary and unavoidable evil around. Be sure that the same people are not blocked for every important scene. It may be impossible to concentrate on one acting area as that where major scenes are played. Major scenes should be moved from one part of the stage to another, thus affording all audience members as close to an equal chance as possible at seeing the important action.

Beginning and ending acts and scenes present a special problem

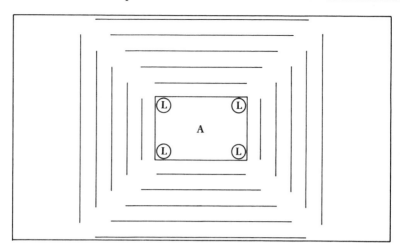

Figure 7.5 A stage area in the center of the gymnasium floor with limited seating on four sides creates a little theater within a gymnasium. Illumination for the acting area in such an arrangement can be provided by four lights (**L**) placed at each corner of the stage area.

when there is no stage. Actors and actresses must assume their positions in full view of the audience. Dimming lights can help create the desired effect; however, the lights cannot be too dim—the performers have to see to move about. Again, you can depend on the imaginative powers of your audience. Most audiences find viewing a play in arena fashion different and fun and are willing to make several compensations.

Lighting.   While lighting can always be counted on to cause problems in play production, problems are increased in alternative methods of staging. The use of overhead lights is practically eliminated and many other types of traditional stage lighting are rendered practically useless.

Keep one point in mind: illumination is the only demand the audience will make. If they can see the action on stage they will forego other aspects of effect and motivation lighting. For arena staging, four floodlights placed at each corner of the set may be adequate. Try to avoid as much as possible the presence of glaring lights shining in the eyes of audience members seated directly across from a floodlight. Four floodlights on stands placed at the four corners of the acting area in Figure 7.5 indicates one possible method of lighting a set in a gymnasium.

Since the audience is seated very close to the action staged and since use of lighting will be limited, other elements of technical production should be toned down. In alternative methods of staging, for instance, the need for stage make-up is significantly diminished.

Even though we have made an effort in this chapter to present information geared to those production groups with limited facilities, much of what we have discussed may be beyond the reach of many groups. Innovative imagination and improvisation can be a workable substitute for virtually any facility which is lacking.

SUMMARY PROBES

1. What is the one advantage to a production group who must stage a play in a gymnasium or cafeteria?
2. How can a production group create a theater within a gymnasium?
3. What special problems are posed in attempting to light a set with audience seated on all four sides of an acting area?

LEARNING ACTIVITIES

1. Tour whatever facilities are available to your group for production of plays. Try to locate as many of the stage items identified in this chapter as possible. Discuss ways to compensate adequately for the absence of facilities.

2. Select a play and make a scaled drawing of the set and a lighting plot using only those facilities available to your production group.

3. Find a play that requires the use of both effect and motivating lighting. Determine how your group could best achieve the lighting requirements using available facilities.

4. Visit a gymnasium and draw a plan for staging a production in it, at the same time overcoming problems posed by acoustics, blocking, and lighting.

EIGHT

GOALS   After completing this chapter you will be able
to:

1. Identify the various components in the
organizational structure involved in the production of a play.

2. Understand the relationship of the assistant director to the director of a show.

3. Grasp the immense managerial responsibilities of the technical director.

4. Identify the primary functions of seven
production crews.

5. Understand the vital contribution made
by the business and house managers of a show.

Play Production Staff

In earlier chapters of this unit, we have examined elements of play production facing the acting staff and those who have the responsibility of designing and staging the play. While these two components of the total production of a play are vitally important, there are many other groups of people who make direct contributions to the success of a play. We will refer to these groups of individuals as the production staff of a play.

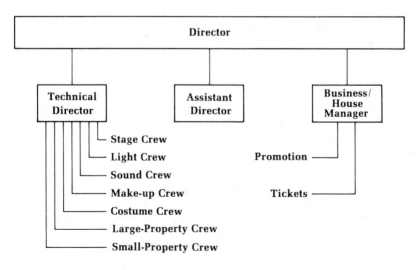

Figure 8.1 Organizational chart of a typical production

153

In Figure 8.1 an organizational chart of a typical production is outlined. While specific situations presenting problems peculiar to some production groups may make it necessary to alter the organizational chart, Figure 8.1 is a recommended plan for organization. In this chapter we will describe some of the functions of each production group, often referred to as *crews*.

ASSISTANT DIRECTOR

Some production groups may choose not to utilize the services of an assistant director. In shows with very small casts, the director may opt to handle the task singlehandedly; however, if it is at all possible, an assistant director is advised. In educational play production, the assistant director is often a student, thus referred to as a *student* director.

The primary responsibility of the assistant director is to act as director in his or her absence. Situations may arise during rehearsal periods which require the presence of the director at some place other than the stage area. Consultation with the technical director or some other crew chief often necessitates the absence of the director.

It is normally the assistant director's responsibility to make a director's manuscript or production book for use at rehearsals. Such a book is a copy of the script with plentiful margins for notations and instructions involving blocking and arrangement of actors and actresses on stage. Every change in movement or direction of any performer, regardless of how insignificant it may seem, should be noted in the production book.

It may be necessary to draw sketches of the stage design on each page of the production book so that blocking and movement can be indicated clearly. The assistant director should follow the script in the production book as rehearsals progress and note any discrepancies in lines or movement of actors and actresses.

A normal procedure for preparing a production book is to cut windows in regular size sheets of plain white paper in which to insert the dismantled pages of a playscript. Notations are made in the remaining margins, as illustrated in Figure 8.2.

The assistant director should constantly remember that he or she is indeed an *assistant* director. While many directors of productions will actively seek creative suggestions and input from an assistant director, the assistant's primary function is to implement and execute the wishes of the director.

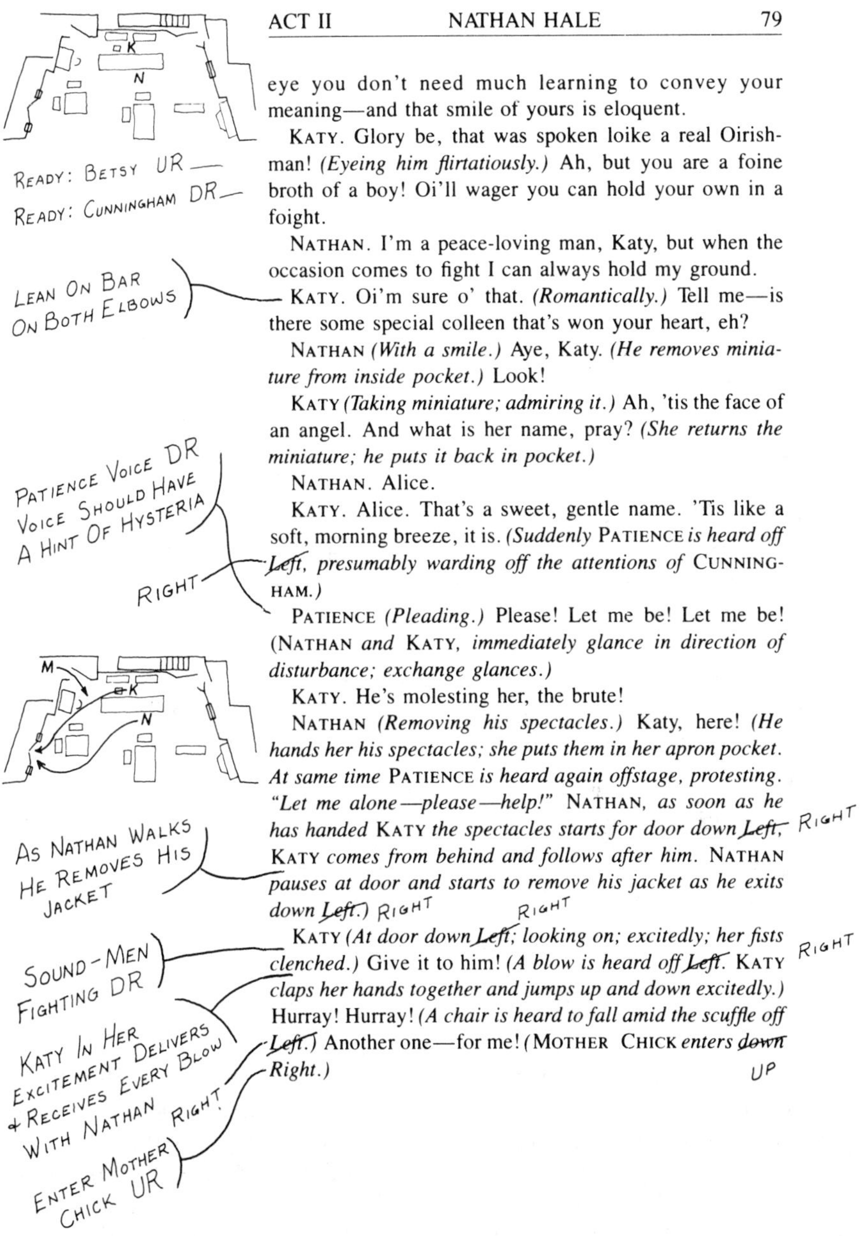

ACT II   NATHAN HALE   79

READY: BETSY UR —

READY: CUNNINGHAM DR—

LEAN ON BAR ON BOTH ELBOWS

PATIENCE VOICE DR VOICE SHOULD HAVE A HINT OF HYSTERIA

RIGHT

AS NATHAN WALKS HE REMOVES HIS JACKET

SOUND - MEN FIGHTING DR

KATY IN HER EXCITEMENT DELIVERS + RECEIVES EVERY BLOW WITH NATHAN RIGHT

ENTER MOTHER CHICK UR

eye you don't need much learning to convey your meaning—and that smile of yours is eloquent.

KATY. Glory be, that was spoken loike a real Oirishman! *(Eyeing him flirtatiously.)* Ah, but you are a foine broth of a boy! Oi'll wager you can hold your own in a foight.

NATHAN. I'm a peace-loving man, Katy, but when the occasion comes to fight I can always hold my ground.

KATY. Oi'm sure o' that. *(Romantically.)* Tell me—is there some special colleen that's won your heart, eh?

NATHAN *(With a smile.)* Aye, Katy. *(He removes miniature from inside pocket.)* Look!

KATY *(Taking miniature; admiring it.)* Ah, 'tis the face of an angel. And what is her name, pray? *(She returns the miniature; he puts it back in pocket.)*

NATHAN. Alice.

KATY. Alice. That's a sweet, gentle name. 'Tis like a soft, morning breeze, it is. *(Suddenly* PATIENCE *is heard off Left, presumably warding off the attentions of* CUNNING-HAM.*)*

PATIENCE *(Pleading.)* Please! Let me be! Let me be! *(*NATHAN *and* KATY, *immediately glance in direction of disturbance; exchange glances.)*

KATY. He's molesting her, the brute!

NATHAN *(Removing his spectacles.)* Katy, here! *(He hands her his spectacles; she puts them in her apron pocket. At same time* PATIENCE *is heard again offstage, protesting. "Let me alone—please—help!"* NATHAN, *as soon as he has handed* KATY *the spectacles starts for door down Left,* RIGHT KATY *comes from behind and follows after him.* NATHAN *pauses at door and starts to remove his jacket as he exits down Left.)* RIGHT   RIGHT

KATY *(At door down Left; looking on; excitedly; her fists clenched.)* Give it to him! *(A blow is heard off Left.* RIGHT KATY *claps her hands together and jumps up and down excitedly.)* Hurray! Hurray! *(A chair is heard to fall amid the scuffle off Left.)* Another one—for me! *(*MOTHER CHICK *enters down Right.)*   UP

Figure 8.2   Director's production book with notations, diagrams indicating adaptations neccessitated by facilities.

TECHNICAL DIRECTOR

The technical director is that person who is responsible for the success of the behind-the-scenes elements of the production. Normally the technical director is responsible for designing the set and seeing that the set is constructed according to specifications.

The relationship of the technical director to the director of the production differs from one situation to another. Sometimes the technical director is autonomous and not answerable to the director of the show. In such situations, the two are equal in authority. In other instances, the technical director may enjoy autonomy to a degree; however, he is ultimately answerable to the director who may make final decisions concerning even technical aspects of the production.

It is difficult to designate one or the other organizational structure as preferable. The relationship between the director and the technical director of a show is highly dependent on the specific situation. Educational institutions involved in play production may find it more feasible to operate with a system of director autonomy in all aspects of the production. Just as in the case of the assistant director, the technical director may be a highly talented student.

In addition to creative responsibilities, the technical director has a significant amount of important managerial responsibilities. While each production crew will have a crew chief, those individuals should be answerable to the technical director who should retain final decision-making authority in all production crew areas. The technical director is in charge of the following production crews: stage, lights, sound, make-up, costumes, large property, and small property. Some shows may require additional crews, some may require less; however, these seven are the ones most often utilized.

Stage Crew

The stage crew, traditionally referred to as stagehands, is responsible for constructing the scenery, painting it, and erecting it on the stage or stage area according to the specifications of the technical director. If a production group owns scenery such as flats and borders from past shows, the work of the stage crew in advance of the actual production may be simplified. If flats already exist, the stage crew simply must paint and erect them with proper window and door openings to meet the requirements of the show in production. If scenery does not exist from past use, the stage crew may face a long and difficult task of constructing the scenery from raw materials.

While the responsibilities of the stage crew prior to production may vary greatly depending on the amount and quality of available scenery, the crew's task during the production itself is a more constant one. The stage crew must check all scenery before each performance to assure that it is stable and ready for use. Any scenery changes required during the course of the production are the duties of the stage crew.

Scenery changes occurring between acts or at other periods affording long segments of time may present the stage crew with little difficulty. On the other hand, in some situations—those requiring fast and quiet changes in setting—the stage crew may be required to perform with as much precision and concentrated rehearsal as the performers on stage.

Light Crew

Like the stage crew, the light crew must implement the specifications of the technical director in the area of lighting the set. Once lighting plans as discussed in Chapter Seven have been completed, the work of those individuals making up the light crew begins.

The lights must be set and checked for precision before every rehearsal and performance. The slightest accidental movement of a spotlight can easily throw an entire lighting scheme out of perspective. For most productions lights must be changed numerous times while the play is in progress. Timing and accuracy of lighting adjustments are essential to the overall success of the performance. Perhaps, the most important task facing the light crew is the operating of the light board during the performances.

Sound Crew

The primary function of the sound crew is to provide and operate sound effects wherever they are needed in the play. Precise timing is a crucial element in the successful execution of the duties of this crew. The effect of a production can be nearly destroyed if an actor picks up a ringing telephone only to have it continue ringing after he says, "Hello."

It may be necessary for the sound crew to locate and operate valuable pieces of sound equipment during the course of a production. In some instances expertise and specialized skill in equipment operation and maintenance can be a near necessity for at least one member of this group.

It is essential that both the light and sound crew be provided a copy of the script solely for crew use. The scripts must be marked for light and sound cues with just as much accuracy as the scripts of the performers.

Make-Up Crew

Before specifying the responsibilities of the individuals composing the make-up crew, we should consider some fundamental concepts of stage make-up. It is possible to take entire courses or series of courses dealing with the art and technique of stage make-up. While we will not go into great detail at this point, we would point out that several professional make-up companies provide instructional materials for the amateur dramatist.[1]

It is our belief that most beginning dramatists tend to overdo stage make-up. While some attention to this area is essential, we would caution the student from becoming too make-up conscious. Although make-up is the art of transforming the actor's appearance, the purpose of stage make-up is not to make the actor look different or unnatural. Good make-up will make the actor look natural—just as the person being portrayed should look.

Thus, a good beginning rule to keep in mind when confronting the task of stage make-up is that moderation is the keynote to good make-up. When amateur dramatic groups err in make-up they tend to transgress in the direction of too much make-up or overdoing the art for the part required. Audiences find too much make-up more distracting than too little. When an audience notices excesses in application of make-up it tends to draw their attention to the fact that they are viewing a stage production and not a real-life situation. The successful performance should strive for the effect of realism on the audience.

There are a number of good reasons why make-up is a part of every good play. Stage lights tend to wipe out an actor's natural color, to make him look hollow eyed and pale—even sick. Make-up is intended to restore natural color and make him look healthy. A second use of make-up is to emphasize certain features on the face, to bring out dominating facial characteristics. In the third place, it is used to project features in a large auditorium so that the actor will look his part from the back of the room as well as from the front.

Three factors must be considered when planning make-up for a production. First, the size of the auditorium is a factor. Make-up must be applied in such a degree that it will be suitable for the majority of spectators in an audience. In order for make-up on performers to be appropriate for the greater portion of the spectators, the people sitting in the first few rows may be able to see what appears to them to be make-up excesses. If make-up is applied to appear realistic to front-row viewers, the actor will appear "washed out" to the majority of the audience. When make-up is tested for adequacy, it should be viewed under full lighting from about one-half the total distance from the stage to the last row of audience seats.

The intensity of the lighting is the second important factor in assessing make-up needs. More intense lighting will remove a greater degree of natural color from the performer's complexion, thus requiring more make-up. Make-up planners should keep in mind that lighting intensity will most likely change significantly from one scene to another during the performance. When assessing suitability of a performer's make-up, the judgment should be made under the most intense lighting—not the least intense.

A third factor affecting make-up is the proximity of the audience. This factor is especially important when the production group is faced with an alternative method of staging the production. An example might be a production staged in arena fashion with members of the audience sitting practically in the playing area and even those audience members farthest from the actors not more than twenty yards away. In such situations, the amount of make-up required will be significantly less than in auditorium settings.

The duties of the make-up crew are to be certain that the needed supplies are on hand and to assist actors and actresses in applying make-up at each dress rehearsal and performance. Make-up work lists for each actor should be prepared by members of the crew in consultation with the performers and the director. Following are samples of two make-up work lists:

Character A: The following character is a very healthy young man. In this act, however, he should show some sign of mental and nervous strain. He is in a very precarious situation.

1. Cleanse face.
2. Dry face thoroughly.
3. Apply the base; grease paint # 5½ with a small amount of 8A blended in.
4. Apply moist rouge to the cheeks.

  5. Shadow eyes.
  6. Apply light shadows in the depressions of the cheeks, at the temples, and across the forehead. Shadow neck and ears.
  7. Apply very thin wrinkles across the forehead.
  8. Outline the eyes.
  9. Apply face powder # 9.
 10. Brush surplus powder from face.
 11. Apply a little rouge to the lips.
 12. Outline the eyebrows with pencil.
 13. Retouch features.

Character B: This character is a very fair-skinned attractive girl of 16. She has blonde hair.

  1. Cleanse face.
  2. Dry face thoroughly.
  3. Apply base; grease paint # 4½.
  4. Apply moist rouge to the cheeks.
  5. Shadow eyes.
  6. Apply frown lines; perhaps some wrinkles across the forehead.
  7. Outline the eyes.
  8. Apply face powder # 7R.
  9. Brush surplus powder from the face.
 10. Apply lip rouge.
 11. For a special effect, make a light beauty mark on cheek. This should be done with black pencil.
 12. Retouch features.

Costume Crew

Very early in play preparation, members of the costume crew should read the playscript very carefully and prepare complete costume lists for every performer. In consultation with the performers, costume crew members should locate suitable costumes for each part. The actors and actresses may be asked to assume a portion of the burden of locating some items of costume required for their roles.

For some specialized productions, it may be necessary to make costumes, i.e., a production requiring twenty Roman togas. Many production groups will find themselves short of financial resources to rent costumes from professional companies and may have to improvise in costume creation.

It may be necessary for members of the costume crew to conduct research to determine appropriate costumes for specific productions. For example, productions which occur in historical time periods may

Looped hat

Strong fustian

Vest

Nankeen breeches

Hose

Shoes

Palisade

Flowered chintz or dimity

Quilted petticoat

Figure 8.3 Sketches show costume research for Revolutionary War production.

require such research. In Figure 8.3 are sketches done after research for proper costuming representing the revolutionary period in America.

Perhaps, the most crucial point of the work of the costume crew is in the initial compiling of costume lists. Samples of costume lists for a stage production are listed below.

Character A:　She should wear a fashionable everyday costume of a young lady. Her gear should consist of a flowered chintz or dimity looped over a quilted petticoat. Over this she should wear a cloak and a hood which can be thrown back. This cloak might be dark green. She should wear a fashionable frilled cap known as a palisade over her head. Her shoes should be stylish and similar to that of other females in the show. They should buckle rather than lace and her hose need not be seen.

Character B:　He should wear a coat of strong fustian over nankeen breeches. His coat should be dark grey or black and his breeches cream or white. His shoes are the buckled type and are black. The hose are also black. His vest should match his breeches. His hat is either grey or black and is looped.

When costumes have been acquired for the performers, it is the responsibility of the costume crew to care for them during the duration of the show. Costumes may be entrusted to the actor or actress for care; however, a more likely and preferred procedure would be for this responsibility to be assumed by the crew.

Large-Property Crew

The primary function of this crew is to secure all furniture and large items to be used on stage during the performance. Depending on the demands of the setting, the task of the large-property crew may be easy or difficult. If the setting of the play is a historical period, furniture suitable to that period may be difficult or impossible to find, thus some form of construction becomes necessary.

Most schools and institutions are quite limited as to the furniture available to them for use on the stage. Many times large properties must be borrowed or rented from local business enterprises or private individuals. A great degree of responsibility accrues to this crew if valuable items are borrowed or rented for use in the production. Obviously, large pieces of furniture cannot be locked in cupboards after every rehearsal and performance; however, it is the obligation of the large-property crew to secure them in the best way possible.

Small-Property Crew

This crew is responsible for all properties used by the actors themselves as a part of their business in the show and for small decorative things on the stage. A normal method of distinguishing large and small properties is that small props are any items that can be carried on or off the stage by one person as a hand item.

Again, the immediate task of the crew is to compile a list of properties needed by each performer in the production. Most playbooks include property lists; however, the script should be double checked for completeness and accuracy. Actors and actresses should be consulted after they have become familiar with their parts to determine if there are any properties needed that crew members have missed.

Performers can be made responsible for securing many of their own small properties; however, the great and demanding task of the property crew is to keep the props after they have been brought to rehearsal for the first time. The small-property crew is responsible for seeing that the right property is available to an actor at the exact location he needs it—whether that location is on stage or off stage to be carried on.

SUMMARY PROBES

1. Why is it important for an assistant director to make a production book?
2. How might the relationship of the technical director to the director of a show differ from one situation to another?
3. What are the usual seven production crews for which the technical director has responsibility?
4. How do the duties of the stage crew differ in preparation for a show and in actual performance?
5. What is an important beginning rule to keep in mind when beginning a study of stage make-up?
6. What are the three factors to be considered when planning for make-up?
7. Briefly describe the difference between the duties of the large-property crew and the small-property crew.

BUSINESS AND HOUSE MANAGERS

The most creative and intense efforts of the best director, performers, technical director, and production crews will be for naught if there is no audience to view the performance. A most important figure in the organizational structure of play production is the business and house manager.

The business and house managers may not be the same person in all situations. The business element of this position rests in seeing that tickets are printed, that intense promotional efforts are made on behalf of the show, and that some well-organized scheme of ticket distribution and sales is implemented. House elements in the position are primarily contained in providing for the convenience and comfort of audience members by securing an adequate number of ushers and ticket takers to serve the situation.

Groups working under the direction of the business and house manager are normally a promotion and sales committee, ushers, and ticket takers.

Promotion and Sales

Most amateur production groups do not have financial resources to conduct expensive media advertising campaigns. There are several promotional devices available to amateur groups at relatively low costs. Many play publishers provide promotional posters for a show at a low cost. Such posters can be helpful, but often original posters—created for cost of materials by student artists—can have a greater effect when displayed in prominent places in the community.

Local radio and television stations are usually most willing to provide public service time to educational institutions to promote dramatic productions. It is the responsibility of the business manager to make the necessary arrangements; however, members of a promotional crew might be expected actually to originate ideas for media use to sell the production. In many communities, service clubs will be happy to have groups of student performers appear as part of a program to promote an upcoming production.

While the business manager and his promotional and sales staff may have little or nothing to do with the actual production of a show in terms of what happens on stage, they are essential elements in the total effort to make a production a success.

Ushers and Ticket Takers

Part of the tradition of the theater is that audiences expect to be ushered to their seats. The business and house manager is responsible for assuring that an adequate number of such individuals are on hand to take care of the audience. Audiences do not like the inconvenience of having to stand in a long line outside a theater to wait to be seated.

Certainly our treatment of the various elements involved in the successful production has been an overview. Any one of the production areas discussed could be expanded into much greater detail. For the beginning student of play production our purpose has been to create an awareness of the many segments necessary to earn that eager and enthusiastic audience applause when the final curtain goes down.

SUMMARY
PROBES

1. **What are the primary responsibilities of the business manager of a show?**
2. **What are several inexpensive methods available to a production group to promote a show?**
3. **Why are ushers and ticket takers essential to a production?**

LEARNING ACTIVITIES

1. Select either a one-act play or a single act of a three-act play and make a production book as illustrated in this chapter. Mark the book for elements of blocking and cues.

2. Using the same script you used for exercise 1, make costume lists, make-up lists, and prop lists for at least three characters.

3. Check the available sources in your community for inexpensive promotion of a show. Write up a complete promotion plan for a hypothetical production.

Debate

NINE

Introduction to Educational Debate

During the history of democratic society, debate has grown and diminished in parallel with the health of fragile democratic societies. This chapter will offer the values of educational debate and survey its fundamental concepts.

DEFINITION

Debate is a decision-making process founded in human rational thought. Because the process is founded in human rational thought, it is a "critical" process, that is, it involves drawing conclusions after thorough examination of available evidence and acceptable motives. Debate is process because it has several component parts which usually interact and are ongoing.

The process of debate may occur in several locations. Debate can be a personal process of decision-making or it may be intrapersonal in setting. Life is filled with the need to make choices. The decision to follow a particular career is one of the most momentous decisions you have made or will make. Marriage may also be a decision following very careful weighing of evidence and emotions. Before you make a decision of whether or not to travel abroad, the expenses must be weighed critically against the possible personal and professional values. At each juncture you are confronted with the choice of action from critical rational thought or action from uncritical feeling.

Debate is often a decision-making method used by and for small and large groups of people. An issue of public concern such as building a lake-reservoir near a community will likely bring industrial, commercial, and local government representatives to argue the case for lake development. That group will likely be opposed by conservation and property owner groups who argue a case against lake development. On college campuses, the issues of allocating student activity fees, regulation of housing, and student security are real issues which need critical rational advocacy just as much as issues in the nonacademic world.

Debate has even appeared in what might be considered entertainment in the media. During the pregame show before the 1975 American Football Conference playoff game, two commentators engaged in an organized debate to determine who would win the game.

Debate may be best known as a curricular or an extracurricular experience in our educational system. As such, it is intended to provide controlled simulated acquisition of the fundamental skills of debate necessary to being a successful citizen in society.

Thus far, we have suggested that debate is a process involving critical thinking and is important in many aspects of life. An understanding of the meaning of debate can be expanded if we consider

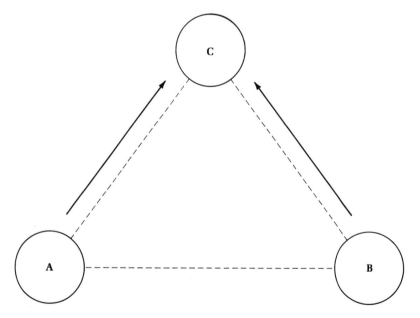

Figure 9.1 Transactional communication: Parties **A** and **B** attempt to influence **C**.

several important characteristics of the debate process. Properly under-stood, debate is characterized as: 1) a transactional communication; 2) an instrument of investigation; and 3) a competitive as well as a cooperative enterprise.

A Transactional Communication Experience

Consider the model in Figure 9.1. Party A and party B are both trying to influence party C. If that is to succeed, party C must be able to understand parties A and B. That means communication symbols must be presented so that they can be received and decoded. It means that symbols exchanged by parties must fall within shared fields of experi-ence or backgrounds. Some feedback must be provided at times by party C to parties A and B and between parties A and B. A reaction by party C ought to enable the speaking party to adjust communication either in content or delivery. Much of the high school and college debating today often ignores this most fundamental characteristic of debate. Debate utilizes oral communication and thereby is governed by the characteristics of the oral communication process.

An Instrument of Investigational Communication

The debater is concerned that decisions be reflective and that method be correct. He is interested in augmenting decision with inves-tigation and reflection for devices of censorship, open threat, and indi-rect persuasion.

A Competitive as well as a Cooperative Enterprise

The competition involved in debate is a conflict of ideas rather than a conflict of personalities. It is a competition to locate the best way to make clear, to organize, to dignify reason. Otherwise, debate is cooperative. It is cooperative if the following conditions stipulated by both parties in a debate are present: 1) Each party has an equal oppor-tunity to be heard; 2) Each party is willing that judgment be suspended until the facts are in; 3) Each party agrees to abide by the decision of an external arbitrating agency.

In debate, conflict occurs on the level at which means are in service to ends. The conflict is used for socially constructive, not destructive, purposes. The failure to recognize the appropriate relationship between competition and cooperation is a serious threat to the vitality of the debate process. There is no situation to warrant using debate as an ego-satisfying activity.

There is a distinct difference between substantive debate and educational debate. In substantive debate, propositions are those in which the advocates have special interests: The lawyer seeks to defend a client, or the political candidate seeks to defeat an opponent. Educational debate is conducted on propositions in which the advocates have more of an academic interest than a special interest. Educational debate is presented before a judge, who does not have power to render a decision on the resolution, but who may render a decision on the merits of the debate to assist the advocates in improving their use of the fundamental debate processes. It is customary that those asked to judge are instructed to disregard the merits of the proposition and to offer their judgment solely on the debating done by the parties.

Educational debate is usually conducted under the auspices of some educational institution. Today, a high school or a college is the most common fostering institution, whereas in the past centuries, literary societies were the sponsoring institutions. The purpose of educational debate is to enable a speaker to become a more effective practitioner in substantive debate.

VALUES OF EDUCATIONAL DEBATE

The list of values that the individual and society derive from educational debate could be lengthy and profound. Here, we will keep the list short, but not to lessen its significance.

Social Values

First and foremost, debate is preparation for effective participation in a free society. The guarantee of freedom of speech is to insure that government does not deny the opportunity to present all sides of an issue. The Jeffersonian concept of an educated, liberated person requires the protection of such opportunity and assumes the person will seek the means to become an active participant in substantive controversy. Citizens who are educated in debate can hope to attain truly effective participation in a free society.

Second, debate is preparation for effective judgment of controversy in public affairs. Exposure to good debate experiences will help you to: 1) develop proficiency as a critical thinker and listener; 2) synthesize knowledge from related fields of inquiry; 3) become knowledgeable about certain important issues.

Personal Values

There are several ways in which educational debate can be of personal value to you. First, it affords an opportunity to develop effective oral communication skills of composition and delivery. Good debating places a premium on extemporaneous delivery which is clear and concise. Good debating requires adaptation to audiences and situations.

Second, debate develops social maturity. Through debate activity, you will be in contact with opponents, judges, and audiences from different communities. The contact with other people and their perspectives will give you a broader social awareness. Educational debate often takes place in a tournament situation. Amid the competition, you must learn to accept victory and defeat with a social dignity and grace.

The validity of social and personal values of educational debate can be found in the testimony of business, professional, and political figures over decades of history. Edmund Muskie, United States Senator from Maine, has testified, "Dealing, as one must, with everchanging opinion, one can hope to be successful in a career of leadership only to the extent that one practices effectively the art of debate."[1] The late Senator Everett Dirksen of Illinois always felt a great indebtedness to his high school debating.[2] Austin Freeley has reported the results of a survey of government leaders:

> A survey of 160 Senators, Congressmen, Governors, Supreme Court Justices, Cabinet members, and other leaders revealed that 100 of the leaders had high school or college debate experience. All of the 100 found their debate experience helpful in their careers, and 90 classified the experience as "greatly helpful" or "valuable." Of the 60 who did not have debate experience, 26 expressed regret that they had not gone out for debating while in school or college.[3]

SUMMARY 1. **What are the social values of educational debate?**
PROBES   2. **What are the personal values of educational debate?**

3. In what way is educational debate a communication transaction?
4. How can debate be both competitive and cooperative?

FUNDAMENTAL CONCEPTS

Educational debate, that is, debate under the auspices of educational institutions, has a long tradition in American society. Over one hundred years ago, the Adelphic Society of Northwestern University debated the Athenaeum Society of Chicago University in Evanston, Illinois, on November 29, 1872 in one of the first educational debates on record in the U. S.[4] The debating today between thousands of high schools and colleges is conducted within a rather rigid framework of rules and procedures. Many of the rules and procedures are intended to promote success as a result of masterful use of certain fundamental concepts.

Debate Propositions

The subject for debate between two teams is the proposition. The proposition is a carefully worded statement expressing judgment or opinion about a controversy such as, "Resolved, that the federal government should regulate the use of natural resources."

There are three kinds of propositions. Propositions of fact present a controversy over the fact of something such as, "Resolved, that a cause and effect relationship exists between smoking and cancer." The central issues are related to what exists or doesn't exist. Propositions of value present a controversy over the value of something such as, "Resolved, that smoking pot is not dangerous to health." Propositions of policy present a controversy over whether or not some course of action should be pursued. Such a proposition might be, "Resolved, that a reservoir should be constructed to satisfy the water needs of Middleburg."

Debates of any of the three types are useful educational experiences which present the opportunity to gain mastery of fundamental concepts. However, because propositions of policy are oriented more to the present and future, and because action is a theoretically logical outcome of concluding the debate, the debating of propositions of policy has greater interest. Propositions of policy are nearly always the propositions used for college and high school debating. The following are propositions of policy similar to those debated recently in colleges and high schools throughout the United States:

> Resolved, that the method of electing the President and Vice President of the United States should be changed.

> Resolved, that natural resources should be controlled by an international agency.

The proposition is always worded affirmatively. That is, it is worded so that the affirmative can and must support the resolution. Also, the proposition is worded such that if adopted it would change the present status of things, the status quo.

Obligations

Prima-Facie Case. The affirmative side in a debate must present a prima-facie case. That means it must present a series of arguments and supports which, if unchallenged, would cause a reasonable person to agree with the resolution.

The affirmative has the obligation to present the prima-facie case because the presumption of right is with the status quo. The affirmative wishes to rearrange the status quo. It is not reasonable to rearrange the status quo unless two conditions are proven: 1) That some facet of the present system has inherent shortcomings; and 2) That the affirmative proposal will improve the conditions in question. The affirmative presents a prima-facie case when it advances contentions and proof to establish those two conditions.

In educational debate, as in substantive debate, failure of the affirmative to have a prima-facie case is sufficient cause for concurring with the negative position.

Burden of Proof. The burden of proof is the requirement to prove a claim or statement. Since the affirmative is advocating change, that side must always carry the burden of proof. This means the affirmative bears a risk of not being able to prove what is advocated.

Burden of Rebuttal. Although the burden of proof always rests with the affirmative, a burden of rebuttal shifts back and forth between the two sides. The burden of rebuttal is the obligation to: 1) engage in refutation, which is the destruction of opposing proofs; and 2) defend one's own case against an opponent's attack. Assumption of the burden of rebuttal by both the affirmative and the negative provides a debate with considerable give and take of controversy. That kind of controversy is fundamental to debate since it allows the advantages and disadvantages of a proposal to be thoroughly examined in relation to each other.

Procedure

The debate is opened by the affirmative team, which agrees to support the resolution. The negative team replies by opposing the resolution. Present-day debate usually has four constructive speeches alternating between affirmative and negative. During the constructive speeches, each side presents its case with supporting evidence and reasoning.

After the constructive speeches are complete, the negative team begins the rebuttal speeches. Each side has two speeches to refute the case of the opponents and to defend or rebuild its own case.

Time

As educational debate has evolved, certain time limits have become normal procedure for debating. Any set time limits agreeable to affirmative, negative, and judge or audience would be workable. The following pattern is one commonly used in college debating:

Constructive Speeches	Time
First Affirmative	10 minutes
First Negative	10 minutes
Second Affirmative	10 minutes
Second Negative	10 minutes

Rebuttal Speeches	Time
First Negative	5 minutes
First Affirmative	5 minutes
Second Negative	5 minutes
Second Affirmative	5 minutes

In high school and college debate, cross-examination is common. After each constructive speech, the opposing side is allowed to question the speaker. The following is the most commonly used format in high school debating:

Constructive Speeches	Time
First Affirmative constructive	8 minutes
Second Negative cross-examination	3 minutes
First Negative constructive	8 minutes
First Affirmative cross-examination	3 minutes
Second Affirmative constructive	8 minutes
First Negative cross-examination	3 minutes
Second Negative constructive	8 minutes
Second Affirmative cross-examination	3 minutes

Rebuttal Speeches	Time
First Negative	4 minutes
First Affirmative	4 minutes
Second Negative	4 minutes
Second Affirmative	4 minutes

Duties

It is the duty of the affirmative team to support the resolution with a prima-facie case. It is also the duty of the affirmative to defend the prima-facie case against negative argument. It is the duty of the negative to defend the status quo with an attack on the affirmative's prima-facie case. On rare occasions, the negative might opt to defend only very limited aspects of the status quo and advocate an alternate proposal.

The affirmative must obtain a "yes" to ALL of the issues in a debate. An issue is a vital and inherent question upon whose answers the acceptance or rejection of the proposition will depend. Whether there is a need for a change is one such issue. There are several ways the affirmative might treat that issue, but the fundamental question of necessity for change will remain and must be carried by the affirmative.

Both the affirmative and negative are obligated to present their cases or positions in the form of contentions. The contentions are specific arguments advanced for positions relative to an issue. The decision is won by substantiating a preponderance of the arguments relative to that given issue. Carrying the issue is vital to the life of an affirmative or negative position.

On a topic like, "Resolved, that the CIA should be disbanded," the affirmative must carry the issue of necessity for change. The affirmative might contend that the CIA is abusive of power in violation of human rights, or the affirmative might contend that the CIA functions could be better performed by contract with a private agency.

The remainder of this section will help to prepare for debating through analysis and research, to prepare affirmative and negative cases, to develop a case with evidence and reasoning, to give refutation and rebuttal, and to use cross-examination and present a case effectively.

SUMMARY
PROBES

1. How do issues and contentions differ?
2. What is an issue on the topic, "Resolved, that the United States should withdraw from the United Nations"?
3. Why does the affirmative have to carry ALL issues in a debate?
4. What is meant by the following terms: *prima facie, burden of proof, burden of rebuttal, resolution?*
5. Why is the affirmative team given both opening and closing speeches in a debate?

LEARNING ACTIVITIES

1. Prepare an oral or written report on the history of educational debate.

2. Prepare a five-minute speech suitable for presentation to prospective debaters in which you set forth the values of educational debate.

3. Select a recent or current political campaign. Prepare a report of the issues developed by the candidates.

4. Prepare a brief report in which you list examples of the following:

a. Use of rational decison-making to make a personal decision.
b. A group discussion in which a decision of public importance was made.
c. A persuasive speech using argument and proof to gain acceptance of an idea.

5. Investigate the significance of debate in the following instances:

a. Ratification of the United States Constitution.
b. Lincoln-Douglas Debates.
c. Woodrow Wilson's arguments for the League of Nations.
d. Ratification of the Nuclear Test Ban treaty.

6. Prepare a list of the ways in which debaters have to cooperate in order to make a debate possible.

7. Discuss debate as a thinking activity.

8. On a selected proposition, complete the following:

    a. Evaluate the strength of the negative presumption.

    b. Describe the relationships of the stock issues to the proposition.

TEN

GOALS   After completing this chapter you will be able to:

1. Dissect a proposition for careful analysis.
2. Identify the stock issues for selected debate propositions.
3. Recognize the importance of defining terms.
4. Employ several methods to define terms.
5. Locate sources of material for research purposes.
6. Find and record information systematically.
7. Complete the analysis and research for a resolution on one of several selected topics.
8. Understand a method for information storage and retrieval.

Preparing through Analysis and Research

Once a proposition for debate has been agreed upon, the two parties to the debate must follow several rationally determined steps. Step one is to carefully analyze the proposition. Step two is to conduct thorough research. The purposes of analysis are to locate issues and to categorize and select those that are substantive and critical. Ehninger and Brockriede identify four parts to completing the analysis step: "(a) discovering the immediate issues of the controversy; (b) understanding the historical background; (c) defining the terms of the proposition; (d) determining the issues."[1]

ANALYSIS

Discovering the Immediate Causes

One of the first questions you should ask yourself is, "What are the causes for the controversy which are inherent in the resolution?" The immediate cause will be a recent condition which has made people question the wisdom of some aspect of the present order of things. Every time some person has confessed to a crime for which another was executed, there have been challenges to the criminal statutes which allow the death penalty. Most likely you will discover this to be one reason to question the death penalty, if you begin a search for immediate causes on the proposition of abolishing it. A search for immediate causes for the proposition to control auto exhaust emissions would probably reveal startling factual studies of the carbon monoxide levels during rush hour times in large metropolitan areas.

You may search for immediate causes in three basic ways. First, you may be an interested party and have firsthand experiences which reveal the immediate causes. Second, you may find immediate causes by reading contemporary literature. Finally, you may be able to locate what people perceive to be immediate causes by conducting surveys.

Understanding the Historical Background

Once you have found the immediate causes of a controversy, the next question you must ask is: "What is the historical background?" On any controversy, there will likely be a considerable number of events related to the controversy. As an example, consider the controversy over a policy of open housing. Groups may have expressed dissatisfaction with housing policies. Some modifications may have been tried and found to be failures. You need to know about the historical circumstances concerning (a) dissatisfaction and (b) past efforts to change.

After examining the historical background, you will be able to determine which specific research questions to pursue. Your next steps will be to formulate contentions for issues and to prepare a case with organized arguments and evidence to gain acceptance of a plan.

Defining the Terms

The third part of the analysis step is to arrive at definitions for terms. This is an important part of analysis because it is critical to the actual debate which will follow. During the debate itself, the affirmative has the right and obligation to define terms, within reasonable bounds. The debate cannot proceed to substantive issues until the intrinsic and extrinsic terms of the resolution are identified and defined.

Example. One of the clearest methods to define terms is to use example. The example used must be one which is commonly known. A form of definition by example, common to many debates, is what is often labeled "operational definition." In such an instance the affirmative defines a term with its plan as the example.

Authority.   Some terms are best defined by quoting the definition established by some well-qualified authority. *Black's Law Dictionary* is often used for an authoritative definition of legal terms. In debates on negative income tax, the term could best be defined by a quotation from the Department of Labor. A definition for nuclear weapons could be obtained from a source such as the Atomic Energy Commission.

Explanation.   A brief explanation of how something functions will be the clearest method of definition. The term *harmful emissions* can be defined by explaining the nature of some emissions which have occurred and how they affected people.

Negation.   A term may be defined by explaining what it isn't. The term *major pollutors* can be defined by stating that "we don't mean the deposits of ash into the air from campfires in national parks or the natural decaying of animals which die from natural causes in the forests."

Comparison and Contrast.   Sometimes a comparison or contrast with something known will provide clear definition. In debating the proposition, "Resolved, that the President should be elected by direct vote of the people," the affirmative might define direct vote by contrasting it to the electoral college.

Definition of terms can be an issue itself in the debate, but that is usually a rather poor and uninteresting debate. It is important that the affirmative select a reasonable definition of terms and select the method which will provide the clearest and most understanding definition. The affirmative team who intentionally selects the most complex and confusing method in order to "trap" the negative is violating the ethics of debate.

The negative debater should be prepared to accept or reject the affirmative's definition of terms. If the affirmative definition is reasonable, the negative would do well to accept that definition and proceed with the debate. If the affirmative definition is not reasonable, the first negative debater must make the challenge and offer a reasonable alternate definition.

Determining the Issues

The fourth part of the analysis step is to determine the issues in a controversy. No matter how startling your evidence will be or how

clearly you organize, the identification and selection of the real issues
are fundamentally necessary if you hope to persuade a critical listener.
The first point of competition in educational debate is competition
between the affirmative and negative advocates to identify and select
the real issues in the controversy behind the proposition.

The structure of issues becomes more complex from one type of
proposition to another. The structure of issues is more complex in
propositions of policy than in propositions of fact and value.

Propositions of Fact. A proposition of fact may contain issues
over definition of terms in the proposition or the designated state of
being which is implied in the proposition. A term like *control* may not
be an issue in a proposition of fact. The term *reduction in crime* may be
an issue in a proposition of fact.

In order to analyze a proposition of fact, you should make an inventory of data related to the controversy. Seek alleged facts. Search for
disputes over the status of alleged facts. Examine issues over fact which
are important (vital) to the proposition in question.

Propositions of Value. Every proposition of value contains a term
implying a value, such as, *best, good, useful, rewarding.* The definition
of terms is a central issue in the debate of value. The term may be
defined most clearly by the method of comparison. Compare the thing
in question with some acceptable norm (criterion). The comparison
will probably yield a relative answer.

Designated issues in propositions of value arise when you ask:
"What is the referent in the proposition?" The term *economical* in a
proposition, "Resolved, that the Chicago metropolitan area has an
economical transportation system," raises the question "economical to
whom?"

Propositions of Policy. The central issues in propositions of policy are usually related to action. The stock issues' analysis is most often
used by debaters on propositions of policy.

You would likely discover subordinate issues relating to the following stock issues: (a) Is there an inherent problem with the present
policy? (b) Will the proposed change remedy the undesirable conditions in the present situation? (c) Can the remedy be applied without
serious disadvantages?

One additional controversy is sometimes considered an issue, that
is, whether the proposition change is likely to be implemented. This is
what debaters call the "should-would" issue. It is our point of view that

the affirmative is not obligated to prove "would" unless the special policy of the affirmative plan would result in a great social disruption and other disadvantages if it were tried without success. Since that possibility is theoretically present with any proposal, the issue of implementation is an issue which should be examined by the debaters during the analysis step. The decision of whether it should be made an issue in the debate is relative. In some congressional plans to take action eliminating existing health care centers in order to reallocate present funds, there is a risk to present health levels as a result of the change. The disadvantage could occur if the totality of the affirmative proposal failed to materialize. Under those conditions, the probability of the proposal being given existence is, as we see it, a legitimate issue.

The number of issues will vary from one proposition to another. The issues can be discovered by careful analysis and research. Usually, the number of issues is small. You can expect three to six issues in the typical high school or collegiate educational debate. If an advocate claims a large number of issues, he may be confusing supportive contentions with issues. There is presently an unfortunate practice by many debaters to "spread" the debate with a multiplicity of issues. The practice is deplorable. Many of the "issues" are not really issues, and the proponents know that to be true. More often, issues are alleged but never fully developed. The proliferation of issues usually produces a shallow debate. The practice of proliferation has become so widespread, it constitutes a major threat to the vitality of educational debate and even substantive debate practices.

SUMMARY
PROBES

1. What is involved in the analysis step of preparation to debate?
2. What are the ways to define terms in a debate?
3. How can the definition of terms be an issue?
4. What are the three common stock issues in propositions of policy?
5. How many issues are likely to develop during a debate?

RESEARCH

The essence of good debate, both educational and substantive, is to know what you are talking about. Without support information, ideas are often rather sterile. The location and retention of information is the research phase of debate. The process of analyzing a controversy for issues and the exploration for information are interrelated phases. Your efforts are likely to be directed at both phases simultaneously. Research is a two-part process: location and retention.

Location

The most logical place to turn for information is the library. There are different kinds of libraries, each with different emphases. Public libraries contain most general references and some specialized materials. Large metropolitan areas usually have law libraries containing specialized legal references. The law libraries usually are not open to the general public except by special arrangement. College and university libraries are usually good research centers; larger institutions often have specialized libraries ranging from medical and law to science research centers.

Books are still the basic source for research. They may be located efficiently by consulting the card catalog where books are listed alphabetically three times: by author's last name, by title, and by subject. Many volumes are now placed on microfilm for the sake of economical storage.

Magazines are the next common source for information; several indexes are available to help find desired articles. The *Reader's Guide to Periodical Literature* is an index of popular and common magazine articles. More specialized indexes are *The Education Index*, *Agriculture Index*, *Engineering Index*, *Psychological Abstracts*, and *Catalog of the United States Government Publications*.

Newspapers and pamphlets must be consulted for current information. Unfortunately, except for the *New York Times Index*, newspapers are not indexed. The debater will make a practice of reading the paper daily in order to remain current on the topic which is going to be debated.

There are several other reference sources available. *Facts on File* will contain some useful statistical data. More sophisticated data is available from *Statistical Abstracts of the United States*. Factual data can be located in general works like *Information Please Almanac*.

Retention

As information is located, it must be stored in such a way that easy and quick access can be made at a later time. A filing system is mandatory. The filing system should include: (1) the physical equipment of a file box or boxes and file cards, and (2) an indexing system for filing and locating information.

The physical equipment may be simple or elaborate, depending upon the extent of participation in educational debate intended. A very simple minimal effort would include the availability of a four-by-six-inch file box of any depth, the use of four-by-six-inch index cards, and index dividers.

More elaborate equipment for the more thorough debater would include a four-by-six-inch metal two-drawer file, the use of four-by-six-inch index cards of two different colors, index dividers, and a subject index. The different color cards enable you to place affirmative material on one color card and negative material on a different color card. Dual color cards have been found to be an aid to filing and locating cards. The index divider cards are used to establish categories in a filing system. Using a logical filing system with many categories is necessary in order to locate material quickly during debate. Certainly, it is an aid to refutation and rebuttal.

A most elaborate set of equipment is to use a suitcase, IBM cards of several colors, and a subject index. As the information is typed on the IBM cards, they are categorized for filing topically in rows in the suitcase.

(Category) Role of Fed. Gov't.
(Subcategory) Consequences of
categorical aid

One consequence of this categorical approach has been the exclusion from Public Assistance of many who are unquestionably in need of help. Part of this exclusion has been by design, as in the case of the employed or employable poor. Other exclusions result because it is impossible to design categories which can cover all cases of need, anticipate the wide variety of human circumstances, and change in response to new manifestations of need.

(Source) The President's Commission, *Poverty Amid Plenty*, p. 48.

Figure 10.1 Sample affirmative card on the topic, "Resolved, that the federal government should enact a program of comprehensive welfare for United States citizens living in poverty."

The evidence placed on four-by-six-inch or IBM cards needs to be accurately recorded and labeled according to categories and subcategories. A sample affirmative card is shown in Figure 10.1 on the topic, "Resolved, that the federal government should enact a program of comprehensive welfare for United States citizens living in poverty."

The exact system for indexing and filing information should be designed specifically for yourself; it should include several categories and subcategories of the topic to be debated.

The following set of categories and subcategories for filing was developed for an extensive and rather sophisticated filing system on the topic, "Resolved, that Congress should develop a comprehensive program to control land use in the United States."

Public Lands
    I. The lands
        A. Public
            1. ⅓ of total land
            2. Most in West
            3. Managed under federal systems
        B. Private
            1. 59% rural
            2. Various uses

    II. Resources
        A. Energy
            1. Control by FG
            2. $1 billion production
            3. Coal production
        B. Leasing
            1. Lease of 10%
            2. Multiple use maintenance
            3. Force production
            4. Stimulation of development

    III. Management
        A. BLM
            1. Management control
            2. Lack of authority
            3. Multiple use
        B. Multiple Use Act
            1. Multiple use mandate
            2. Public interest balance
            3. Expiration
            4. Still followed

C. Mining Law of 1872
   1. Exploitation
   2. Exemptions
D. New Mexico State Controls

IV. PLLRC Report
   A. Not environmentally sound
   B. Promotion of dominant use
   C. Retention of Mining Law of 1872
   D. Political bias
   E. Not expert study

SUMMARY PROBES

1. **Where could you locate information on fertilizer production in the United States and India?**
2. **Why is systematic retention of information necessary?**
3. **List the categories for the topic, "Resolved, that the federal government should adopt a program of compulsory wage and price controls."**
4. **List several subcategories for a possible category in probe 3.**

LEARNING ACTIVITIES

1. Locate ten articles or books which might prove useful for research purposes with the following debate resolution:

Resolved, that the federal government should guarantee a minimum annual income to all citizens.

2. Using whatever means necessary, locate all relevant definitions for terms in the following debate resolution:

Resolved, that the law enforcement agencies in the United States should be given greater freedom in the investigation and prosecution of crime.

3. For each of the following debate resolutions, locate two articles from the *Reader's Guide*, read the articles, and then prepare a list of eight categories for retaining information:

a. Resolved, that the United States military forces should engage in combat only following a declaration of war by Congress or nuclear attack on United States territory.

b. Resolved, that the United States should turn over the Panama Canal to the government of Panama.

4. For the current high school or college debate resolution prepare a complete list of affirmative and negative categories and subcategories for an information retention system.

5. Divide into sets of two. Each pair of individuals will select a proposition of value or policy. One person should act as affirmative speaker and present a three-minute speech in which he or she: (a) states the proposition; (b) defines the terms; and (c) states the issues. The other person, acting as a negative speaker, should: (a) accept the definitions or offer alternative ones; (b) accept the statement of issues, revise the issues, or offer additional issues.

6. Assume that you are assigned the task of finding evidence for a speech dealing with control of crime in the United States. List sources you would use and the order in which you would consult them. Justify the list and its order.

7. List what you believe to be the five best general sources of debate evidence. Also, list one liability for each source you have listed.

References

Ehninger, Douglas, and Brockriede, Wayne. *Decision by Debate*. New York: Dodd, Mead, 1970, p. 226.

Freeley, Austin. *Argumentation and Debate*. Belmont: Wadsworth, 1962, p. 31.

Kruger, Arthur. "The Underlying Assumptions of Policy Questions: Presumption and Burden of Proof." *Speaker and Gavel* 2(November 1964), p. 4.

Marsh, Patrick O. "A Model for Arguing Directive Propositions." *The Journal of the American Forensic Association* 6(Winter 1969), p. 3.

ELEVEN

GOALS   After completing this chapter you will be able to:

1. Understand the requirements for an affirmative case.
2. Recognize the requirements for a negative case.
3. Grasp the need to organize carefully.
4. Select arguments to construct one of three structures for an affirmative case.
5. Select arguments to construct one of six approaches for a negative case.
6. Construct an affirmative case.
7. Construct a negative case.

Developing Affirmative and Negative Cases

To overcome the presumption of the negative discussed in Chapter Nine, the affirmative must present a prima-facie case, that is, one which will stand on its own merits. The affirmative case does not emerge accidentally or spontaneously, but must be carefully prepared in advance. Considering possible lines of attack and strengthening critical positions in the planning stage is valuable strategy indeed.

Although the novice may assume that the negative case must be spontaneously developed, that is the farthest possible thing from the truth. In reality, the negative must also prepare a case designed to defend the present condition. It is always necessary to modify and adapt to the actual affirmative case.

This chapter will describe the process of carefully preparing an affirmative and a negative case. For each position you will find treatment of both traditional and comparative advantage cases.

PREPARING THE AFFIRMATIVE CASE

Traditional Case

The traditional case should be developed around three stock issues: (1) the need for a change from the status quo, (2) the workability of the affirmative proposal in meeting the need, and (3) the benefits produced from adopting the proposal.

When examining the first issue, you will probably discover that the best way to organize support for it is with sign and causal reasoning. Suppose you are a member of an affirmative team supporting a proposal for direct election of the president and vice-president. You would employ sign reasoning to support the first issue that:

A. There are serious problems in the method of electing the president and vice-president.
   1. Example: minority presidents have been elected (sign of the problem).
   2. Example: minority presidents lack confidence to deal with Congress (sign of the problem).

You can use causal reasoning to support the issue that problems are effected by certain basic characteristics of the present system:

B. These problems are caused by basic characteristics of the electoral college system, for
   1. Characteristic number one:
     a. Evidence
   2. Characteristic number two:
     a. Evidence
   3. Characteristic number three:
     a. Evidence

It is important for you to remember that one of the characteristics, probably the last one you name, must be the *characteristic of inherency*. The affirmative must argue and establish that the flaws in the system are the result of the inherent functioning of the present system. Many affirmative teams fail to come to grips with the issue of inherency.

The second stock issue with which the affirmative must deal is the *workability of their plan*. The plan itself should be outlined for presentation. In outlining the plan, key parts of the outline should be as follows:

II. The affirmative proposes the following plan:
   A. Structure of the plan
   B. Functioning of the plan
   C. Method of enforcement
   D. Financing of the plan

The form of support most likely to be used is explanation and description. Sufficient explanation of each of the four parts should be provided so that the audience and listeners can understand how your proposal would work. Some plans may be familiar to the audience and thus require very little description. If the plan you propose is technical or complex in nature, then additional explanation or possibly comparison and contrast with known entities will be necessary to make all four parts clear to the listener. Remember, the obligation is with you—the source of the message—to provide clear, orderly, and understandable explanation of the issue. At the end of your presentation of the plan, you should be able to state honestly to the listener in summary that "We have provided evidence that the affirmative plan would be workable."

The third stock issue for the affirmative is that, if adopted, *the plan is likely to produce benefits in excess of any cost or other disadvantage.* At this point in the debate, your case will shift from reliance on sign, description, and causal reasoning to prediction. You will predict the likelihood of certain things occurring. If your prediction is to be believed, it must strike a reasonable person as being highly reliable, that is, very likely to occur time after time if it could be tried over and over.

One method is to use opinion of experts as testimony to the likelihood of the advantage. The reliability of such prediction is dependent upon the reliability of the source. You will want to ask:

1. How close is the source to the situation?
2. What degree of control does the authority have over the situation?
3. Is the source honest enough to prevent bias from distorting accuracy of prediction?

You may further wish to give any historical precedent in which similar proposals under similar circumstances were tried and proved to be workable. Has it worked before? The probability of success again under present circumstance will be highly dependent upon the similarity of the fundamental parts of the past and present plans.

In preparing the part of the case which deals with the third stock issue, you will want to structure support around two kinds of advantages: (1) the correction of evils in the need, (2) additional benefits which will accrue. The organization of this part of the affirmative case may be outlined as follows:

III. Many benefits will result from the affirmative plan, for,
    A. The plan will correct evils cited in the present system, for,
        1. Evil number one will be corrected, for,
           a. Evidence

2. Evil number two will be corrected, for,
   a. Evidence
B. The plan will accrue additional benefits, for,
   1. It will. . . .
      a. Evidence
   2. It will. . . .
      a. Evidence

Comparative Advantage Affirmative Case

The comparative advantage case centers around the affirmative plan. In so doing, the affirmative captures the initiative on the portion of the debate most vulnerable to negative expansion—or "spread"—tactics. Essentially, the comparative advantage case consists of an affirmative proposal for change from the status quo and resulting advantages from the change if it were to be adopted.

The plan is presented immediately by the affirmative followed by the advantages. The advantage usually consists of four parts: (1) a demonstration that the present system cannot produce the advantage; (2) a description of the extent of success with the present system; (3) an explanation of how the plan will secure the advantage; (4) an explanation of the inherent and significant nature of the advantage.

The advantage case emphasizes defense of the plan by an early establishment of issues related to the plan and may even negate part of the effect of the usual negative attack.

The comparative advantage and the traditional case are similar in the ends they seek to serve. Both approaches must confront the same fundamental stock issues.

A major difference between the comparative advantage and the traditional case structure is that the comparative advantage case accepts the philosophy and success of the status quo. The affirmative, then, does not question that the status quo achieves some of its goals. The affirmative may question the success of the status quo in relation to capability or potential. The comparative advantage case will focus on the relative potential of consequences if a certain change is made. The traditional case does not accept the successes of the status quo. The traditional case also focuses on the necessity to change rather than on the proposed change itself.

A second difference between the comparative advantage case and the traditional case is the location of treatment of inherency. In the traditional case, inherency is considered as part of the status quo. Structurally, it is treated with the need for change: something in the fundamental make-up of the status quo makes it impossible to alleviate harm without fundamental change. In the comparative advantage approach, inherency is considered as a part of the proposed change. Structurally, it is treated with the advantage. Something in the new plan or approach is likely to accrue the desired change without producing new disadvantages.

To simplify the relationship above, consider the following hypothetical case:

Topic   Snow removal
Proposition   X organization should adopt a new means of snow removal from their place of business.
Affirmative plan Buy a mechanical snow plow

The affirmative would probably want to recognize that individuals with snow shovels can remove snow. The status quo is workable in achieving the desired goal. The affirmative, however, might point out that much money might be saved for greater business profit if the task could be completed quicker. That advantage is likely to result only if the snow plow is purchased, therefore, the advantage is inherent in the affirmative plan.

The risk for the affirmative is in the challenge they will face to build upon sound prediction. The whole case focuses on the future.

The comparative advantage case, like the traditional case, must be integrated in order to establish a prima-facie case. The agreed goals, the plan, and the comparative advantages must be developed to dovetail perfectly. The interrelationship is suggested by the model in Figure 11.1.

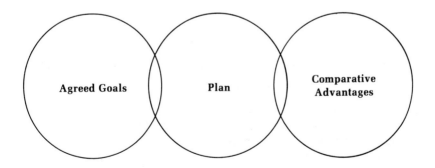

Figure 11.1 Comparative advantage case rests on integrating the agreed goals, plan, and comparative advantages.

You will need to identify the agreed goals. It is unlikely you will accept all the goals of the status quo; however, you must identify specifically those which you do accept. The plan must be tailored to the agreed goals and presented in sufficient detail so that it is obvious how your plan will relate to the advantages in a way different from the status quo. Your comparative advantage must be inherent in the plan as discussed above. The advantages must be significant.

There are several ways to organize the comparative advantage case. One way is to begin by showing that the absence of certain qualities is a cause for action. You would then argue that this absence from the status quo would prevent the attainment of certain benefits. Then, you would argue that the affirmative proposal would produce the benefits.

Using the above pattern, you might organize your case around the following main blocs:

First Affirmative

1. Introduce the problem with definition of terms.
2. Present the plan.
3. Present advantages.
   a. Point out absence of a certain quality.
   b. Absence is responsible for an undesirable condition.
   c. Affirmative plan will accrue the advantage.
   d. The advantage is inherent in nature.

Second Affirmative

1. Restate the affirmative position briefly.
2. Offer defense against the negative attack.

Criteria Case

A contemporary refinement of the comparative advantage approach is the criteria case. Philosophically, the criteria approach is similar, if not identical, to the comparative advantage approach. The affirmative attempts to focus the debate on goals. Although the validity of goals can be a fundamental issue in any debate, it usually isn't allowed to become such an issue. In the criteria approach, the affirmative claims certain advantages in relation to identified goals.

The case structurally would be the same as for the comparative advantage case except that before the plan or advantages are given, the first affirmative would state as a contention the existence of a goal or goals. The validity of the goal(s) must be established by some kind of support.

SUMMARY
PROBES
1. How does the affirmative confront the stock issues differently with traditional and comparative advantage cases?
2. What kind of support is best for proof of the advantages of a proposal?
3. What does the term *inherency* mean?
4. Where is inherency treated in the affirmative case?
5. How does the criteria case differ from others?

PREPARING THE NEGATIVE CASE

The negative must be prepared with selected lines of argumentation because the affirmative team will present a prima-facie case which will overcome the presumption of the negative. The negative team in a debate has six different approaches available for regaining the presumption.

Before discussing the available approaches, there are several basic considerations important to the negative case development which should be remembered. First, you must select wisely from available approaches and arguments. You will have more avenues of attack than you can possibly employ. The common error is to develop a shotgun strategy and try to take a "quick shot" at a lot of areas. You must select the most cogent arguments available and concentrate your efforts.

Second, you must test the affirmative case with as much direct clash as possible, given the topic, case, arguments, and evidence. Direct clash means to take specific issue with specific arguments. The reasons given by the affirmative must be challenged. In preparing to clash directly, you will formulate certain arguments. The debater should be wary that this formulation of arguments does not lead to "canned" negative speeches. Direct application to the specific affirmative case must be demonstrated. Failure to clash directly by a negative team is often a reason for affirmative decisions by judges.

Third, prepare and state a negative philosophy. The philosophy is a basic position statement made in the first negative speech with a broad enough umbrella to cover all subsequent negative arguments.

Fourth, the negative must work as a team. Therefore, to avoid duplication and to keep a logical sequence, your arguments must be coordinated with those of your colleague. For example, the first negative would attempt to establish the value of the status quo, whereas the second negative would charge that changing the status quo would jeopardize the values which exist because of the mechanism of the status quo.

In summary, you must select wisely, clash directly, state a philosophy, and work as a team in order to regain and retain the presumption from the affirmative.

Depending upon your analysis of potential weaknesses in various affirmative cases, you would select one of the six basic negative approaches. Each of the six is designed to focus your attack at the point of weakness in the affirmative.

No Need

The first approach for the negative team is to concentrate their emphasis on the position that there is no justifiable reason for making major changes in the status quo. With this approach, the negative team will be defending the status quo as workable and desirable. The negative will also be attacking the affirmative case on the first stock issue.

If you choose to use this approach, you will need to be prepared to make your arguments fit the particular style of the affirmative case structure. If the affirmative has a traditional case structure, you will want to present arguments and evidence around contentions selected from the following:

1. The harmful effects have not been proven to exist.
2. The harm is not significant.
3. The harm which does exist is not a result of some inherent aspect of the status quo.
4. Whatever harmful conditions do exist can be eliminated by small administrative modifications in the status quo.
5. The status quo has been beneficial.

Naturally, not all of the above would be compatible for use against the same affirmative case. Using this approach, you would devote all of the first negative constructive speech and possibly a portion of the second speech to contentions aimed at the need stock issue.

If the affirmative has a comparative advantage structure, you will want to present arguments and evidence around contentions selected from the following:

1. The advantage is not significant.
2. The advantage is not unique to the affirmative plan.
3. The alleged advantage isn't an advantage at all.
4. The advantage will not result from the affirmative plan.

After concentrating heavily on the first stock issue, the prudent negative debater will also present a short, carefully focused attack at each of the other two stock issues, if they present any vulnerability. Perhaps time will allow for one argument against the workability of the plan and for identification of one disadvantage of the affirmative plan.

Allocation of time is often neglected. If you are going to use the "no need" approach, the proportional relationship of time devoted to the three stock issues should be like that represented in Figure 11.2.

Inadequate Plan

The second approach available to the negative is to concentrate emphasis on the position that the affirmative plan is not workable. The potential contentions for this approach are the same against either the traditional or the comparative advantage case structures. The available contentions would include:

1. The operational mechanism as described will not work.
2. The affirmative plan is structurally unworkable.
3. The plan lacks a workable enforcement mechanism.
4. The cost of the plan is incorrectly determined.
5. There is precedent that similar plans have failed.

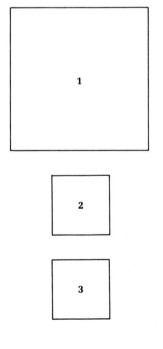

Figure 11.2 Proportion of time devoted to the three stock issues in the "no need" approach

Figure 11.3 Weight of relative time emphasis for the "inadequate plan" approach

Essentially, you will argue that the plan is structurally unsound; or, if sound, will not meet the necessity to change.

Again, the prudent negative will not ignore the other two stock issues. If you listen carefully, you will likely discover some area of inadequate need development which is worthy of challenge. If you contemplate any plan carefully, it is bound to contain some potential disadvantage—the potential for an undesirable consequence—if adopted. It might be costly or dangerous to some existing value.

The weight of relative time emphasis for the "inadequate plan" approach is suggested in Figure 11.3.

Disadvantageous Plan

The third approach available to the negative is to concentrate emphasis on the position that the affirmative plan should be rejected because of its disadvantages.

Specific contentions must be developed in accordance with specific affirmative plans. You must be careful not to use "canned" or preplanned contentions which do not apply. However, through careful analysis and practice against several affirmative cases, it is possible to anticipate possible affirmative plans. Then, you may "block" outline contentions and supporting evidence or reasoning.

The perspective for attacking advantages and disadvantages will vary slightly between traditional and comparative advantage cases. Against traditional cases you might argue the disadvantages are reasons enough to reject the affirmative plan. Against the comparative advantage case, you might argue that the disadvantages comparatively outweigh any advantages.

The weight of relative time emphasis for the "disadvantageous plan" approach is suggested in Figure 11.4. (See page 204.)

Total Rejection

The fourth approach available to the negative is to concentrate equally on all three stock issues and argue for complete rejection on all grounds. Negative speakers argue that there is no reason to change, that the affirmative plan would not meet the need even if the need existed, and that the plan would produce more harmful than beneficial effects.

For beginning debaters this is probably the best approach to test the soundness of the affirmative proposal, for the "total rejection" approach is sound. With experience in assessing cases, the beginning debater will begin to feel confident of his ability to assess and select. Then the debater will want to try other approaches.

The weight of the relative time emphasis for the "total rejection" approach is suggested in Figure 11.5. (See page 204.)

Minor Repairs

The fifth approach available to the negative is to argue that there are certain shortcomings in the status quo, but they can be corrected with relatively minor changes in the present system. Essentially, the negative will argue that any existing problems are not inherent in the system. For example, if the affirmative argues that a national welfare system should be adopted because present state and local funds are excessively wasted, the negative team can argue that, while waste does exist and is undesirable, it can be eliminated by certain small administrative changes. The negative might even suggest expanded use of computer monitoring for eligibility. In other words, there is not inherent reason why the present system cannot reduce waste; the minor repair would be the use of computer monitoring within the state and local systems.

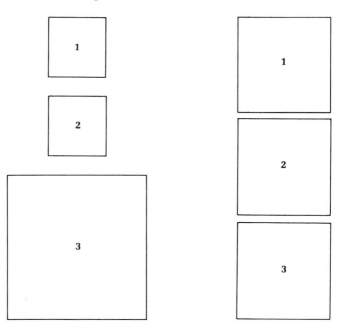

Figure 11.4

Relative time emphasis for the "disadvantageous plan" approach

Figure 11.5

Weight of relative time emphasis for the "total rejection" approach

Counterplan

The sixth approach available to the negative is to offer a counterplan. This approach is strategically dangerous and philosophically fuzzy.

When using this approach, the negative admits that needs exist. In fact, the negative may contend that the need is even greater than presented by the affirmative. The negative may also contend that additional causative factors operate to produce the harmful effects. In other words, the affirmative has erred in two ways: (1) identifying the actual severity of the need, and (2) accurately analyzing the scope of causative factors. At this point in the debate, the negative is compelled to take the offensive and offer a counterplan. In effect, the negative must become affirmative debaters in nature and outline a plan which will satisfy the requirements of: (1) meeting the need, (2) workability, and (3) advantages greater than disadvantages.

If the negative uses this approach and presents the counterplan in the first negative speech—as must be done—the debate should hinge principally upon the question of which plan can better fulfill the goals.

The counterplan approach can be effective when there is a workable proposal outside the intent of the proposition. If there is no proposal outside the intent of the proposition, then an attempt to use a counterplan would be logically unsound and strategically unwise. One such counterproposal—which is an example of *not* being outside the intent of the proposition—is one on the control of natural resources, which simply proposed that the affirmative plan be studied by a blue-ribbon committee and either dropped or adopted as they see fit. That clearly is not outside the intent of the proposition.

The negative will need to adapt the various approaches to fit the unique structure of the comparative advantage case. It may be helpful to you in organizing your thinking to ask yourself the following questions:

First Negative Speaker

1. Are there advantages?
2. Will the alleged advantages occur?
3. Are the alleged advantages inherent in the affirmative plan?
4. Do the alleged advantages stem from the debate proposition?
5. Are the alleged advantages significant?

Second Negative Speaker

1. Will the plan work?
2. Will disadvantages accrue from adopting the plan?
3. Will disadvantages occur as a result of excluded programs or policies?

SUMMARY PROBES

1. **What is direct clash?**
2. **What is a negative philosophy?**
3. **List six possible negative approaches.**
4. **How does the "no need" approach vary between the traditional cases and comparative advantage cases?**
5. **Which negative approach would be best suited to use against the comparative advantage case?**
6. **What is unique about a counterplan?**
7. **What are the risks of using a counterplan?**

LEARNING ACTIVITIES

1. Select three debate propositions. Define terms operationally for one proposition. Define terms by stipulation for a second proposition. Define terms both operationally and by stipulation for a third proposition.

2. Assume that you have presented a need for censorship in the United States. Propose a plan which would institute a system of federally controlled censorship of literature. Develop advantages which would result from implementing your proposal. Now, develop three arguments an opponent would most likely use to attack your proposal.

3. For the current proposition, discuss whether a traditional case or a comparative advantage case would be most logical. Also, consider whether it would also be the most strategic to use.

4. For the current proposition, list some possible contentions that would support your position.

5. Attend an interscholastic debate and prepare an outline of the affirmative case. Attach to this outline a written critique of the affirmative case, in which you evaluate the organization and the development.

6. Attend some public debate of a controversial topic and prepare an outline of the arguments presented by one of the speakers either in support or opposition.

7. Locate a sample debate in Ehninger and Brockriede's *Decision by Debate*. Outline the affirmative and negative contentions developed in the constructive speeches.

8. Select a proposition of policy and formulate the following kinds of negative cases:

    a. Defense of the status quo
    b. Modification of the status quo
    c. Counterplan

9. Using the current proposition, prepare an affirmative case outline for each of the three types of affirmative cases considered in this book.

10. After completing the preceding activity conduct a discussion in which you consider the following questions: Which type of affirmative case is most effective in general use? Which type of case is least effective in general use? Which type of case is most effective with an audience of people who have studied debate?

11. Attend an interscholastic debate and prepare an outline of the negative case. Attach to this outline a written critique of the negative case in which you evaluate the organization and development.

12. Using the current proposition, prepare a negative case outline for each of the possible negative approaches considered in this book.

13. After completing the preceding activity, conduct a discussion in which you consider the following questions: Which negative approach would be most effective in general use with this topic? Which negative approach would be least effective in general use with this topic? Which negative approach would be most effective with an audience of people who have studied debate?

References

Freeley, Austin. *Argumentation and Debate*. Belmont: Wadsworth, 1971, pp. 215–19.

Nebergall, Roger. "The Negative Counterplan." *The Speech Teacher* 6(September 1957): pp. 217–20.

Wood, Roy. *Strategic Debate*. Skokie: National Textbook, 1972, p. 84.

TWELVE

Developing the Case
with Proof

The first time you debate, someone will probably ask, "What proof do you have for that contention?" The challenge to produce evidence and reasoning is frequently issued in debate. An affirmative case without evidence and reasoning fails to change the negative presumption. A negative response to an affirmative prima-facie case without evidence and reasoning fails to regain the negative presumption.

This chapter will (1) present the relationship between evidence and reasoning with the Toulmin model of proof, (2) discuss definitions, types, and tests of evidence, (3) discuss the types and tests of reasoning.

RELATIONSHIP BETWEEN EVIDENCE AND REASONING

One of the most helpful ways to comprehend the relationship between evidence and reasoning is to examine and understand the Toulmin model for proof. In the following discussion, you should particularly note that evidence is an integral part of reasoning structure.

In the Toulmin model, the unit of proof has six elements: evidence, warrant, claim, support for warrant, reservation, and qualifier. The first three—evidence, warrant, and claim—are absolutely essential elements to affecting belief of a rational person.

Evidence

Evidence will be defined in depth later in this chapter. At this point, it is sufficient to understand that it is the initial information and factual foundation for proof appeals. No unit of proof is possible without the informative data provided by evidence. Reasoning will evaluate and interpret evidence and give it perspective.

Not all the information you collect will be evidence. Two conditions must be met. First, some principle of reasoning must justify the connection between bits of information and a conclusion or claim. If it isn't relevant, it isn't evidence. Second, the informative statement must be believable to a listener.

Warrant

A warrant provides the method by which a proof is derived. It provides an answer to the question of "so what?" Its function is to bring believed data to bear upon a claimed statement.

Warrant is different from evidence by the fact that it "does" rather than "is"; it is "form" rather than "matter."

Claim

The claim is the explicit appeal justified by the warrant which has been supported by the evidence. Strategically, a claim may be stated and then supported; or, the support may be stated which leads to the claim. In most cases the first method is preferable.

A claim may be a final proposition in an argument, or it may be an intermediate statement which itself serves as the evidence for a subsequent claim as proof in a controversy.

The relationship of the three indispensable parts—evidence, warrant, and claim—in the Toulmin model are represented in Figure 12.1. In addition, consider the example given in Figure 12.2

Support for Warrant

In the Toulmin model, support for the warrant means the indirect explanations which imply something but do not constitute actual data.

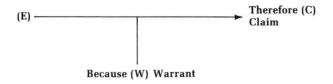

Figure 12.1 Relationship of evidence, warrant, and claim

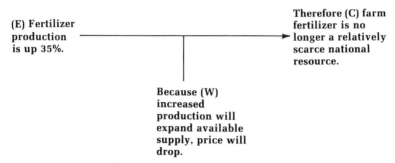

Figure 12.2 Example of relationship between evidence, warrant, and claim

Sometimes clarification or amplification of actual data or how it constitutes a warrant is necessary. Such clarification and amplification are support for a warrant which may increase believability among doubters.

The acceptance or rejection of argument based on the Toulmin model is likely to be a result of the nature of the warrant. Individuals perceive and react from very different a priori beliefs and attitudes. Therefore, the nature of the warrant as presented and perceived is likely to exert profound impact on the outcome of the entire course of argument.

The warrant is the basis for the data-claim relationship. Therefore, the warrant must be accepted by the receiver. Why might a receiver accept a warrant given? Within educational debate, receivers are likely to accept one of three kinds of warrants: 1) that which satisfies a particular motivational need, 2) that which is derived from a highly credible source, 3) that which is substantively and structurally appealing.

The first type of warrant is motivational. The appeal to the desires of humans, if accurately analyzed and carefully applied, is likely to obtain a favorable response. If the appeal to motive takes into account attitude, ego involvement, and dogmatism, the actual data or evidence may not have much impact one way or another. The fact that most warrants influence reaction to argument so heavily cannot be disputed. That same fact raises for the debater a whole new set of questions which are of an ethical nature. The debater must be judged on whether or not he has made a motivational warrant excessively dependent upon base human emotions.

The second type of warrant is that of source credibility. Often it is not *what* is quoted as much as *who* is quoted. Some people respond primarily to an authoritative source with whom they can closely identify. All people respond to some greater or lesser degree to the appeal of an authoritative figure.

The third type of warrant is the substantive warrant. Some individuals have learned to base their opinion and behavior primarily upon structure or precise rules and guidelines. Here, the appeal is dependent upon the structural accuracy of the warrant in relation to the other elements of the argument. Such questions as "Is it introduced properly?" "Is it stated in the correct order?" "Is a relationship stated?" are typical fundamental questions to a person who responds to a substantive warrant.

The debater who has gained some experience in other fundamental debate techniques and skills would do well to explore further and in depth the whole area of persuasion variables. Suggestions of additional references useful for exploring the bases of persuasion are to be found at the end of this chapter.

Reservation

Even when the warrant authorizes you to move from the evidence to a claim along the main proof line, the authorization is only general. Specific circumstances or special conditions surrounding proof may set aside or reduce the force of the warrant on the claim. Then, you will have to append reservations to the statement of the claim.

Three kinds of reservations are applicable to certain types of proof: (1) an intervening or counteracting cause may completely or partially block the main line of proof; (2) special circumstances in the factual context surrounding the specific relationship between evidence and claim may not conform to the general relationship expressed in the warrant; (3) counterproofs may have greater validity or force than the proof under consideration.

Qualifier

A qualifier provides a degree of belief, claim, or perceived probability. Many statements must be qualified to be honest reflections of the true conditions. Until something is accepted, the reservation may still exist, but the qualifier need not be used.

EVIDENCE: DEFINITIONS, KINDS, USES

The previous section considered evidence in relation to reason according to the Toulmin model. Now we should consider the definition, kinds, and uses of evidence in educational debate.

Definition

Evidence can be defined in law according to customary practices that are rather technical and stable over a period of time. The legal definition of evidence is not identical with the definitions in educational debate.

There are essentially two definitions of evidence which pertain to nonlegal substantive debate and to educational debate. There is a psychological definition and a message-based definition.

Psychological. The psychological definition states that evidence is what is perceived and believable to the listener. Such a definition is receiver based. Whether or not a bit of information is evidence is strictly in the mind of the listener. It is believed that through observation and research of how and why people respond, it is possible to formulate some generalizations about what will be accepted as evidence and what will not be accepted.

Considerable research exists to suggest that most general audiences are rather indiscriminate in what they are willing to accept as evidence. Some recent studies revealed the uncritical nature of the average audience's listening behavior.[1]

In obtaining and using data as evidence, you must consider two questions: (1) Can I apply the principles underlying the psychological definition of evidence to the educational debate situation? (2) Can I assume that those who evaluate educational debate constitute a fair sample of general population auditors?

Message Base. It is usually assumed in most educational debates that the judge or listener is something different from the general population auditor. It is assumed that the person is usually trained in listening, critical thinking, and research methodology. Therefore, a definition of evidence for the educational debate setting must account for the critical nature of those who evaluate.

The definition of evidence for the debate with expert judging is evidence with source-based assertions and empirical data offered by an advocate, who, in good faith, wishes to support and advance a given position. The definition suggests some knowledge on the part of the judge that what is advanced as evidence must meet certain critical tests.

Unfortunately, the assumption of expertise by the judge has caused some high school and college debaters, today, to develop a cavalier attitude toward the way they "blurt" out some data or assertion and eliminate the steps of relating the evidence to argument. Those debaters seem to feel the trained critical listener will provide the necessary mental connections. Such a trend is unfortunate since it undermines the value of educational debate. It tends to take educational debate out of the realm of realism and into the realm of sterile sophistic exercise. Therefore, you should be cautioned not to forget that source assertions and bits of data, even though considered evidence, must meet critical tests and must be used properly.

Functions

One function of evidence is to establish the likelihood that an argument used reflects the reality of the situation. Testimony might be used to fulfill this function. If the best expert can describe a situation a certain way, the probability of its being true is high. If several qualified sources agree on a particular view of a situation, the probability of truth is high.

A second function of evidence is to increase the credibility of the speaker. Since considerable research testifies to the fact that source credibility is an indispensable factor in persuasion, it must be an important function of evidence. The use of evidence suggests to the listener that the debater is being objective and not relying on subjective personal opinion. Most audiences, expert or nonexpert, will give higher credibility to such argument.

Tests of Evidence

Before you select evidence to support a position, you will want to subject it to one or more tests to be certain of its value. You can be certain that the opponent and the critical judge will probably subject your evidence to such tests. During the debate, the outcome of testing the evidence should not come as a great suprise to you. Following are some of the more important tests of evidence.

Recency. The data should be recent; otherwise, it may be inaccurate. The true nature of things changes rapidly. Data about geographic or economic conditions which was true ten years ago may be totally untrue under present conditions. It is very likely that the changes would have been considerable. The opinion that a source might give about noise pollution may very well have changed in five years as more knowledge has been gained. Another example would be the changing of expert opinion about the safety of nuclear power reactors. You should ask yourself: (1) Is there more recent information? (2) Have conditions been likely to change considerably since the data was obtained or the opinion stated?

Consistency. The piece of evidence should state or imply the same thing at the beginning as at the end. Furthermore, the piece of evidence taken out of context should not vary from the position or data to be found at other locations in the same source. Inconsistency of evidence is a great danger to the debater. Sometimes research is rushed and the context of some information or opinion is not checked for consistency. You should ask yourself: (1) Does the quotation contain an internal inconsistency? (2) Is the piece of evidence consistent with the rest of the information from the same source?

Relevancy. The evidence you select to use must relate to the point. Data about highway accident rates would not be relevant to insurance rates unless they were auto insurance rates. Data which is general in nature, or a "blurb" as debaters call it, isn't really relevant to a specific argument or contention. You should consider this test of evidence as most useful in preparing to refute an opponent's argument. Experience has shown the authors that failure to use relevant data in high school and college debating is probably the most frequent error in the use of evidence.

Competency. To be competent, one must have some expertise. A source who is quoted must be knowledgeable and wise in order to offer competent opinions. A source who is quoted must have the opportunity and technical knowledge of a field in order to report data accurately. The question of competency as a test of evidence is asking whether or not the source is in a position to receive information and whether or not the source has intellectual capacity to evaluate information.

If you wished to offer evidence relating to trends in the gross national product (GNP) as an economic indicator, a private economist or the secretary of commerce of the United States would be in a position to qualify as a competent source; so would the president of a local bank. However, a newspaper journalist would not be in a position to qualify as a highly competent source. The same journalist, however, might be a highly competent source if he had just completed a six-month intensive study of economics.

Objectivity. To test the evidence for objectivity, you would ask whether the source has affiliations which might bias his judgment. A member of the board of directors of a major steel producer might not be very objective about a question of pollution levels in certain streams.

There are many individuals in public relations positions with firms who issue statements relative to company or industry problems. They may be intentionally or unintentionally biased. Their statements must be suspect as evidence to prove an argument.

The debater should be aware of the pressure exerted by special interest groups who will likely give biased, although true, information. Some of the more powerful such groups today include the American Legion, the American Medical Association, the American Farm Bureau, the AFL-CIO, the National Education Association, and the National Rifle Association.

An obvious case of failure to meet the test of objectivity is to use information from product advertising. As an example, it has been reported that debate teams have been known to use data as support for a key claim in an affirmative case on environment from a product advertisement for herbicide in the *Farm Journal* magazine.

Reliability. Reliability raises the question of consistency. This test asks whether the source provides the same data or conclusion every time. Over a period of time, some sources may come to be known as highly reliable. Other sources come to be known as erratic or highly unreliable.

Validity. Empirical data should be tested for its freedom from several potential sources of threats to its validity, or "truth." Much research has been conducted in this area in the various social sciences. Thus, questions must be raised about the conditions of the research. Was the sample size adequate? Was the sampling done randomly? Were there extra factors which could be responsible for the observed effect? Was the correct statistical method used to analyze the data? Is the data statistically significant? Was the observed effect only an isolated case?

REASONING

As indicated earlier, there is a vital relationship between evidence and reasoning. Both are vital to making inferences and probability statements worthy of asking a neutral party to accept them as the basis for decision-making.

Kinds

Depending on the claim to be supported and the nature of the listener, the debater will wish to rely upon one of three kinds of reasoning: (1) deductive, (2) inductive, and (3) sign.

Deductive. Classical syllogistic reasoning is deductive. One starts with a general logical premise and proceeds to a more specific premise and finally to a very specific conclusion. As an illustration, consider the chain of deductive reasoning in Figure 12.3.

It is highly unlikely that you will take the time to go through all three parts of the deductive syllogism when constructing an oral argument. More than likely you will use a shortened form called an *enthymeme*. The enthymeme has one or more premises omitted.

The danger of abbreviating the deductive process is that some people will omit all parts of the deductive chain and just suggest the process with a statement of one word or short phrase. Some debates recently have degenerated to a series of one-word "blurbs" standing as proxy for deductive reasoning. The practice threatens to undermine the value of educational debate. Since educational debate is preparation for substantive debate, the continued practice of substitution of form for substance would ultimately find its way into substantive debate. Should that occur, a society will have opened itself to decision based

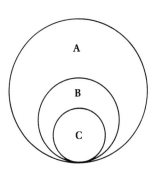

(A) Major premise: Private educational costs are high.

(B) Minor premise: John wishes to attend a private school.

(C) Conclusion: John's education will be expensive.

Figure 12.3   Chain of deductive reasoning

on hearsay and rumor rather than substantive logic and evidence. Therefore, you are encouraged to develop sound argumentation skills.

It is likely that you will want to use the deductive reasoning process as a means of testing the support offered by an opponent for their claim given to urge adoption of the resolution.

Inductive.   Inductive reasoning is best illustrated by the example of the weatherman who checks the skies in all four directions and concludes it isn't raining. Several specific facts provide a reason to draw a conclusion. The person who reasons inductively is actually sampling wisely and making an inference.

The debater will use inductive reasoning by gathering specific pieces of evidence relative to a particular point and making an inference from what appears to be some consistent pattern. You might find that: (1) rabbits died from eating grass sprayed with DDT; (2) cattle died from eating corn sprayed with DDT; (3) birds died from drinking water sprayed with DDT. That evidence might cause you to reason inductively that DDT was dangerous to animal life in general.

As a debater, your task is to assess whether or not a particular argument is supported sufficiently well to be accepted. Here, you would want to raise some of the questions of sufficient sampling to test the validity of evidence.

Sign.   Reasoning by sign consists of inferring relationships or correlations between two things. You would argue that the presence of one thing is evidence of the presence of the other thing. The one attribute is a substantial part of the totality of the whole.

Some economists have noted a correlation between economic recession and tight money policies. They even suggest a cause-effect relationship. When one item is observed—tight money—the inference is made that a recession is in progress. One is taken as a sign of the other.

A sign may not necessarily imply a cause-effect relationship, but nonetheless an event may be a sign by being part of a whole. The Cuban missile crisis of 1962 was a sign of the Cold War. Grain sales to Russia in 1975 is a sign of détente. Blockage of American access to Soviet oil in 1976 is a sign of an end to détente.

If you plan to use sign reasoning, consider the tests which should be applied to determine if reasoning is sound. Freeley has described several useful tests.[2]

1. Is the alleged substance relevant to the attribute described?
2. Is the relationship inherent?
3. Is there a counterfactor that disrupts the relationship?
4. Is the sign reasoning cumulative?

SUMMARY PROBES

1. What is the meaning of evidence, warrant, and claim?
2. What is the difference between psychological definition and message-based definition?
3. How is a quotation by George Meany considered evidence?
4. What is the relationship between evidence and reasoning?
5. How does the debater use deductive reasoning? Inductive reasoning? Sign reasoning?
6. How can you use the tests of reasoning in planning to debate?
7. How can you use the tests of reasoning during a debate?

LEARNING ACTIVITIES

1. Develop your argumentation skills by participating in a balloon debate. In groups of four to five people pretend you are in a leaky balloon with only one parachute available. Each of you, in turn, must give a single reason why you should have the chute. The rest of the

class will listen and judge which debater gave the "best" rationalization, and the winner from the first group can then join winners of other groups to form a "super balloon" group.

    2. Complete the following task on evidence below. Apply the tests of reasoning and evidence to these statements:

        a. Want headache relief? Take St. Vitus Compound. Five New York doctors recommend the ingredients in St. Vitus Compound.

        b. Of course you'll do well in philosophy; I got an "A" in the course.

        c. Governor Smith will win the next presidential election. He carried his state by a landslide when he ran for governor and he had a clear lead over all other announced candidates in his party in the preconvention national public opinion polls.

        d. Gloucester cigarettes are better for you; they contain more expensive tobacco.

        e. Communications stocks are a sound investment. American Telephone and Telegraph has paid good dividends for years.

        f. Married couples just aren't getting along as well as they used to. In 1920 only one in six marriages ended in divorce; today one in four ends in divorce.

        g. Miss A, the great movie star says, "Sudsy is the best soap for your complexion."

        h. Parental care of children is becoming more and more lax. The head of the FBI reports that juvenile delinquency is on the increase.

        i. The president of the United Mine Workers says, "The workers of America have never gotten their fair share of the fruits of industry."

        j. The premier of Russia testifies, "Russia wants only peace."

        k. If 35 per cent of the consumers, 60 per cent of management, and 90 per cent of labor are for the repeal of law X, we can readily conclude that the American people are overwhelmingly for its repeal.

        l. In a study of stutterers, Professor Mildred Berry of Rockford College found more twins in the families of stutterers than in the families of nonstutterers. Therefore, there must be a relationship between stuttering and twinning.

        m. We can readily conclude that people today are having trouble paying for hospital care. The president of the Association of American Hospitals reports, "Due to increased costs, we have had to double our charges on hospital services over the past ten years."

n. In order to make sure that we have enough and better teachers with high qualifications, we must pass the new minimum wage law calling for a minimum salary of $7000.

o. Our city would have a more efficient form of government if a city-manager system was adopted. Every department of city government in Cincinnati became more efficient after adoption of the city-manager system.

3. Develop a five-minute speech on a proposition of policy. See that most of your speech is developed in accordance with sound principles of argumentation and debate. However, include two carefully concealed fallacies. Present the speech to fellow debaters and invite them to find the fallacies.

4. Select a letter from the "letters-to-the-editor" column of your local newspaper. Locate the claim being made, isolate the data used to support the claim, and determine the warrant underlying the data-claim relationship.

5. Attempt to justify the contention, "For the sake of national security, the President may violate the law," using as many reasoning structures as possible. Invite another person to challenge any of the reasons given with a brief explanation of the challenge.

6. Present a three-minute speech on an issue using complete syllogistic reasoning. Discuss how the syllogisms can be used in a shortened form in an actual debate.

7. Locate the text of a debate in Ehninger and Brockriede's *Decision by Debate* or Austin Freeley's *Argumentation and Debate*. Analyze the evidence used and how it was refuted.

8. Try an experiment. Prepare two five-minute speeches on a topic. One speech (called speech A) should have evidence and reasoning. The other speech (called speech B) should have assertion. Divide a class randomly into two groups. Give one speech to one group and the second speech to the other group. Before each speech ask the audience to complete the opinion form below. After the speech have the audience complete the opinion form again. Compare the change in Group A with the change in Group B. Write an essay to explain the change.

OPINION SCALE

My feelings toward (topic) are best represented on this scale as:

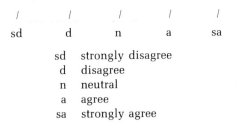

/	/	/	/	/
sd	d	n	a	sa

sd strongly disagree
d disagree
n neutral
a agree
sa strongly agree

References

Andersen, Kenneth. *Persuasion: Theory and Practice*. Boston: Allyn and Bacon, 1971.

Ehninger, Douglas, and Brockriede, Wayne. *Decision by Debate*. New York: Dodd, Mead, 1963.

Fishbein, Martin, and Ajzen, Icen. *Belief, Attitudes, Intention, and Behavior: An Introduction to Theory and Research*. Reading: Addison-Wesley Publishing, 1975.

Klopf, Donald W., and McCroskey, James C. *The Elements of Debate*. New York: Arco Publishing, 1969.

Scheidel, Thomas M. *Persuasive Speaking*. Glenview: Scott, Foresman, 1967.

Whitehead, Jack L. "Factors of Source Credibility." *Quarterly Journal of Speech* 54(February 1968): pp. 59–63.

THIRTEEN

GOALS   After completing this chapter you will be able to:

1. Recognize the difference between refutation and rebuttal.
2. Execute the steps of refutation.
3. Understand the tasks of rebuttal for affirmative and negative positions.
4. List lines of argument for the first negative and first affirmative rebuttal speeches in the actual debate.
5. Grasp the function of cross-examination in educational debate.
6. Distinguish between appropriate and inappropriate questions.

Rebuttal, Refutation, and Cross-Examination

The constructive speeches in debate allow for the introduction of an affirmative case and the negative plan of defense. Most topics of a controversial nature cannot be resolved quickly and simply. Evidence must be tested again and again. Priorities must be established. In fact, most controversial questions which are disputed with just a statement of the case for each side are dull and uninteresting. Even worse, they are probably intellectually sterile. The probing, examining, weighing which takes place in refutation, rebuttal, and cross-examination are vital to good debate.

REFUTATION

To refute means to hold up for examination and prove false. The process of refutation is done by examination, challenge, counterargument, and support for the counterposition. The refutation is not a haphazard, impromptu response to an opponent. The probable issues in a case are anticipated and a response is planned.

Refutation may occur at any time in debate after the first affirmative speaker has finished his constructive speech. If there is cross-examination, the refutation cannot begin until after the cross-examination of the first affirmative has been completed.

The purpose of the refutation is to answer a challenge or attack in such a way so that the original position is re-established. The affirmative in the second affirmative speech seeks to regain the presumption by offering greater support for, or understanding of, the original position in light of the negative attack. Likewise, the negative seeks to regain its original presumption by offering greater support for, or understanding of, the original negative position.

In order to prepare for refutation, you must be familiar with all the evidence and reasoning related to the proposition. Your research should be sufficiently detailed so that you will not be taken by surprise. That means continuing to search for information and being alert to current affairs to gain the latest pertinent information.

Aside from preparation, the next best method of preparing for refutation is to debate both sides of a proposition. Debating both sides will give you a wide perspective and a better understanding of the potential use of arguments and evidence.

After researching thoroughly and debating both sides, you will be in a position to plan what you will say in response to arguments and evidence. If the opposition quotes source A, what will your response be? On the other hand, if the opponent quotes source B, what will your response be to that?

There is a basic organization to refutation which should be employed in all cases. The basic organization involves five stages:

1. State the argument to be refuted concisely and as accurately as possible.
2. State concisely the objection you are making to the argument.
3. Introduce counterevidence and counterreasoning to support the objective.
4. Summarize the counterevidence and reasoning.
5. Explain how this refutation has weakened the opponent's case.

The final stage, step five, should never be omitted or shortened. It is a vital part of persuasive argument. You do not want to act as though you assume the connection is obvious. With substantive argument, it will not be obvious until the transfer is made with reasoned explanation. Since educational debate is preparation for substantive debate, you should practice the method which will be necessary in "real" situations.

Within the basic structure for all refutation, you have some latitude in selecting the best method to refute an argument or evidence. The choice of method depends upon the reasoning, or lack of reasoning, and upon the evidence, or lack of evidence. Following are some of the more common methods you might use in the refutation process.

Evidence

One of the best ways to refute an argument is with evidence which shows that something claimed is untrue or highly unlikely to be true.

Dilemma

The dilemma is a situation in which only two positions are possible and both positions are unsatisfactory. It is necessary when using this method to, first, establish that only two positions are possible, and second, to explain why each is unsatisfactory.

Reducto ad absurdum

This method involves carrying an argument to an ultimate logical conclusion and demonstrating that the ultimate conclusion is absurd. In order to use this method, you will often have to locate the general principle underlying the opponent's reasoning and then demonstrate the continuation of that principle to its extreme. For example, the affirmative might observe that one aspect of a negative response on capability of the status quo to prevent wire tap would cause police to be completely unable to function. The affirmative would suggest that situation would be an open invitation to crime.

Exposing Inconsistencies

This method necessitates taking two parts of an opponent's argument or evidence and comparing them. For example, a first affirmative might argue that his revenue-sharing plan has never been tried, and the second affirmative might argue that the affirmative revenue-sharing plan is financially feasible because a similar program was inexpensive.

Turning the Tables

This method involves taking the argument of the opponent and demonstrating that it is really an argument for your position. This opportunity will be presented when the opposition has failed to analyze his own position carefully.

SUMMARY
PROBES
1. What does it mean to refute?
2. When does refutation occur during a debate?
3. What is the function of refutation for the affirmative? For the negative?
4. How can you prepare for refutation?
5. What are the stages to effective refutation?

REBUTTAL

Rebuttal refers to the specific refutation which is relegated to separate structural speeches. In this case, rebuttal is, in fact, refutation. Here, we will consider what is customarily done in the way of refutation during the formal rebuttal speeches.

It is customary in high school and college debate for each side to be given two opportunities to probe the issues in rebuttal speeches.

Since all issues must be introduced during the constructive speeches, the rebuttal speeches will be devoted solely to attack and defense of established issues. A good debate is one in which arguments are either refined, extended, or dismissed. During this time, the key issues should receive most attention. Think of the entire debate as a large funnel. During the rebuttal speeches, arguments are funneled down to a few key considerations. Debaters should avoid the temptation to continue to spend time with each issue and extension. It is necessary to develop the skill to recognize and select the issues important to the logical and emotional decision-making.

First Negative Rebuttal

The first negative speaker presents the first rebuttal speech. Since the second negative constructive immediately precedes the rebuttal period, the first negative rebuttal completes a substantial concentration called the "negative block." It is usually expected that the first negative rebuttal speech will deal with the extension of arguments related to case issues. Case issues are issues which have developed over the need for change or the advantages to be realized from making a change. In addition to addressing these issues and extending the negative arguments, you identify inconsistencies which have been found in the affirmative case. If your side has presented dilemmas for the affirmative team, you can extend that argument in two ways: (1) additional support for the validity of both aspects of the dilemma situation; (2) significance of the inability of the affirmative to resolve the dilemma satisfactorily.

First Affirmative Rebuttal

The first affirmative rebuttal speaker has two primary tasks to complete. First, the affirmative case must be defended against attacks made in the two preceding speeches. The best way is to review the original case contentions and answer the most damaging (notice, *not all*) attacks on the case. Avoid the temptation to spend a lot of time "smashing" weak negative attacks.

Second, the negative arguments from the constructive period not directly related to the first affirmative case must be answered. In particular, the first affirmative rebuttal should make a reply to the allegations that the plan is unworkable and disadvantageous. Attention to this second task is essential since it is the first opportunity of the affirmative to reply to some critical negative challenges.

The first affirmative rebuttal speaker has four or five minutes to counteract twelve to fifteen minutes of negative attack. Obviously, you cannot deal with each negative argument. In no other speech is selectivity, clarity, and conciseness so crucial.

Second Negative Rebuttal

The second negative rebuttal should concentrate on three or four key arguments which are still crucial to the debate. Those arguments already won should be summarized briefly. The negative should avoid the tendency to make "shotgun" attacks on every point of clash in the debate. This speech should conclude with a concise reason for agreeing with the original plea to reject the proposition.

Second Affirmative Rebuttal

Like the first negative rebuttal speech, the second affirmative rebuttal speech represents the last opportunity for defense of the case since the goal of the second affirmative is to re-establish the case for the proposition.

The second affirmative speaker will usually begin with an attack on negative contentions, follow with a defense of the affirmative case, and conclude with a plea to adopt the proposition.

1. What issues are likely to emerge during rebuttal speeches?
2. What does the first negative rebuttal speaker usually do?
3. What does the first affirmative rebuttal speaker usually do?

CROSS-EXAMINATION

Today, most high school debates are the cross-examination type. As explained earlier, there is a three-minute cross-examination period following each constructive speech. Cross-examination style debate seems to be returning to junior college and college debate.

Cross-examination debating has several desirable effects. First, it creates the fear of having to face embarrassing questions if the advocate has not prepared carefully. Secondly, the cross-examination creates some fear of facing embarrassment if one is being untruthful. Finally, the cross-examination debate is more interesting to the audience because of the greater direct clash.

There are at least three purposes for cross-examination questions. The first purpose of the cross-examination is to clarify positions on the issues. Clarity might be obtained by re-examination of a plan or by associating two apparently disconnected positions which are actually contradictory and, thus, a dilemma. Through clarity, the clash of ideas and arguments will be heightened.

The second purpose of cross-examination is to gain admissions. If the debater can get the opponent to admit a flaw in his own case, there is a logical basis for rejecting the claim of the opponent's position. Actually, this seldom happens, but it is a worthy goal for the cross-examination period.

The third purpose of the cross-examination is to obtain data for later speeches. Care should be taken later to specifically point out that the information was obtained during cross-examination. Otherwise, it will seem that time has been wasted.

If the questioning periods are to be an integral part which aids the debate process, debaters for both sides should remember certain principles.

First, plan a series of questions in advance. Begin with common ground or admitted matter and proceed to areas of disagreement. Assume all possible answers and plan subsequent questions for those responses. The questions for testing evidence and reasoning can provide a helpful beginning, but they must be adapted to each case.

Second, utilize the information revealed in the question period in subsequent speeches. Confine the cross-examination time to questions alone, thus avoiding the temptation to make presentations or present constructive material. Do not press for admissions of faulty analysis or weak evidence. Use the rebuttal time to draw these conclusions.

Third, be reasonably sure of the possible answers. Unexpected answers to crucial questions may cause obvious embarrassment to you.

Fourth, use a summary question to conclude a line of questioning. Sometimes the original question will serve: "Do you still believe that. . . .?"

There are also four principles for the witness in cross-examination to keep in mind during a debate. First, be prepared for the different kinds of questions which might logically be asked about your case or position. Give some prior thought to how you will answer those questions. The question period should not be full of surprises for you.

Second, be as direct and fair as possible when answering the questions. Obvious dodging suggests that something is being hidden. Your credibility will be seriously shaken by obviously dodging questions. It is all right to admit lack of knowledge of certain facts. A debater should never be afraid to say, "I don't know."

Third, refuse to answer blatantly unfair questions. If you do refuse, it would be wise to explain briefly why you are refusing to answer.

Fourth, do not try to play the role of questioner when you are being questioned. To do so is trite and suggests something other than a good debater.

SUMMARY PROBES	1. What are the effects of cross-examination on the debate?
	2. What are the purposes of cross-examination?
	3. How do refutation, rebuttal, and cross-examination improve the debate?

LEARNING ACTIVITIES

1. Complete the following activity with the stipulation that before a person speaks, he must restate the argument of the previous speaker:

The people in your group represent a panel of doctors. Each of the patients listed below is in need of the services of a kidney machine to do the work of his own failing organs. There are only enough machines available to treat three patients. It is impossible to purchase additional machines. It is the job of your panel to decide, based on the information given, those patients who will receive treatment and those who will not. The patients who do not receive treatment will die.

Professor Tom Swanson: He is thirty-five years old and a professor of social sciences at a major university. Presently he is doing research on the urban poor. He is very active in organizations that help underprivileged children. He is planning to be married in three months.

Betty Harlan: She is a forty-one-year-old divorcee. She has no children but helps to support her bedridden mother. She works as a public health officer, giving seminars in diet and health to various groups. She holds an M.S. degree in social work and is attending school in the evening to complete her Ph. D.

Johnny Bailey: He is an extremely bright ten-year-old who has severe emotional problems. He rarely talks with other people and has been removed from the public school system.

Father James O'Donnell: He is a fifty-seven-year-old Catholic priest. He has been counseling young people for many years and has established three local missions for alcoholics.

James C. Washington: He is a nineteen-year-old freshman at a large university. He has been arrested on a number of minor charges, but has never been convicted. He is a member of a black radical group that believes in revolutionary tactics. He works at various jobs to support himself and finish school.

William Zeigler: He is thirty-nine years old, married, and the father of four children ranging in age from two to fourteen. He owns and operates a small television repair business.

Jean McBride: She is twenty-three years old, single, and works as an undercover agent in the narcotics division in the city's police department. She gives a large part of her salary to drug-care centers.

2. Prepare in written form your refutation of an editorial appearing in a recent issue of a daily newspaper. Hand the editorial and your refutation to your instructor.

3. Discuss which element—attack or defense—is more important to the affirmative team, the negative team. Why?

4. Present a single proof for an argument. Invite another person to refute that argument. Extend your original position by refuting what the other person has said.

5. Present a dilemma to a group. See if the group can offer and support an additional alternative or can accept and support one of the choices you supplied.

FOURTEEN

GOALS   After completing this chapter you will be able to:

1. Recognize the importance of oral communication to effective debate.

2. Identify the mode of delivery most appropriate for debate.

3. Identify vocal aspects of delivery significant to the debater.

4. Understand the importance of visual aspects of effective delivery for a debater.

Communicative Persuasion

The decision in a debate most often rests on the debater's ability to communicate rather than on his ability to perform. This means you as a source must accept the responsibility of communication. To do that, you will need to be a forceful, clear source who accepts feedback given by the judge and the opposition during the debate. Besides being a forceful, clear source, you must also be a careful listener. You must listen to the opponent carefully in order to organize and deliver your own reply. The following section will provide suggestions for being a debater who communicates orally in an effective manner. This chapter will discuss: (1) fundamental concepts regulating delivery, (2) the appropriate mode of delivery for debate, and (3) physical aspects of delivery important to debate.

FUNDAMENTAL CONCEPTS REGULATING DELIVERY

Delivery must be natural. Observe people around you as they engage in everyday informal conversation. Have a friend observe you for a few days and tell you how you behave physically during natural communicative discourse. When conversing and speaking in informal, nontense situations we do all the physical things that we are unable to do when we stand before an audience. We use good vocal delivery and variety, we look at the people to whom we are speaking, we use fluent and meaningful hand gestures, we communicate with our body. In short, we practice delivery in speaking that is effective for us and that blends with our individual personalities.

The ideal delivery in the debate situation would be one that duplicates our delivery mannerisms in conversational and informal situations. Rather than strive for rehearsed, canned movement in debate, make an effort to render yourself comfortable with the arguments, with the evidence, and with your listeners, so that you aren't aware of the movement that will certainly occur.

Delivery must always be viewed as an aid to the communicative purpose of the debater. When delivery becomes the end goal of the speech rather than one of many means to attain the goal, it is not "good" delivery. Thus, the speaker who rehearses vocal inflections and gestures may be just as guilty of inadequate delivery as the tense debater who trembles, suffers voice breaks, and who never looks at his listeners.

MODE OF DELIVERY

The extemporaneous mode of delivery is by far the most acceptable for debate. When the debater speaks extemporaneously, an outline of ideas is used which may be committed to memory—as is the case by the first affirmative—but rehearsed words in expressing ideas are not meaningful. The extemporaneous speaker organizes ideas in outline form and makes notes to himself of what proof will be used and, then, speaks from a short outline.

The greatest advantage of this approach is that it allows the advocate to plan what he wishes to say and the way in which he wishes to say it without committing exact words to memory. All the advantages of building the case and speech composition may be brought to bear in the extemporaneous speech. Another advantage of the extemporaneous speech is its flexibility. Since the speech is planned, but not frozen, the advocate can modify his presentation to adapt to the situation and to the statements of previous speakers. He can watch the listener closely and adapt to feedback found in the reaction and responses.

If notes are used, there are certain points for consideration by the debater which will increase his effectiveness. First, the debater should use no more notes than is necessary. The first affirmative will be likely to have a thoroughly outlined case. Other speakers will use their flowsheets, which are notations of the flow of issues and arguments through the debate. Sometimes a debater will choose to make a short one-page longhand outline of information taken from the flowsheet and then speak from the outline rather than the flowsheet. Both methods are excellent, and you will have to find the method which suits you best. Naturally, you will need to have cards with direct quotations which you plan to use.

Don't try to disguise the fact that you are using notes. Regardless of how hard you try to fool the listener, it will be recognized if you are using notes.

PHYSICAL ASPECTS OF DELIVERY

The physical aspects of delivery fall into two categories: vocal and visual.

Vocal

Probably the single most important vocal communication variable for debate is the rate of speaking. It is imperative that you speak at a rate so that your words can be understood. Some people can articulate words faster than others with the same clarity. If you cannot be clearly understood at 160 words per minute, but someone else can, you should not try to do the impossible. Remember, no communication is occurring unless the receiver can decode and understand the signals given.

Closely associated with the normal rate of speaking is vocal variation. Different points in your speech will no doubt require different variations in voice. The debater who speaks in the same rate, pitch, and tone will quickly put an audience to sleep. Listen to friends in conversation; notice how their voices "talk" in addition to their words when the emotional content of the message varies.

Vocal variety is enhanced by using either impromptu or extemporaneous methods of delivery. Reading a speech can often result in a monotonous vocal delivery. Memorizing a speech can often result in voice mannerisms that are completely separate from the meaning of the message being communicated.

Visual

Probably the single most important visual communication variable for debate is eye contact. Closely following are gesture and movement.

Eye Contact.   Audiences like to be looked at. One of the most crucial components of physical delivery is establishing good eye contact with audience members. Most debates occur in a relatively small room with very little distance between speaker and listener. Under such circumstances, it is expected that eye contact be more sustained. The tendency to speak to your notes or flowsheet weakens the speaker's credibility.

Eye contact can also be an effective device for holding the attention of the audience. If audience members know that you are going to be looking directly at them, they will truly feel that you are speaking to them as individuals, and they feel an obligation to return the contact. It is difficult to go to sleep on a speaker who is looking at you.

Gesture. A relaxed, natural public speaker will automatically make frequent use of meaningful gesture. He probably will not be aware of every gesture. Audiences like naturally appearing hand, arm, and body gestures. In conversational settings we talk constantly with our hands and many other parts of our body. A relaxed debater will make effective use of the same kinds of movement. Developing a variety of natural-looking gestures will be an asset to you in debate. If you will look at high school and college students who have been debating for some time, you will notice several common gestures which always seem to appear. They become distracting because they are so common and trite. You will want to develop a variety of ways of expressing meaning and giving emphasis with visual symbols.

Timing of gestures can be a crucial factor in their meaning. Natural gestures are normally perfectly timed to coincide with verbal message content. One grave danger of rehearsing gestures is that they will appear to be off in timing. Such ill-timed movements usually result in some distraction from message content and sometimes diminish the speaker's credibility.

Movement. Some movement during the speech is a natural phenomenon for most people. The amount and degree of movement utilized by a speaker in a given situation should be adopted to his need for relaxation. Don't force yourself to move. The old oratorical tradition of carefully plotted steps at strategic points in a speech does not lend itself to clear communication in any kind of public speaking situation, especially debate.

If you are using a lectern, and you feel like moving out from behind it—do so. If you feel that moving away from the lectern will increase your self-consciousness or reduce your security—don't do it.

Natural, spontaneous movement during the course of a speech normally results in more spontaneous communication and reception of content on the part of the speaker and listener. However, movement should be used in moderation. The key to a speaker's developing effective movement during a speech lies in his ability to bring himself to a relaxed and comfortable mental state in front of his audience.

SUMMARY
PROBES

1. What is an ideal mode of delivery for debate?
2. How is rate of speaking related to debate?
3. What are the aspects of visual delivery important to debate?

LEARNING ACTIVITIES

1. Select a complex term or concept with which you are familiar as a result of special study (balance of trade, for example). Paying careful attention to word choice, sentence arrangement, and the order and pace of thought progression, prepare a three-minute speech in which you make this concept as clear as you can to the listeners.

Test how successful you have been by seeing whether, as a result of your speech, your listeners can now state the meaning and significance of the concept correctly.

2. Arrange with your instructor to prepare a videotape recording outside of class. In the recording, present a three-minute speech supporting or opposing the current debate resolution. Use the various means of the visible code to make the delivery most effective. View the recording and make observations about your delivery.

3. Tape record one of your debates. Listen to the tape and check the following: (a) words per minute, (b) number of grammatical errors, and (c) nonfluencies (vocal pauses). Make some observation as to whether or not you have a conversational nature.

4. Arrange to present a prepared debate before an audience of people who have never been trained in debate. After the debate, ask them questions like the following:

a. Was I talking too fast? Too slow?
b. What were my arguments?
c. Could you understand everything I said?

IV

Competitive Public
Speaking

FIFTEEN

GOALS   After completing this chapter you will be able to:

1. Recognize the unique features of extemporaneous speaking.
2. Prepare generally and specifically for extemporaneous speaking.
3. Organize the extemporaneous speech.
4. Utilize effective delivery techniques for extemporaneous speaking.

Contest Extemporaneous Speaking

With the exception of interpersonal communication, extemporaneous speaking is a contest simulation activity which comes closest to duplicating the real conditions under which most people are most likely to communicate. Allowing only a short preparation period, the activity requires the speaker to present a five- to eight-minute speech on a given topic of current interest. Customarily, the speaker draws three topics, selects one of the three, and prepares for delivery during a forty-five- to sixty-minute period.

Asking people to get up and "think on their feet" is a relatively common occurrence. Everyone may be asked at one time or another to organize quickly and support a point in such situations as: selling products, upholding an idea at a PTA or church meeting, or in teaching. In such situations there will seldom be time to write a speech. It will be assumed that the speaker must and can speak extemporaneously, sometimes impromptu.

Besides preparing for a very real and practical communication situation, the speaker will also become knowledgeable about important contemporary social, economic, and political issues. In fact, the high school and college "extemp" speaker is usually one of the best informed individuals on subjects of a contemporary nature.

As a contest event, extemporaneous speaking is usually the most challenging, interesting, and rewarding activity. This chapter will offer suggestions to help speakers prepare, develop, and present an effective extemporaneous speech.

PREPARATION

Preparation for extemporaneous speaking falls into two categories: (1) general preparation *before* the speaking situation; and (2) specific preparation *during* the brief time just before the speech is to be given.

General Preparation

One of the first stages in general preparation is to become familiar with the topics upon which you might likely be asked to speak. Familiarize yourself with economic, political, and social questions which have been in the news during the most recent six to nine months. The topics will probably be broad in scope and concerned with state, national, and international issues, and usually, the topics will necessitate explaining a position or arguing a point of view.

It is important to obtain and read material on all likely topics. To facilitate later preparation, it is a good idea to prepare an index of issues. To do so, you should take a small notebook and divide it into subject categories for listing articles and sources which will be in your file. Such a categorical index might have the following main divisions:

State Topics
Economic
Political
Social

National Topics
Economic
Political
Social

International Topics
Economic
Political
Social

After you complete a categorical indexing system, then begin listing topics in each category as you think of them, or as you discover them in the news media. As you locate related articles, you should not only list the topic, but also write down the magazine, pamphlet, or book which contains the information. To illustrate this aspect of general preparation, consider the following list of current topics which are listed in a categorical index system:

State

Economic
1. State finance of education
2. Finance of higher education
3. Development of lake reservoirs

Social
1. Mass transit in cities
2. Capital punishment

National

Political
1. Future of the Republican party
2. Carter administration
3. CIA investigations

Economic
1. Land use policies
2. Alternative energy research and development
3. Unemployment
4. Inflation

Social
1. Invasion of privacy
2. Food stamp programs
3. Swine flu vaccination

International

Political
1. U.S. involvement in Africa
2. United Nations
3. Value of détente

Economic
1. World bank
2. Bribery by international corporations
3. International monetary reform

Social
1. Famine in the world
2. Disease epidemic

After beginning a thorough index system, the second stage of general preparation may be started. General preparation involves locating, reading, and retaining information on all current topics of human affairs. The best kind of sources for the extemporaneous speaker are current news magazines and newspapers. You will need to read *Time*, *U. S. News and World Report*, *Newsweek*, *Nation*, and *Congressional Quarterly* regularly; the Sunday edition of the *New York Times*, which contains a summary of the week's news, is also an excellent source. Two other very useful newspapers are the *Christian Science Monitor* and *The National Observer*. The *Wall Street Journal* is useful for economic news, but is inclined toward the business community's perspective. You should subscribe to one or two of the weekly news magazines and to one or two of the newspapers so that you can literally take the articles from the source.

The person preparing for extemporaneous speaking must read widely and frequently. You must develop your own personal form of speed reading. If the reading material is your own, you might develop the habit of underlining important points, useful data, or unique interpretations.

Retaining information must be a personalized part of preparation. Some people who want to speak extemporaneously prepare a card file system just like the debater. They place all the information on index cards and file according to topics. If you plan to use the card file system, refer to Chapter Ten in the debate section.

A second system is the "article file" system. Those using this system actually remove articles from sources, or copy articles and place the articles or copies in manila folders with each topic having a separate folder. There are at least two advantages to this system. First, it saves the time of writing or typing all the information, and second, you have all the information on hand with no chance for transcribing errors. Reading time is the same with either system.

Specific Preparation

The specific preparation begins as soon as you select the topic. You will have forty-five to sixty minutes to complete specific preparation of the speech. We suggest that, as a rule of thumb, you divide your available time according to the following guideline:

$$\text{Preparation} = 1/5R + 1/10T + 2/5D + 3/10P$$

1/5R   This part of preparation refers to reviewing material available on the topic. No doubt you have read the material before; scan it again.

1/10T   This segment refers to thinking about the question asked in the written topic and the overall response you want to make to that question.

2/5D   An element of preparation: developing the speech. The speech should be organized with an introduction, body, conclusion, and supporting material for the arguments presented.

3/10P   The final segment of preparation should be devoted to practice in presenting the speech. Use an outline on one or two notecards. Go through the speech quietly to yourself at least two times and think about any small changes you may care to make in organization, support, or delivery.

DEVELOPMENT

Developing a thoughtful speech quickly and concisely is the unique challenge of extemporaneous speaking: it is the skill you are trying to master by being involved in the activity, the skill you want to demonstrate when you speak during most occasions in real-life situations. The key to successful extemporaneous speaking is to have simple, clear organization of ideas and supporting material. Since the topic drawn will be in the form of a question, the speaker's task is to develop and deliver a brief, but effective, speech aimed at presenting a thoughtful and documented answer to the question.

The first part of the speech is an introduction. The introduction's purpose is to gain attention, to outline the speech purpose, and to present the speech theme. For the contest speaker, the most important function is gaining attention, which helps the judges to remember the individual performance, and introducing the theme, which presents an organizational pattern to be used.

There are several attention devices available. Following are five which have proven useful to extemporaneous speakers: (1) the striking statement, (2) the story, (3) the quotation, (4) the rhetorical question, and (5) an allusion to an important incident.

The striking statement should not be so shocking as to antagonize the listener before you are able to explain what the point of the speech actually is. A slightly milder striking statement does have impact, though, and serves to gain the immediate attention of the listener. Using a story or anecdote can be effective if it is brief, vivid, and easily related to the theme of the speech. Using a quotation by a famous person can lend an air of authority to the speech if the person quoted is truly an authority in the area of concern and the quotation is easily related to the speech.

A rhetorical question is one used by the speaker to create effect rather than gain an answer. It is a useful device because it causes members of an audience to think about what you want. An example of a rhetorical question which could be used effectively to open a speech on air pollution is, "Would you like to see the earth run out of air to breathe in your lifetime?" Obviously the speaker using such a question does not expect an answer from the audience. The answer is rather obvious; the question is used for purposes of effect and thought provocation.

The speaker who chooses to allude to an important event often provides a good historically based, or personally interesting, introduction to current problems. As with other attention devices, however, the speaker must be certain that the event actually relates to the specific question involved in the extemporaneous speech.

When selecting the device, the speaker should keep in mind that the introduction must gain attention and must present an implicit or explicit theme. In fact, the explicit theme will usually be more successful. Specific topics lend themselves better to certain types of introductions, as well as to selected speakers. The constant factor is that the introduction will furnish a hook on which the rest of the speech will be hung.

After formulating the introduction, a smooth transition from the introduction to the body of the speech should be developed. One good technique is to use the topic statement, or purpose statement, as a transition.

For most extemporaneous speaking topics, there are at least four types of organization available for the body of the speech: (1) the series; (2) the extended analogy; (3) the repetition of a pattern; (4) the problem-solution.

Using a series of reasons, component parts, or implications is often a good method for extemporaneous speaking. Breaking down a topic or policy to examine its philosophical bases, its different parts, or its relationships to other policies generally gains favor. It is incisive and vivid rather than general or vague. Using this method, you may relate abstract topics to audience interest.

The extended analogy is the most interesting organizational pattern. Tracing an idea by developing a parallel theme is interesting and clear. Fables, biblical allusions, historical events—all make good analogies. Remember that the analogy must remain subservient to the topic at hand. It must not become so involved that it attracts attention away from the topic or main point of the speech.

Repeating a pattern develops a theme by examining in sequential order its aspects on different levels. Examples of such patterns include: past, present, future; economic, social, political; federal, state, and local. This type of pattern is rather mundane, but it is clear, concise, and easy to follow. Therefore, it is well suited to extemporaneous speaking.

The problem-solution pattern is perhaps best suited for controversial topics. The speaker states a problem, then offers proposals which may solve it. This pattern of organization is discussed at length in the following chapter on oratory. Often when this pattern is chosen, the extemporaneous speaker spends the entire speech analyzing the problem and never tends to solution. Even if solution is discussed, it has become common practice to "cop out" and avoid any really controversial position for fear of offending the critic judge. Such practice is unfortunate. Some topics demand emphasis on solution. Further, it requires courage to take a position in an extemporaneous speech. In addition, skill is essential in arguing for a particular position without becoming offensive to some people. To be able to do so is the true test which separates the adequate extemporaneous speaker from the really outstanding one.

After the organizational pattern of the body of the speech is decided, select the main headings and supporting material. The main points should be stated clearly and concisely. Use the active voice rather than the passive and avoid complex or compound-complex sentences.

The transition between the body and the conclusion depends on the type of conclusion used. If the conclusion is a summary, very little transition is needed other than a brief introductory clause or phrase. If a conclusion of application is chosen, the rhetorical question is a smooth, although elementary, transition. Whatever method is used as transition, the conclusion should do essentially two things—summarize and provide direction to the listener's thoughts.

PRESENTATION

Clear organization, emphasized in the preceding pages, and direct delivery are the two unique features of extemporaneous speaking. Direct delivery is a style achieved by several specific characteristics.

First, the extemporaneous speaker establishes eye contact with all of his listeners. The speaker establishes eye contact as much as 95 percent of the time he is involved in giving the speech to the audience. Eye contact should be sustained with specific individuals in the audience for short periods of time.

Second, the extemporaneous speaker communicates in a conversational rate and volume level. The speaker should always try to talk with individuals rather than at them. A casual and conversational approach to the listener in extemporaneous speaking is one of its unique characteristics.

MODEL EXTEMPORANEOUS SPEECH

Following is the text of a winning extemporaneous speech in the Illinois High School Association state final individual events contest in 1971. The speech was recorded as delivered. Comments appear in the margins to identify features which were discussed in this chapter and to identify other aspects of organization and development.

Is there evidence that the United States is embroiling itself further in Southeast Asia?

Terry Lenhardt
Thornridge High School
Dolton, Illinois

For the last twenty years, the United States has been involved in a war in Southeast Asia in one form or another. It began with the Korean conflict in the early 1950s. Most recently, and the topic about which most of us are very much concerned, of course, is the Vietnam War in which we are now involved. The last two presidential administrations have made the commitment to bring us out of this war in Vietnam through one means or another. But recently, in reading the newspaper, we all found that an invasion of Laos was made by South Vietnamese troops with American support. And many of us have asked the question: Was Nixon telling us the truth? Is he really going to get us out? And the question I have been asked to answer today stems directly from this: Is there evidence that the United States is embroiling itself further in Southeast Asia?

Constant use of "we" and "let's."

Now I think in order to answer this question, we are first going to have to look at this evidence which seems to indicate that we are embroiling ourselves further in the conflict—getting ourselves more involved in Southeast Asia. Once we have considered this evidence, we're going to have to analyze it further to see whether or not it really constitutes evidence that we are getting ourselves in deeper in South Vietnam. And I think we are going to find that it doesn't indicate this. And because I feel this, I am going to go one step further and point out evidence that shows that we're not only lessening our involvement there, but we are pulling ourselves out all the time.

Let's take a look at that first area, then. What exactly is the evidence that makes us feel that we're endangering ourselves in South Vietnam, bringing ourselves into more trouble in Southeast Asia? As I mentioned before, all of us read in the newspaper that we were recently involved in an invasion into Laos. The Americans were involved in two primary ways. First, we provided the tactical air support—the bombing—which helped cut off the supplies to the Ho Chi Minh Trail from the communists down to the south. Secondly, we had our own men involved inside the South Vietnamese border, shelling. About nine thousand men of ours were shelling the communists' positions in Laos. Thus, we were involved in two ways: first, in the air, and second, on the ground. And in connection with this, President Nixon announced that there will be no limits placed on the use of tactical air support in a Laos incursion. The encouragement was just recently finished, and this is the primary piece of evidence that makes people wonder whether or not President Nixon will keep his word and get us out of Vietnam before he comes up for reelection. But, as I said before, there are some reasons to doubt that there is actually such evidence.

Internal summary.

Let's go on to that second point. Let's take a closer look at the Laotian incursion and see how in fact it does not really constitute evidence that we are engaging ourselves further in Southeast Asia. Let's first of all take a look at the reasons behind the incursion into Laos. Let's, second, look at who is actually involved in the Laotian incursion which has just recently been finished. And third, consider the results of the Laotian incursion.

Listener guideline to second main point.

Stating substructure to follow.

In the first area, why did we go in? We can turn to President Nixon on a March 4 press conference as viewed from across the country and he stated two primary reasons for our going into Southeast Asia in the Laotian incursion. The first reason, was, of course, to cut off the supply lines of the communists to give our men more time to withdraw, not to get ourselves further involved, but to withdraw from the Southeast Asian conflict. And the second reason that President Nixon made clear for this Laotian incursion was that he wanted to give the South Vietnamese more time to solidify their control of the countryside over the people which they supposedly rule. Two reasons for this Laotian incursion, neither of which seems to indicate that the United States wanted to get itself further involved.

Internal summary.

Now, let's take a look at that second point that I mentioned, who is actually doing the fighting? There were actually signs posted at the South Vietnamese border saying, "No U. S. personnel shall cross this point." All American ground support troops stayed within South Vietnam in accordance with what President Nixon stated earlier. It was the South Vietnamese troops, twenty-three-thousand strong, that went into Laos for this incursion—for this invasion of Laos. Our men stayed behind the lines providing only tactical support. However, we do have the pilots going in, but they were not fighting on the ground. President Nixon promised to get our ground troops out. He seems to be keeping his promise.

Transition and listener guideline for second subpoint.

Let's go on to that third area, and consider that this is not really evidence that we are getting ourselves further involved in southeast Asia. Let's take a look at the results that have come about because of this Laotian invasion. The first, and most important to us here at home, is that President Nixon in that same March 4 news conference stated that as a result of what had happened up to that point, and that was almost four weeks ago, the withdrawal plans were proceeding at a faster rate than before, and there was nothing to impede the withdrawal plan. And after the last four weeks we can look to General Creighton Abrams who commanded our forces in South Vietnam who states that the results, although with problems involved, the results have been better than expected. We can look secondly at one of those main reasons why we did undertake the Laotian incursion. The communist supply lines into the South had been cut, or at least reduced dramatically, giving the South Vietnamese up

Listening guideline.

Overuse of phrase "take a look" or "can look".

to ten months before the rainy season is over to strengthen their position at home. We can find evidence, thirdly, of how the communists have suffered because of this. The number of organized attacks brought about by the communists have been reduced up to 25 to 30 percent. Terrorism is also down in all areas of Southeast Asia. Therefore, we can see that this would supposedly indicate that we're getting ourselves deeper in Southeast Asia is not really true. President Nixon has stated that we will be coming out as fast as ever.

As I said before, we'll go one step further. We'll not only see how there is no evidence that we are not embroiling ourselves, but that there is indeed evidence to the contrary—that we're pulling ourselves out faster. We can look first at the successes of the Vietnamization program President Nixon proposed about two years ago. We can again look to General Creighton Abrams who stated that the first part of the Vietnamization program—that of turning the war over to the Vietnamese—is coming along very well. The South Vietnamese fighting forces, although not perfect, are at least holding their own against all the combat forces they've had to go against in Southeast Asia. Second, we can look at the casualties which we ourselves are incurring in South Vietnam. We find over the course of the last two years during which time this has taken place, there has been a 50 percent reduction in our American casualties in South Vietnam. And third, and finally, if you look at how many troops we have deployed in South Vietnam, from an all time high 543,000—that's 1967—we are now down to a low of 330,000 men. President Nixon has promised that by May 1st an additional 50,000 men will be withdrawn and that all combat troops will be out by the end of the summer and that in total, 125,000 will have withdrawn by the end of 1971.

So, in answering that question, "Is there evidence the United States is embroiling itself further in Southeast Asia," I think we are going to have to answer it, no, because this Laotian invasion just completed that is supposed to be pulling us into the war so deeply, has

History has raised doubts about this source. It seemed valid in 1971.

Summation leading to

not done that. It achieved its goal. There were losses, yes, but the goals were maintained and achieved. And President Nixon is continuing to promise, and indeed if we look more closely at the question we are going to find that not only is there no evidence that we are embroiling ourselves more deeply, but there is positive evidence that we are withdrawing ourselves completely. President Nixon seems to be keeping his promise and we are seeming to get out of Viet Nam.

concluding position.

SUMMARY PROBES

1. What is unique about extemporaneous speaking?
2. What kind of general preparation do you need to do in extemporaneous speaking?
3. Compare the filing systems available in extemporaneous speaking.
4. How do you compare the available organizational methods?
5. What is meant by directness of delivery?

LEARNING ACTIVITIES

1. Using the model speech provided in this chapter, suggest where language could be improved.

2. Identify the main points in the model speech.

3. Prepare a categorical index system for topics which are currently in the news.

4. Read widely and then under simulated conditions present an extemporaneous speech to a group.

SIXTEEN

GOALS   After completing this chapter you will be able to:

1. Grasp the unique features of oratory.
2. Prepare an oration.
3. Organize the oration.
4. Develop the speech with carefully chosen language.
5. Recognize effective delivery style for oratory.

Oratory

Oratory is the oldest and most formal of the public address forms. The orator's subject is always of some vital concern to society. In all cases, oratory is persuasive speaking. There is always some idea, feeling, or course of action that the speaker wants the listener to accept. Planning to select the best means of persuasion requires careful selection of ideas and support, meticulous organization, judicious choice of words, and thoughtful planning of delivery.

VALUES OF ORATORY

Oratory is valuable because of the emphasis it places on choice of language to express ideas with precision and eloquent grace. The skilled orator will testify that precision and grace with words is difficult to achieve.

It is also valuable because it demands careful and complete preparation. The orator develops the habit of thinking carefully and thoroughly before taking a position on an issue. Debate and extemporaneous speaking stress ability to make cogent verbal responses under pressure of time. Although the student in these speaking situations must prepare thoroughly in general as well as in specific detail, the final form and language are determined at the moment of speaking. The orator, by contrast, lives with ideas and materials for weeks or months, continually thinking, planning, and refining the ideas and words to communicate those ideas.

In addition, oratory is valuable because it requires the speaker to assume great responsibility. The orator has those responsibilities to the listeners to express the ideas. In turn, the listener expects the speaker to offer objective thought and wisdom as opposed to biases of one small faction or group. The listener anticipates that the speaker has conducted critical evaluation. Just as the debater needs to read widely on both sides of any proposition, so must the orator complete wide and varied research. The listener considers the orator to be an enlightened source of knowledge on a given issue.

PREPARATION

The orator prepares in several stages, some of which are basically the same as the extemporaneous speaker. The first stage of preparation is to select a topic which requires that you consider your interests, the interests of the part of society which might constitute the audience, and the availability of information through research. The topic selected should constitute a specific entity rather than a generalization. Following are sample topics which have been selected to prepare interesting and worthy orations:

The Aged in American Society
Deceitfulness of School Busing
The Crises of Confidence in Government
The Essence of Blackness
A Torn Society
As the Twig is Bent
What To Do with the Killer Drunk?
What Are We Loyal To?

Searching for information constitutes the second stage of preparation for oratory; the search should be as thorough and as complete as possible. Possible places to look are suggested and discussed at length earlier in Chapter Ten and in Chapter Fifteen of this section. Most important, the orator should investigate many sources and gather a considerable amount of information on the topic selected before beginning to organize and write the speech.

After selecting a specific topic, stage three—writing a thesis for the oration—should be completed. The thesis, a statement which gives purpose and direction to the speech, should be stated as a declarative sentence, as concisely and as strikingly as possible. You may state your thesis explicitly in the oration; you may even state and restate it several times. On the other hand, you might choose not to state the thesis, but rather to imply it so strongly that the listeners will be able to supply the actual statement in their own minds. If you wish to imply the thesis, it is still very necessary that you know specifically what it is you intend to suggest, lest you lead the listeners to an incorrect conclusion. Because of that danger, beginning orators should state the thesis explicitly.

An example on the topic of controlling inflation might be "We must find a means to ease the effects of runaway inflation."

Stage four in preparation is to organize the speech. Since several outline drafts will be necessary, the first draft will probably be a very rough outline of ideas and information as they have been located without too much attention to persuasive structure.

The second draft should be an outline in the form of the structure you have chosen to use for the oration. One of the best organizational patterns for many persuasive speeches is the problem-solution pattern developed from John Dewey's reflective-thinking process.[1] Dewey's description of basic human thought processes led to the five-part pattern:

1. definition of a problem
2. problem analysis
3. criteria determination
4. suggestion of possible solutions
5. determination of best solution

In adapting Dewey's reflective-thinking process to a structure for an oration, it is possible to develop two main points with several logical points of substructure. Begin your outline with the two concepts of problem and solution. On the topic of inflation you would have the following:

I. Inflation is a serious problem to many segments of society.
II. A solution to inflation must come from sacrifices and from mutual efforts of the individual, the state, and the nation.

Consider the following skeleton outline for using the problem-solution organizational pattern.

Introduction

I. (Attention-focusing statement) Give the statement.
II. (Statement of purpose) Agree that tax reform by Congress is necessary.

Body

I. Present income tax policies are unfair because loopholes are not equally available.

  A. People are not given equal opportunity to use loopholes.

    1. The poor can't depreciate capital investment.

      State the kind of support.

    2. Middle income people can't benefit from large donations to foundations.

      State the kind of support.

  B. The size of the inequity is large.

    1. State subpoint.

      State the kind of support.

    2. Stage subpoint.

      State the kind of support.

  C. The inequity leads to undesirable consequences.

    1. Loss of faith in government.

      State the kind of support.

    2. Loss of revenue for the government.

      State the kind of support.

    3. Governmental programs suffer.

      State the kind of support.

II. Any reform should do two things.

  A. Provide sufficient income to the government.

    State the kind of support.

  B. Provide equity.

    State the kind of support.

III. A plan of negative income tax will provide needed reform.

  A. Explain negative income tax plan.

    Subpoints or "planks" in plan.

  B. The tax reform plan will be workable.

    1. It will give sufficient income.

      State the kind of support.

    2. It will be equitable.

      State the kind of support.

Conclusion

I. (Summary) State the points which will be summarized.

II. (Direction to audience) State the appeal to be made asking for agreement.

The final stage in preparation for oratory is to write the actual speech. In developing the manuscript, clear, graceful, and striking language style must be the objective.

Clarity

Clear style depends upon a good foundation of precise purpose and good organization. Choosing the right word to express ideas is very important; the words selected should be simple and precise.

There is often a tendency to interpret formal communication like oratory as an invitation to be verbose with unnecessary, overblown words. Overlarge words which call attention to themselves will divert attention from the central meaning of the message without adding any grace. Instead of big words, strive for words which are likely to be common to most of the listeners.

Concrete language is generally clear whereas abstract language can be often confusing. The word *cloth* is abstract whereas *satin* is concrete; *auto* is abstract whereas *sedan* is concrete.

Grace

Graceful style requires attention to words which will give ease to expression. Being simple and direct will facilitate ease. Instead of saying "There are three steps to be taken to solve a problem," say, "We should take three steps to solve our problem." Sentences should be of medium length rather than rambling or complex.

Striking

In addition to clarity and grace, the orator must remember that the oration is a persuasive speech which must appeal to an interest of the listeners. Without sacrificing clarity and grace, the orator must also have striking language.

Fresh words rather than trite words will add interest. Colorful adjectives—used carefully—are very striking. Rhetorical devices such as alliteration and parallel phrasing add interest to an otherwise colorless text. Alliteration, the use of two or more words in succession which begin with the same sound, is illustrated by "The arsenal contains woefully weak weapons." Parallel phrasing is the use of similar opening clauses for two or more sentences relatively close together. An example of parallel phrasing is to begin one sentence with, "Inflation hurts the young by. . . .", begin a second sentence with, "Inflation hurts the working man by. . . .", and, finally, begin a third with, "Inflation hurts the elderly by. . . ."

DELIVERY

The final stage in oratory is to plan and practice delivering the oration. The oration should be memorized so that most attention can be given to the techniques of delivery.

The best way to memorize the speech is to go over the entire speech time and time again until you find yourself becoming more and more free of the manuscript. Concentrate on one paragraph for brief periods of time, and then go back and go through the entire speech. It is also possible to memorize by concentrating on one sentence at a time and then going over the entire speech until it has been memorized. The latter method is less desirable because you will lose the continuity and meanings behind the words; a mechanical rote recall is very likely to be the end result.

Varying your vocal tone and using controlled gestures and body movement will give the actual delivery a quality of dynamism and vitality.

In addition, there are some suggestions which may help improve your feelings of confidence just before presenting the speech, assuming you have been faithful to yourself in careful planning and preparation. Just before you are called or introduced to speak, try to recover the desire or impulse to communicate which you must have felt at some time before or during the preparation. Think to yourself, "Here's my chance to do a real job for the people who will be listening. I have something important to say, and I believe I can help them understand my thoughts." In other words, try to make the audience the essential stimulus that prompts you to deliver the speech. Whatever you do, do not spend your time trying to remember what you are planning to say. You have already done that. Mental attitude toward an audience is most important during the few minutes before the speech.

Make a positive physical approach to the front of the room or platform. Proceed vigorously, but don't run. After facing the listeners, look at them for five seconds or so before you begin speaking. Give them time to adjust to you and for you to feel warmly toward them. A smile will help both you and your listeners.

MODEL ORATION

The text that follows was a winning oration in 1973; comments in the margin illustrate noteworthy points.

WHAT ARE WE LOYAL TO?

Christy Reed
Eastern Illinois University
Charleston, Illinois

Many of us, in our education on the subject of patriotism and loyalty, were taught the meaning of the familiar quotation: "Be there a man whose soul is so dead, who never unto himself has said, 'this is my home, my native land?' " In any discussion of patriotism and loyalty to America today, we must be cognizant of the many problems we face. But as we look at ourselves in the midst of our problems let us ask the question, what are we loyal to?

Attention is focused with a quotation.

Statement of purpose.

From academic studies in psychology, sociology, and history we have learned that every man has a loyalty. Henry A. Murray in his book, *Explorations in Personality*, has listed *affiliation* or loyalty as a basic human emotion. His concept of loyalty includes: "To be loyal to friends, to participate in friendly groups, to form strong attachments." Alan H. Monroe, in writing on the basic motive appeals, has listed four kinds of loyalty every man possesses, including: "Loyalty to family, loyalty to social groups, and loyalty to a nation." Every modern textbook on psychology and sociology reaffirms that every man has a loyalty. Just for example: in prison, the convicted criminal is loyal to his fellow convicts. In a sorority, a girl is loyal to her sisters. On a football team, a player feels a loyalty to his teammates. Every man has a loyalty, but our question remains: What are we loyal to?

Begin analysis of problem (Main point # 1).

Source of information.

Examples drawn from common knowledge, so quote or source is not needed.

In our own American history there are many examples of strong national goals and the loyalty which led to these goals. During our infant years, the Pilgrims had the goal of settling and developing the untouched land. Their goal made them strong, resolute, determined. During the Revolutionary War, our forefathers had the national goal of independence. For that goal, they were determined, self-sacrificing and loyal. Even during the four years of a terrible Civil War, both the North and South were loyal in their devotions to different causes. Later, during our period of western expansion and railroad building, our loyalty to worthwhile goals developed strong personal character and an even stronger national image. Finally, during two World Wars, Americans fought loyally to preserve the American dream of freedom and of self-determination. Today we are free; free to be loyal to whatever we want to be loyal to. But, just what are we loyal to?

Transition which high- lights overall theme.

Loyalties can be put on a hierarchy or ladder. At the bottom of the ladder is personal loyalty, loyalty to one's self. The ladder then progresses to friend and family loyalty, community loyalty, and finally national loyalty. The first step, personal loyalty, must be reached before friend or family loyalty can be attained, and so the hierarchy progresses. Stanley Niehaus in his article, "Anatomy of Loyalty," summed it up well when he said, "Before we can have any sort of national loyalty there must be a personal loyalty, something close to the person so it can expand, like the rings from a pebble thrown into the water."

Some authority for this hier- archy would be helpful.

Today, all of us have our personal loyalties or individual goals. But too often that is where the cycle ends. We seem to be unable to expand our loyalties upward to higher levels. Our personal loyalties are basically selfish, concern for pleasures, and for money. Take the example of mothers working, or fathers holding down two jobs. This seems to be the great American game, to better yourself and your social position by making as much money as possible. The accumulation of wealth supercedes all else. A new car is a must, not in view of utility, but of what the neighbors might think. Another personal loyalty common today, is one's own employment, his fun. Now having fun is a natural and worthwhile part of life. But when by far the most of our leisure hours are spent in playing golf, bowling, playing cards, watching T. V., or bending the elbow at our favorite cocktail lounge, we should ask with some alarm, What are we loyal to?

Now when we are tied only to personal, pleasure-loving goals, we are unable to progress up the ladder to family loyalty, community loyalty, and national loyalty. We need to ask: What is a plan for improving our sense of loyalty? A simple three-point plan could include the following: Point I: Involvement with family life must supercede our personal pleasures. For example, parents can guide their children into creative activities such as Boy Scouts, Campfire Girls, Rocket Club, or playing a musical instrument in the grade school band. And family loyalty does not stop by paying for trumpet lessons for Junior. It includes going to the grade school band concerts to listen with appreciation to Junior and his friends while they squeak out the tunes on the John Phillip Sousa marches. Years later, the true strength of family love will be enhanced by remembrances of those earlier family experiences between parent and child. Point II: Involvement with community life must supercede our personal pleasures. When our lodge calls for volunteers to help in a fund-raising project, when the Boy Scout Master invites fathers to serve as merit badge counselors, when the county environmental committee calls for helpers to clean up the parkways, where do we stand? Do we answer the opportunity to serve in our community? Point III: Involvement with the life of our nation must supercede our personal pleasures. In spite of all the growing problems in American democracy, we still have the opportunity to participate directly in the solutions to those problems. We can vote. We can sign petitions to initiate certain actions, to recall certain officials and to request a referendum on laws passed by legislators. We can join a political party and help that party as a precinct committeeman or as a county organizer. And we can show outward personal pride whenever our nation achieves goals of any kind whether in space exploration or in environmental cleanup.

Ralph Nader stated, "Citizenship must include the duty to advance our ideals actively into practice for a

Begin analysis of solution (Main point # 2).

Listener guideline provides clarity.

Again, the listener guideline helps clarify.

better community, country, and world, if peace is to prevail over war."

Other visionaries, in the history of civilization, have said essentially the same thing. In his famous funeral oration over 2,500 years ago in ancient Greece, Pericles declared, in speaking of the virtues of the Greek civilization, "There is visible (in our citizens) an attention to their own private concerns and to those of the public. For we are the only people who think he that does not meddle in state affairs—not indolent, but good for nothing."

In the thousands of ways that we can become of service to our family, of service to our community, and of service to our nation, how do we stand? Are we loyal to our personal selves? Are we indolent? Are we good for nothing?

Every man has a loyalty. With each of us the question remains, What are we loyal to?

SUMMARY   1. Why is oratory persuasive speaking?
PROBES   2. How do the values of oratory compare with other forms of oral communication?
    3. What is included in the first stage of preparation?
    4. What is the advantage of writing and memorizing the oration?
    5. What role does language play in the oration?
    6. What is the thesis of an oration?
    7. What are guidelines for stating the thesis?
    8. In what ways can you use striking language?
    9. What can you do just before speaking to provide a compelling presentation of the speech?

LEARNING ACTIVITIES

1. Locate an issue of *Vital Speeches*. Read three speeches and write a thesis statement for each. Can you make a clearer and more interesting statement than you found in the speech?

2. Locate two speeches in a source like *Vital Speeches* on a similar subject. Analyze the language in terms of clarity, grace, and striking

impact. Outline both speeches and compare the language and organization of the two speeches.

3. Select three general topics. Read two articles related to each topic; list two specific thesis statements suitable for each general topic. Select one specific thesis statement for an oration.

4. Complete the research for the topic selected in the preceding activity; outline the speech and write a text. Memorize the oration and present it to a group.

SEVENTEEN

GOALS   After completing this chapter you will be able to:

1. Recognize the unique features of contest activities such as impromptu speaking, declamation, informative speaking, persuasive speaking, radio speaking, and after-dinner speaking.

2. List the major criteria for determining excellence in each of the listed speaking activities.

Special Public Speaking Contest Events

There are several forensic activities in addition to extemporaneous speaking and oratory which have some popularity in certain areas of high school and college participation. All of them are specialized forms of public speaking in which the basic skills of speech communication are practiced and developed with specific modification. Some of the more common forensic events—other than extemporaneous speaking and oratory—are declamation, impromptu, informative, persuasive, radio, and after-dinner speaking. This chapter will provide a brief description of each, suggest criteria which are considered important by judges, and offer ways to prepare for each of the six activities.

IMPROMPTU SPEAKING

Impromptu speaking is a contest activity intended to help develop a skill in mental quickness. Each person draws three topics, just as in extemporaneous speaking, but has only three to five minutes to outline thoughts to be expressed. No outside references are allowed.

The challenge is threefold: (1) to organize quickly, (2) to recall support material, and (3) to speak coherently. The impromptu speech needs an introduction, body and conclusion. The body of the speech must be clearly organized.

Preparation for impromptu speaking is very similar to preparation for extemporaneous speaking except for two features. First, the topics are drawn from one subject area; therefore, reading and analysis can be concentrated in that single broad area. It might be a subject area such as tax reform or trade with communist countries. Second, it is not necessary to build a file of information. It is necessary to read widely about the general subject from which the topics will be selected.

The speech will be evaluated on the basis of organization, originality, fluency, and appeal to an audience. There is a danger to those engaging in this activity. Sometimes participants read very briefly and superficially and then speak very glibly. When that happens, the speaker is probably doing himself more harm than good. Such a person will be learning how *not* to communicate well. You can avoid this dangerous pitfall by reading extensively and practicing frequently. By following this advice carefully, you will develop communication skills in the kind of public speaking situation most frequently used in life.

DECLAMATION

Some contests still maintain a version of declamation—the delivery of another person's speech. Most of those contests will encourage some combination of emphasis on both selection of material and delivery of the selection. The emphasis depends on whether declamation is viewed as interpretation or public address.

In all declamation contests, the individual is allowed to make a short statement about the selection that is going to be presented. The short introduction is intended to allow the interpreter to provide the relevant circumstances of the occasion, audience, and author, and to state the central message, theme, or point which is going to be demonstrated by the memorized presentation. The delivery of the speech—or a smooth cutting from the speech—should be in a style and manner appropriate to communication of the meaning and feeling of the original author of the message.

In some declamation contests, the individual actually prepares a speech of rhetorical criticism. During that speech, the contestant will use some valid system for rhetorical analysis applying the system to a speech, drawing illustrative passages from the speech, and arriving at a conclusion about the impact and value of the speech. In reality, this amounts to a speech about a speech.

Standards of excellence for declamation include the following: (1) the material should be a logical cutting to allow the interpretation intended by the author to emerge; (2) the delivery should indicate the speaker's familiarity with the material by direct eye contact and a clear, direct voice; (3) the organization should be clear and focused on the purpose of the author's original speech.

INFORMATIVE AND PERSUASIVE SPEAKING

In recent years, two new categories of public address have developed in speech contests. These two categories seek to provide a competitive outlet to practice development of public speaking skills studied on a theoretical basis in the speech classroom.

The two events have several differences as well as several similarities. The differences are primarily in purpose and method of organization. Those two differences are likely to result in a third distinction in type of support material selected. The informative speech seeks a response from the listener which in effect says, "I understand." Each contestant may describe, explain, and demonstrate a concept, process, or product. The persuasive speech seeks a response from the listener which says in effect, "I agree." Each contestant will argue a point of view to urge a course of action.

Since informative speaking seeks to exposit and to explain, the best organizational pattern would be chronological, spatial, or topical—one of these three would provide the clearest exposition of meaning. On the other hand, the persuasive speech seeks to influence opinion or action. Some kind of psychological organizational pattern would be most appropriate. A problem-solution organizational structure like that suggested for oratory would be fitting; the motivated sequence would be another appropriate organizational pattern.[1]

Although the above differences are very fundamental, there are some very real similarities between the two contest categories. First, it is helpful to use audio-visual support material in either category. In fact, audio-visual material may be used the same way in both categories.

Second, the preparation is similar. Both types of speaking necessitate selecting a topic, narrowing the topic, gathering information through research, organization, and practice speaking with note cards. Informative and persuasive speeches of this type should not be memorized.

The situation may be very formal or very informal, before a large audience or before a small audience. Contestants are expected to demonstrate thorough understanding of their topics. Regardless of which category a speaker is involved in, any information about communicating with an audience directly should be helpful in both informative and persuasive speaking.

RADIO SPEAKING

A very unique and timely public speaking event is radio speaking; this activity is quite common in high school contests and in classroom activities. The purpose of the activity is to improve speaking and organizing skills under a tightly controlled simulated situation. A key feature of the simulation is emphasis on time. Customarily, the contestant must present a newscast and commerical which is five minutes in length. The absolute requirement of being within a fifteen-second variation is to simulate the importance of time in actual radio broadcasting. Time is money and dead air is costly.

Although the conditions imposed by the simulation are demanding, they are minimal conditions. The real criteria for radio speaking are related to the skill development portion of the stated purpose. Each contestant must take ten to twelve minutes worth of news copy and cut it to about three- and three-fourths minute's of news. To do so requires skill in recognizing which items to select and which to discard. It also requires skill in cutting some information from items. Organizing the items is a very important function. One logical pattern for organizing news items is to itemize by state, national, and international; another would be to rank the news items in importance or impact. Each contestant will also be given a commercial to read which should be about one minute in length. Placement of the commercial can be a part of organization of the total newscast. The commerical should be placed at any point except the very end of the newscast.

AFTER-DINNER SPEAKING

Sometimes we are asked to deliver a speech in which the primary purpose is to entertain the audience and the secondary purpose is to communicate some message, perhaps, a point of view. The goal of the after-dinner speaker is to cause the listener to "feel good" and to, at least, say "I understand your point."

Humor is the heart of the after-dinner speech. While humor is a part of the relaxed informality which people enjoy when their stomachs are full and life seems pleasant, the after-dinner speech can entertain without being hilariously funny. What is needed is light touch wit: a good-humored and optimistic speech which fits the mood and the occasion.

Since humor is highly individual, you must take stock of your own learned humorous tendencies. Some people can tell stories while others fail. How effective are you with exaggeration, irony, understatement, puns? Avoid just copying a style of humor of some popular comedian. It may work for him but not necessarily for you. Remember that good humor has its roots in your own personality.

The most difficult challenge for the after-dinner speaker is to face and recognize the fitness of things. The speech must be in harmony with the audience and the occasion. Just as you will wait until the boss is in a good mood to ask for a day off, you should size up the mood of the audience or the anticipated audience and select ideas and materials accordingly.

In organizing the after-dinner speech, you should plan the introduction and conclusion with care. The introduction must capture the interest and set the mood for the speech. The conclusion must be brief and to the point. The middle—the body—may be filled with illustration, narrations, stories, and comparisons.

The delivery of the after-dinner speech should be somewhat informal. The delivery should be pleasant and lighthearted. Considerable impact can be made by effective use of pause to change a meaning or interpretation. The difference between irony and sarcasm often is with the voice. The opposite meanings are conveyed by what is done with the inflection of the voice and pause.

As a concluding point, if you are entering a contest, or just speaking before a group, prepare for the occasion mentally by answering the following questions:

What is my purpose for speaking to this particular audience?

What do I know about my listeners, their backgrounds, their interests, and their attitudes?

What is the central idea I want to leave with the listeners?

Do I have the proper material selected to help me accomplish my purpose?

Are the materials arranged in a pattern which is meaningful to my listeners?

If you can answer the above questions, you have every right to feel confident as you approach the speaking situation.

SUMMARY   1. What is the challenge of impromptu speaking?
PROBES   2. How do you compare and contrast preparation of impromptu and extemporaneous speaking?
                           3. What is declamation?
                           4. What are standards of excellence for declamation?
                           5. How do you compare and contrast the organizational patterns for informative and persuasive speaking?
                           6. What is the purpose of radio speaking?
                           7. What are minimal conditions for radio speaking?
                           8. What is the after-dinner speech supposed to achieve?
                           9. How do you apply the mental preparation questions?

LEARNING ACTIVITIES

1. Observe one of the public speaking activities in this chapter and answer the following questions:
a. Was it carefully prepared?
b. Did it communicate with an audience rather than at an audience?
c. How did it achieve its basic purpose in terms of content?
2. Select one of the public speaking activities in this chapter and participate in the activity at least once.

Notes

One: Why Should I Read: An Introduction to Oral Reading

1. Jeré Veilleux, *Oral Interpretation: The Re-Creation of Literature* (New York: Harper & Row, 1967), p. 1.

Two: What Should I Read: Selecting Material

1. Wilbur Schramm, "How Communication Works," *The Process and Effects of Mass Communication* (Urbana: University of Illinois Press, 1955), p. 6.

2. Howard Cosell, *Like It Is* (Chicago: Playboy Press, 1974).

3. Etheridge Knight, et al., *Black Voices from Prison* (New York: Pathfinder Press, 1970).

Five: An Introduction to Play Production

1. William Shakespeare, *Hamlet*, Act II, scene 2.

Eight: Play Production Staff

1. We highly recommend the Max Factor Company as an excellent source for materials directed to the beginning student. Of special help is their series of booklets entitled *Max Factor's Hints on the Art of Make-up*. For more information, write to them at 1655 North McCadden Place, Hollywood, California 90028.

Nine: Introduction to Educational Debate

1. Austin J. Freeley, "An Anthology of Commentary on Debate," *The Speech Teacher* 9(March 1960): 121–26.

2. Mrs. Luolella Dirksen, September 1974: personal interview.

3. Austin J. Freeley, *Argumentation and Debate* (Belmont: Wadsworth, 1971), p. 21.

4. Otto F. Bauer, "The Harvard-Yale Myth," *The American Forensic Association Register* 11(Winter 1963): 20.

Ten: Preparing through Analysis and Research

1. Douglas Ehninger and Wayne Brockriede, *Decision by Debate* (New York: Dodd, Mead, 1963), p. 211.

Twelve: Developing the Case with Proof

1. Paul Holtzman, *The Psychology of Speaker's Audiences* (Glenview: Scott, Foresman, 1970), pp. 16–25.

2. Austin J. Freeley, *Argumentation and Debate* (Belmont: Wadsworth, 1971), pp. 128–29.

Sixteen: Oratory

1. John Dewey, *How We Think* (Lexington: D. C. Heath, 1910).

Seventeen: Special Public Speaking Contest Events

1. Alan H. Monroe and Douglas Ehninger, *Principles and Types of Speech Communication* (Glenview: Scott, Foresman, 1974).

Index

Abilities of reader, 23–26
  appropriate vocal emotions, 25
  consideration of personal experience, 25–26
  dialect or accent required, 25
  need for character differentiation, 24
Acoustics, 148–49
  see also Staging the play
Acting area lighting, 145
Acting techniques, 119–35
  and audience awareness, 127
  changing stage positions, 130–31
  common error in, 127–28
  glossary of terms, 133–34
  movement, 129–33
  speaking technique, 127–29
  stage business, 130
  stage poise, 131, 133
  supporting a cross, 131
Adelphic Society of Northwestern University, 174
Affirmative case
  comparative advantage case, 196–98
    treatment of inherency, 196–97
    vs. traditional case, 196–97

criteria case, 198–99
preparation of, 193–99
traditional case, 193–96
  stock issues, 193
    need to change the status quo, 193
    workability of the plan, 193
    benefits from the plan, 194
  use of causal reasoning, 194
  use of expert opinion, 195
  use of historical precedent, 195
After-dinner speaking,
  and humor, 273
  challenge of, 273
  delivery of, 273
  organization of, 273
  preparation of, 273–74
Agriculture Index, 186
Alliteration, 261
Alternative staging, 148–51
  See *also* Staging the play
Analysis of proposition, 181–85
  definition of terms, 182–83
  determination of issues, 183–85
  examining historical background, 182

277

DATE DUE

JY 2 '79			

PRINTED IN U.S.A